STO
TURN
INTO
STAR

STONE TURNING INTO STAR

Prayer and Meditation for Lent

Rev. Joan A. Shelton

Paulist Press
New York/Mahwah

The Publisher gratefully acknowledges the use of an excerpt from *Look Homeward, Angel* by Thomas Wolfe, copyright 1929 by Charles Scribner's Sons; copyright renewed 1957 by Edward C. Aswell as administrator C.T.A.A. of the Estate of Thomas Wolfe, and/or Fred W. Wolfe. Reprinted with the permission of Charles Scribner's Sons.

Illustrations in the text by Eleanor Shelton.

Library of Congress
Catalog Card Number: 85-61749

ISBN: 0-8091-2736-9

Published by Paulist Press
997 Macarthur Boulevard
Mahwah, New Jersey 07430

Printed and bound in the
United States of America

Contents

Preface 1

Beginnings 5

Outer to Inner 16
("Why don't I like a lot of what I'm doing?")

My Reality and God's Reality 25
("What if the words I say on Sundays don't seem real?")

Our Histories and God's History 32
("What am I doing here?")

Object and Subject 40
("My prayer seems so stiff and artificial!")

Feeding 48
("What do I do next?")

Meditations 59

Summary of Benedictine Meditation 61

Notes 143

Bibliography 154

Preface

This book was written because I couldn't find one like it.

As a parish priest who also does some spiritual directing, I have become very aware of the warming spiritual climate of the 1980's. I am often approached these days by people who want to learn to pray or at least learn what praying is all about. They want to know what you need before you start praying as a Christian (they might put it, "what the point of entry is"); they want to know what they can expect, what probably will not happen, and a helpful procedure to use. This book is designed to provide practical, integrated help for the interested layperson and also for the clergy and directors who need a manual to work with.

What do my people look like? They are high school or college graduates, often with advanced degrees; they are technically proficient, competent adults, who have recently felt called to grow spiritually. If this description fits you, I hope this book will fit your needs.

Of course, there is a general sense in which all of us are beginners before the things of God. The perennial questions have echoed through our lives from the earliest recorded questions in the Scriptures. My people have come to me with all of them, repeating the basic human experience of faith's beginnings. But when the questioners are alert, competent, twentieth century Americans, we must take their special needs seriously, in such areas as

Faith development: They are well aware they have patchy or downright shaky faith, but they want to know how to proceed authentically and honestly to work with whatever degree of faith they now have.

Using the Scriptures: In an age when Scripture criticism appears on the pages of *Time,* they are well aware that there is "something technical" about the Scriptures. However, they do not know just what, or how to approach them truthfully.

Problem solving: They are already aware that much in their lives is unsatisfactory. Already working with some presuppositions and a method for dealing with the problems they have now, they wonder about opening a Pandora's box which may contain still more.

The end of religion: They know about the "feel good" or simplistic approaches which television and popular culture supply these days, but know these cannot really meet their needs. How much do we—can we—demand from faith? For the beginner, this is the crucial question. Many of us are ambivalent about knowing God; but my people, at least on most days, seek to know God, so that their lives may have passion, goodness, force, and depth. In other words, they are ready for Christianity in its wholeness, the experience of cross and resurrection.

Readers of this book can expect it to address these special needs in two ways. First, it will lay down some solid, up-to-date theory about what generally happens when people begin praying seriously. Second, it teaches a traditional method for Christian meditation, providing material to work with. The meditations are designed to help readers experience the method, practice it, and open themselves to God, if God so chooses.

My acknowledgments are many. I am grateful to Professors Lydia and John Speller, who made many valuable suggestions on theological approaches; to David Kliest, who proposed useful changes in the flow of ideas; to Ruth D'Aleo of the Moravian College Library for patient help in locating references; to David Scott for advice in publishing matters; and to Ellen, Jody, Bettianne, Jan, Dixie, Ernie, Myrna, Didi, Emmitt, Gwenn, and Alison, who have read it to see whether it might address the needs of people like themselves. My thanks also go to Bishops J. M. Mark Dyer and Lyman C. Ogilbie, who gave me valuable encouragement. Finally, Chip provided encouragement and support in a thousand ways. To him this book is dedicated.

I
Beginnings

Everybody over four years old knows what happens to a fledgling bird after you scoop it up from the grass and bring it into the house.

For a while it eats ravenously: bread pellets, worm pieces, Pablum, water from eye-droppers, milk. But presently the bird's native strength fails to carry it further. It's now that the fledgling's nurse needs some theory about the special needs of this fledgling, plus some method for getting proper nourishment out of the world and into the bird. Without these two advantages it droops; sooner or later—generally sooner—it dies.

Growing spiritually is only too often like that. The urge to journey inward has entered our common-day lives with vitality and the surface ability to sustain itself despite random shocks. It is also winningly attractive, this beginning spiritual urge we find in ourselves. Who among us has not been glad to nurse it along? But after the first spurt of growth we do all the wrong things. In spite of the best intentions we feed it the wrong food, or too much of the right food, or we forget to feed it regularly. We fail to consult the right people, and the telltale warnings set in.

As we find our spiritual lives drooping, we can barely bring ourselves to look as we ram in more of the same nourishment in the hope that perhaps it will help us *this* time.

Again, now is the time we need to do for ourselves what we must do for the fledgling: create a supportive environment and let ourselves be properly fed, so that spiritually we can live and grow.

This book is about prayer because prayer is how human beings try to achieve these goals.

Why Do People Try Prayer?

My people come to me to talk about prayer for two basic reasons. On the one hand, they come because life is presenting a bright side:

> Our souls have sight of that immortal sea
> That brought us hither.[1]

In this case they want to discover—or remember—how to claim the bright side more fully. Experience is urging them to grow or move out into joys like those which surprised Abraham: "Go forth from your country and your father's house to the land that I will show you."[2] Their encounter with life has started these people on a journey toward something more than life, something which can sustain it, so they ask questions like, "How can I grow? How do I cooperate with God who seems to be inviting me further?"

Or, on the other hand, people come out of life's dilemmas: a hopeless marriage, a lost job, a parent or child in trouble, all sorts of guilts, griefs and disappointments. Life is presenting its dark side and they hope to learn how to assuage it. When the pressure gets intrusive they show up in my office with some or all of these questions: "Why don't I like a lot of what I'm doing?" "What do I do next?" "Is this a normal way to feel?" or "Why did this Thing— this wonderful or this terrible Thing—have to happen to me?"

Or, instead of either of these, they sometimes say things like, "Prayer seems so stiff and artificial," or "What if the words I say on Sundays don't seem real?"— which are much the same questions as the others. People are only asking them from the further side of experience. It is the same, perennial question: "What am I doing here? How do I find out what it means to meet with the tremendous, fascinating mystery we call God?"

Such are my questioners. They are coming to prayer out of life because, at the moment, life is asking *them* questions which demand answers. We are all like that; and for every one I meet with, there must be thousands more.

What Do We Mean by "Prayer"?

So far, so good; to talk about prayer means to talk about common day, Monday morning living. But there are plenty of other ways to approach them, with psychological counseling, or more enjoyments, or fresh skills, for instance. Why pick prayer? Because prayer lays claim to another, crucial dimension: to that of a God who exists beside our existence and is said to be concerned with our existence.

At this point, then, we need a tentative definition of prayer:

> *Prayer is*
> a radical response to God,
> expressed by the whole field of personal experience.[3]

7

Before going any further with it, this tentative definition needs a little defining itself. It says prayer is *radical*, that such prayer goes below the surface to the roots of experience. Further, prayer is a *response to God*, that is, some kind of a relationship must already exist from God's side, to be the foundation for a response which can later flow out of it from our side. God's attention has already been there before we attended to it. Finally, it says that prayer is to be *expressed by the whole field of personal experience*, pretty or ugly, delightful or disgraceful, not in isolation from it and not by means of someone else's experience.

Now, even if the tentative definition sounds plausible, it is still merely that. Like all definitions it is an ideal, an abstraction to get us going. It is rather like a definition of ice skating, for instance: skating is gliding across the ice with steel runners attached to the feet, in graceful patterns and without falling down. All true, of course, but an ideal to be developed over time. In the same way, prayer is a mode of moving through existence. Like skaters, experienced pray-ers grow through a process of expending effort for months or years, by trying out new modes of expression, taking chances, and sometimes falling down. They work creatively with whatever their unique endowment may be: ice, steel and a human body on one hand; on the other hand God, a human being, and the delights and dilemmas of existence. So here is a second, expanded definition which takes prayer into account as a way of behaving, adding that more and more of its possibilities are disclosed as we work with it over time:

> *Prayer is*
>   a way of living life
>   as a response to God,
>   expressed by more and more of the range of our
>   personal experience.

Early in Christian experience, Clement of Alexandria defined prayer as the "unceasing conversation with God, by means of knowledge, life, and thanksgiving,"[4] which is the second century way to say much the same thing: that prayer involves the whole person at ever deeper levels of awareness.

But if prayer is expression, how is the expression formed? In all religious traditions including ours there are two chief ways. The first, variously called "vocal prayer," or "common prayer," is probably familiar. This is the kind of prayer which enters a world of words and phrases put together for us by a master craftsman. The Lord's Prayer is the supreme example of this first kind. Using the hallowed words as agenda, we move from reverent repetition to musing, more meditative communion. The problem comes when we are locked into this kind of prayer, unable to bring our unique situation to expression. Everyone knows the story of the mythical G.I. who landed on a Normandy beach in 1944 with bullets whizzing by, scared to death yet unable to say anything to God except:

> Now I lay me down to sleep,
> I pray the Lord my soul to keep.
> If I should die before I wake . . .

Of course, his Lord not only understood but sympathized! Nonetheless, our specific needs are shared best with God when we can launch our prayer from who, and where, we uniquely are.

A very personal business, prayer; the second type allows us a personal voice. You may already know it, too: the mode in which you can be free-wheeling in setting your agenda, and more deliberate in structuring your needs and God's revelations about caring for them. So the definition of prayer needs amending once again, this time to shade it in the direction of the second mode of prayer:

Meditative prayer is
  A conscious attempt to open more and more of
    ourselves
    (whoever we discover ourselves to be)
  in response to God
    (whoever God is disclosed to be)
  expressing the response by more and more of the range
    of our personal experience.

Obviously, meditative prayer is the way above all to open ourselves to the food our God will bring to meet our needs. If we hope to grow we will want to use it, and it is the special focus of this book.

What Happens When People Pray, or Try To?

So far this chapter has touched on some of the problems which prod people to consider praying, and some definitions of prayer in its meditative mode. But it feels very different to lift the eyes from some theories in a book and start praying:

1. Prayer Means Vulnerability, and Vulnerability Means Risk

Up to now we have been able to remain on a theory level: that God just might be a reality among our other realities, one who just might need to be taken into consideration as one of the facts of our existence. But if we kneel down we are behaving as if our hypothesis were fact. It takes a risk of self to do that: if prayer is more and more absorbing of life, then prayer will make us more and more vulnerable to this God whom, as yet, we do not know well enough to trust enough. Far from a sensible, safe undertaking, mature prayer demands that we entrust ourselves to the notions that God may be there, and that God may be good.

2. Ambivalence about Praying Is Natural and Persistent

Every adult Christian who takes Christianity seriously struggles with conflicting emotions circling around its chief business. More than theories about God, we need the meeting with God; we need it, but we also fear it. It can seem very unlike what we have been up to until now, yet our experience is the environment out of which prayer must spring, to be authentic. Which do we trust, then, the daily world or the strange, hitherto uncharted world of the Holy? Moreover, what kind of break with our everyday environment will we have to make if we do plunge in? How vulnerable will we have to become, how much will we have to be changed, what will we have to give up? "I guess I don't have faith enough! From where I stand, that's maybe just as well. And yet . . ."

Of course, although all of us have questions, most of us in our culture have absorbed how prayer is supposed to help answer them. There, in God's presence, they will be met or else will melt away. But sometimes the risk seems more real than the promise.

3. Prayer Will Seem Unreal Until Its Theories Can Be Converted into Personal Experience

Beginning to pray is like setting out with a road map. We unfold it, knowing that its symbols give an abstract idea of the direction to move in, but that once we start the trip things will take shape. The double red line which represents the highway will come real as we drive along it; and when we get there, the yellow symbol labeled "Pittsburgh," "Colorado Springs," or "Seattle" will turn three-

11

dimensional: split level houses arranged on hillsides, office buildings, people hurrying by on a rainy sidewalk, a special note of bustle or importance. In fact, a city will embody itself in its concrete uniqueness. We will only know it because we have "been there."

It is the same when we move into prayer. To pray seriously is also to take a map, or theory, or schema, and proceed accordingly, expecting the abstractions to flesh themselves out as we move into them. Each of us is an explorer, a Columbus, launching out across a theory to discover an unknown continent. We hope to arrive in God's environment, although at this point it is hard to imagine: we have not "been there" yet. And if this is the case, and we have not yet experienced God's dimension, we probably still belong, almost exclusively belong, to the human dimension we know, with its mind set and habits. Thus we may not have recognized some of the means to get to our journey's end. Whenever God and the world of God do not seem real, neither can the grace and power of God seem real. All we have to rely on, it seems, is our own strength, however inadequate, and our own good will, however dubious. Like most Americans we still see ourselves self-made. Strike out and see what follows: this is still most of our method. It is mapped out and given some directions by some theories about what happens when a human being prays, or tries to: a mixture of descriptions from experts who *have* been there and met God (these can seem alluring but unreal), plus some empirical descriptions from the human end of the business: philosophy, psychology, anthropology or the enjoyment of beauty. We will need to be acclimatized and be changed to meet whoever God is, like St. Augustine: ". . . I saw that there was something for me to see, and that I was not yet ready to see it."[5]

12

4. Prayer Must Be Launched from Where We Really Are

It is important that any meditator accept, and work with, what is within him or her, while not trying to force what is not yet there. Some readers of a book like this have already glimpsed the Holy, summoned to prayer by a real taste of God. Others have not yet been summoned by anyone but themselves, as far as they can tell. Some readers may have made their leap of faith already, some never really have (attempting to trust an unmet God can be wonderfully clarifying), and some know they never have. For some God is real; for some, God is unexperienced and thus, for all practical purposes, unreal. Is this an important difference—that is, will something go wrong if we have no feel for God's reality as we start out? No, not if we can hang intellectually onto the theory that maybe—just maybe—God is present, perhaps already working with us to draw us beyond our theories. Try to keep the fresh gaze of the explorer. Not only that: try gently to suspend belief in what you have no experience of, positive or negative. Try putting beliefs and suspicions in brackets, try setting hopes and dreads temporarily to one side. For now the task is not to do what we cannot, but what we *can* do: to set out with our human theories, our best efforts, and the human dimension we hold in common. We are in fact moving toward the meeting with God from our end in the hope that the movement from the other end—God's movement—will be taken care of. "Lord, I believe: help my unbelief!"[6]

5. Prayer Also Transforms the One Who Prays

The fledgling, crouched in a makeshift, shoebox nest, cannot imagine a world where wings are strong and air sustains flight. We, too, have to grow as a child does, in ways the child does not foresee, and cannot fit together in any recognizable framework. As we learn, and grow, over time, certain progressions need to be worked through by almost everybody. Of course, it is not a smooth flowing movement: we double back in the spiritual journey, start over, and find ourselves growing larger and then disconcertingly smaller again, while solid facts unmoor themselves, mysteries multiply, and shapes change. So if I try to chart some of the ways in which prayer transforms the one who prays, I also need to point out that it is really not as clear as I will try to make it! Nonetheless, it seems that we need to move along these progressions, among others:

1. We learn to move from the surface of experience into the depths of ourselves to see what is working or lurking down there.
2. We have been conscious of our own selves—motives, efforts, and actions—as real; more and more we grow conscious of God's presence—in motive, effort, and act—as real.
3. We have been using language to set up or frame out a reality that is "out there" so we can describe it and plan accordingly; we shift to a language which uses image, poetry or story telling so we can re-experience and share a more and more inward truth.
4. We have been approaching God as an Idea to be conceptualized, or power to be reckoned with, in fact as an Object to be dealt with from the outside; we come to know, and love, God as subject.

These are some of the changes that take place on the voyage to God's dimension, along the continuum which is prayer. Living between two environments, we find as we develop that our natures are equally designed for each: the human as well as the Holy. Human experience is amphibious, and we grow through hope and risk: that the Godly dimension exists, as well as the human framework

14

we come from, that we already matter to this God, and that the Holy will somehow become present in the human.

From Theory to Experience

Since theory and experience are both needed, this book is in two parts.

In the first, theory section, the progressions uniting each opposite to its other (the four progressions we have just outlined) will be considered in turn. This section is entitled "Introduction" because of course it prepares the meditator for the second section and exists for it. Obviously the theories have little to offer a reader who is only willing to read them, but not work with them.

The second section is a series of forty meditations on the basic experience of the Christian community, the experience of death and resurrection.

Because all of us are bald, skinny fledglings, still hunkered down in an environment unable to sustain life, we must grow so we can leave it. Perhaps mysteries of grace or growth, or perhaps clumsy or terrifying mysteries, loom all around. But we need not remain passive, like fledglings. Humans can do two things necessary to survive: we can claim a more supportive environment for ourselves—some understanding, or structure, or theory—and then we can begin to take in the nourishment which will sustain us and let us grow.

Most readers of a book like this, though, have already made some other decisions, or formed some allegiances, which we are already expressing through our lives. Supporting the believer, then, what really are the beliefs? This is the first progression we need to consider: the movement from outer, surface behavior to inner allegiance, to the basic faith which is making us who we are. To it we are now ready to turn.

II
Outer to Inner

("Why don't I like a lot of what I'm doing?")

It seems, then, that life is never dull when we take a look at who we really are, in all our complex glory. Generally we find ourselves under pressure, while different levels of ourselves move at various rates of speed toward new worlds we can only guess at. Meanwhile, though, the human end of the continuum goes on. The executive part of ourselves tests reality, makes choices, and deals with the disquieting pieces of data which pop up all around. If the environment seems threatening, we deal with it to change it; or if the problem lies within, we turn to ourselves to change ourselves.

Well, what *are* we choosing to be? Keeping abreast of the various pressures is a frustrating business. Much of the sorting is automatic, while most of our conscious energy is drawn to the surface of endeavor, the common-day "buzz of life." But as the data continue to pour in we often sort most of them unconsciously, with chaotic results. Instead of growing according to any deliberately chosen model, we drift into shapes we never really intended to build.

The first step is to make a thorough acquaintance with our unique hopes and strategies, conscious and unconscious. These structures are rather like the presence of bedrock which subsists under a softening cover of soil, giving a particular mountain its special shape. Just as different species of rock account for differently shaped mountains, so different basic beliefs determine the flavor and color and form of the environment we perceive and respond to.

"Why did it turn out like this?" "Why don't I really like myself these days?" If these are some of our questions we need to get acquainted with what is really shaping our identities and choices.

Three Kinds of Allegiances

There are three basic types of spiritual bedrock, that is, three ways to organize and understand the life we are engaged in:

First, there is the basic trust that *reality (and included in reality, that I myself) possess identity, meaningfulness, and valuability.*[1] It is

> a commitment to goodness, a deep conviction that the world, human life, and one's own life have meaning, purpose, dignity and beauty—a commitment which cannot be made unless one is willing to admit that there is Something in life which transcends life . . . a refusal to concede that human existence is purposeless, ugly and evil.[2]

This theorist is Fr. Andrew Greeley, the modern American sociologist and novelist. He speaks of a bedrock of trust which may be hidden below layers of habit, below surface risks and tasks, even below an environment of cruelty and abuse. A survivor of a concentration camp, Viktor Frankl, remembers his act of faith in these words:

Another time we were at work in a trench. The dawn was gray around us; gray was the sky above; gray the snow in the pale light of dawn; gray the rags in which my fellow-prisoners were clad, and gray their faces. I was again conversing with my wife [in his imagination: she had disappeared long before], or perhaps I was struggling to find the *reason* for my sufferings, my slow dying. In a last violent protest against the hopelessness of imminent death, I sensed my spirit piercing through the enveloping gloom. I felt it transcend that hopeless, meaningless void, and from somewhere I heard a victorious "yes" in answer to my question of an ultimate purpose. At that moment a light was lit in a distant farmhouse, which stood on the horizon as if painted there, in the midst of the miserable gray of a dawning morning in Bavaria. *"Et lux in tenebris lucet"*—and the light shineth in the darkness. . . .

I called to the Lord from my narrow prison and He answered me in the freedom of space.[3]

Here, then, we have faith in life, accepted freely and committed to trustingly, one possible bedrock for human striving. At this point, can we call this faith, a faith in God? Perhaps, says Martin Luther, we can:

"What does it mean to have a God?" or "What is God?" I answer: "A God" means that to which we entrust ourselves for everything good and in which we take refuge in every time of need. Thus having a God means nothing else but believing and trusting in it with all your heart.[4]

Notice that it is not yet clear what kind of a God this is, nor do we know the name of this God. Nonetheless, faith in a God is that first step we noticed in the last chapter, which takes us away from theories and notions. Faith in a God involves us in a risk: the risk of being mistaken. It

18

also involves us in a task: of committing ourselves trustingly to this God as the bedrock for our endeavors.

But of course, there is a *second,* opposite choice of allegiance: that *reality is without meaning.* This choice, too, is a risk and involves a task: of living the details of life in the uncertainty or despair that they have (and, therefore, that I have) no ultimate value. Here is a fictional example, nonetheless true for that. Ben Gant and his friend Dr. Coker are arguing about the meaning of existence in turn-of-the-century Asheville, North Carolina; and in spite of some old-fashioned details, the message is chillingly clear:

> "Where do we come from? Where do we go to? What are we here for? What the hell is it all about?" Ben cried out furiously.... "Say something, won't you?"
>
> "A man must live, mustn't he?" asked Coker with a grin.
>
> "That's what I'm asking you, Coker. Why must he?"
>
> "Why," said Coker, "in order to work nine hours a day in a newspaper office, sleep nine hours, and enjoy the other six in washing, shaving, dressing, eating at the Greasy Spoon, loafing in front of Wood's, and occasionally taking the Merry Widow to see Francis X. Bushman. Isn't that reason enough for any man? If a man's hardworking and decent, and invests his money in the Building and Loan every week, instead of squandering it on cigarettes, coca-cola, and Kuppenheimer clothes, he may own a little home some day." Coker's voice sank to a hush of reverence. "He may even have his own car, Ben, think of that! He can get in it, and ride, and ride, and ride. He can ride all over these damned mountains. He can be very, very happy. He can take exercise regularly at the Y.M.C.A. and think only clean thoughts. He can marry a good pure woman and have any number of fine sons and daughters, all of whom may be brought

up in the Baptist, Methodist, or Presbyterian faiths, and given splendid courses in Economics, Commercial Law, and the Fine Arts, at the State University. There's plenty to live for, Ben. There's something to keep you busy every moment."

"You're a great wit, Coker," Ben said, scowling. "You're as funny as a crutch. . . ."[5]

It seems that Dr. Coker could only pile activities and things between himself and his meaningless existence. "Why must a man live? In order to keep busy every moment," says he. And of course a collection of activities and things does not add up to one whole life. What a contrast to Dr. Frankl, owning nothing at all yet able to wring meaning out of the barest, ugliest existence possible. Light did, indeed, shine in the darkness.

Then there is a *third* possibility: *that we have been straddling the fence,* changing between Dr. Frankl and Dr. Coker, never fully committing ourselves to either. Perhaps life has never exacted any explicit commitment. In that case we have probably pledged allegiance to all sorts of incongruous goals, outdated choices, irrelevant expansions, excesses of all sorts. As Luther goes on in the passage of a few pages back:

> As I have often said, only trust and faith of the heart makes both God and an idol. Provided that faith and trust are in the right place, then your God is right, too; and, on the other hand, if your trust is false and wrong, then the right God is not there.
>
> Well, then, as I say, whatever your heart clings to and entrusts itself to, that is really your God.[6]

And there is an excellent chance that our "trust and faith of the heart" has been divided between an idol or two and God the Father of our Lord Jesus Christ (the only God we like to think we have chosen). In that case we may find ourselves struggling with the strategies we have chosen to promote a mixed allegiance.

Allegiances Embody Themselves in Behavior

"Why don't I like a lot of what I'm doing?"—that is, what God or "gods" have I invited to be the foundations of my self? Am I aligning myself to "gods," for example, like "Getting Even" or "Avoiding Myself" or "Piling Up Experience"? In addition to "the right God," most of us have enthroned a pretty collection, often unconsciously. And just because all these are skulking and fattening down below, most of us must observe the surface of our existence—our day-to-day activities, loves, and hates—with such embarrassed disappointment.

By choice after choice our actions have been revealing our basic goals, ideals, theologies, and priorities, including (but not only) the allegiances we apply to our lives on Sundays. We have been committing ourselves to whatever "gods"—and the God—we have found deeply real to us.

Now, St. Paul said something very close to this when he declared that faith expresses itself by means of works.[7] Believing comes first, he asserted, and achieving follows afterward. Our faith (whatever it is) is expressing itself in our strategies (whatever they are). For instance, how do we invest our freedom to use time, spend money, or choose friends? Have we been investing ourselves to further our status and power? Or to promote "the good life?" Or to buy distractions from our real problems? What really engages our interest? What do our children hear us talking about at the end of the day? And so on.

Faith, then, is what we call the basic, underlying entrustment we have made, perhaps unconsciously, to Christ and all our other "gods" or idols or goals. How should we go on to understand our worship of them?

21

Worship is how we have been acting out our under-lying faith as to what is really "of worth" and what is not. Whether our strategy has been to "have faith in" Christ or in something else—"Safety Through Status," for example—our surroundings and personalities provide the raw material with which we ratify our allegiances or embody our conflicts. By choice after choice throughout the day our actions reveal our basic faiths, goals, theologies and priorities, pointing us toward the God or "gods" which are inspiring them no matter what decorations we apply to our lives on Sundays.

"To work is to pray," runs the old saying; we can now understand just how. We may still be far from traditional prayer; nonetheless, our worship is already in full swing whether we realize it or not. Nor can we choose whether or not to engage in worship, or to have faith. It is just a question of which form of worship or what choice of faith. The bright modern people who boast of "having no faith at all" have only noticed less than the rest. They need to look again.

Realigning Works and Faith

The first business before dissatisfied or frustrated Christians, then, is to examine the outer world of worship—the level of daily loves, hates, choices, and acts—in order to disentangle and deal with the inner world of faith, trust, allegiance, and choice. And since we cannot scrutinize our surroundings, physical or spiritual, while moving briskly along, this means that we need a way to slow down and stop, to disengage ourselves from the pressure of things-to-be-done, in order to rediscover our reason for doing them at all.

Meditation is generally the best method for getting reacquainted with ourselves and the various guests we have accommodated in our spiritual basements, once we decide to risk making their acquaintance. And just as we have been worshiping (however confusedly) the objects of our faith (however unconscious), so at the same time we have been meditating as well. Meditation, at this stage, equals our human pondering, systematic or less systematic, on a problem great or small. Should we accept the invitation to join a club? Does such-and-such a good cause deserve our money, or should we save it for a longer vacation? How about that bad business at work today, or in the bedroom last night? And so on.

Granted, this is meditation from the everyday, practical side of human experience.[8] But whenever we can stay focused, and stay honest, we can open up another fragment of our lives and our world. We can become aware of the choices we have been making, up to today, and how those choices have been giving shape and substance to some basic allegiances. A little light has illuminated a little corner of our spiritual foundations.

Not only can we use our behavior and choices as evidence for the allegiances which evidently underlie them, we can also go further. After moving inward to awareness, after naming our "gods" and our God, we can then return with them to the surface to dialogue with our behavior. For better or worse, certain implications will flow from the meditations: we will join the club, or give the money, or else we will not. Thus we can decide—purposefully, this time—to ratify an old allegiance or to give a first, hesitant incarnation to a rediscovered faith which demands acting out on the level of daily life.

The principle is deceptively simple. Allegiance to God means commitment: liking the things God likes and choosing the things God chooses. In Meditation 1 (p. 63) we find Jesus of Nazareth wrestling with the depths and demands of his own allegiance—in his case, an allegiance which was the ground and center of his life, with life-shattering risks and tasks to embody it, yet, despite its mystery and scale, not unlike our own. On our own smaller

23

scale we find our choices hard because God's world often seems less compelling than the world of our idols, God's competitors. But by meditating on God's relationships as well as our relationships—that is, by meditating on the record of the Scriptures—we come to know God, the God to whom we want to pledge our allegiance. What is God like? What are we being asked by this God? And at the same time, like every human being—like Jesus of Nazareth at Gethsemane—we come to know what our own allegiances really are. Over and over throughout the series of forty meditations we will meet these allegiances in whatever attractiveness and weight they have, with their power to move or not to move us to choose what we see Jesus choosing, our master who rises from the dead.

For better or worse, our lives will have taken a step toward unity. However, though the spiritual basement may be an interesting place to visit, we might have trouble living there. Suppose the Christian faith we thought we had pledged ourselves to has turned out to be unreachable or unavailable, just when we need it the most? The next chapter will turn to the question of what to do when we seem real, but our God does not.

III
My Reality and God's Reality

("What if the words I say on Sundays don't seem real?")

Suppose, then, we need to find some structure and a balanced diet, to grow like a fledgling. Suppose, too, that dissatisfaction with what we see on the surface of our lives—our clutch of habits, possessions, things-to-be-done, and so on—points to some inner alignment which needs investigation. We need to walk around our allegiances, our "gods," to touch them, pick them up, or see which ones are really bearing our weight.

Some form of meditation can be a systematic way to do this because we need to relax the habitual way we see life and make choices. For the moment the methods we are used to are no longer working well for us. This is why shelves of paperbacks regale the browser with Zen, Yoga, Sufism, or witchcraft, while shorter courses on astrology or pop psychology enliven the pages of the newspapers. They witness silently to a widespread need for alternative sources of structure and nourishment as our contemporaries struggle to deal creatively with their networks of reality.

For Christians, however, structure and nourishment

need to agree with the framework of the Christianity we have pledged allegiance to. Most of the readers of a book like this are already familiar with it, if only because some of its very words—splendid ones, like "grace," or "resurrection," or "eternal life"—are part of the environment of any member of Western culture, believer or not. In addition, most of us have formally assented to that set of words, or symbols, or beliefs, just because they put into some communicable form what the Christian community has found deeply true in everyday life since the beginning.

The Community's Symbols Express the Community's Encounters

The symbols which are characteristic of Christian family language sprang from particular encounters with the Holy.[1] At a specific time and place, the community was wrestling with what it means to live in the same world Jesus Christ lives in. For example, they experienced the wonderful, free, unexpected undeservedness of the Holy in their lives, focusing or "thematizing" their experience with the word "grace." Ever afterward, "grace" has opened a special window into the generosity of God. To sing "Amazing Grace" can let us open it afresh, focusing our own experience, touching each other and the earliest Christians, and giving structure and order to experience.

The problem arises when (it seems) we have not yet met with this or that particular Christian experience in our own turn. In that case, to sing "Amazing Grace" only reminds us that we are singing about an experience of God's graciousness when (as far as we can tell) we have not yet had it.

Along with words Christians use many other family symbols of various kinds: crosses, music, light, bread.

They, too, allow us to express the depths of our existence (that is, they allow us to express them if some touch of that common, family experience has already been ours). But of course they do not merely express our own experience: symbols can also convey experience to us. They can carry within them what they signify. Bread, for example, brings strength, nourishment, the family supper-table. So, for many Christians, God seems to have used them to convey what they promise: for example, bread, in the Eucharist, conveys Christ's presence (or perhaps, as far as we know, God does not seem to be using them for us in any way which can be felt as a personal encounter).

Potentially, though, symbols allow us to give expression or to receive it. In either case, insofar as they do help us experience life more fully, symbols are alive and active for us, although they may not always have lived. And even after a pang of experience brings them to life the sense of their aliveness seems to come and go: this can be disconcerting.

This chapter is for readers who are struggling with words, or other symbols, which are not living now or which maybe never have come truly alive or active: for readers who need and want to encounter God, yet who for the most part only meet themselves longing to encounter God.

When the Community's Symbols Do Not Yet Convey Experience

Some Christians stick in this uneasy state for years, repeating the splendid words, maybe reading earnestly to learn what they are supposed to convey. Meanwhile the symbols remain inert, mere concepts. Not that we are insincere: we believe, or at least we want to. We may desperately want to! But the words, or symbols, or the concepts behind them—our "Sunday beliefs"—may not come alive on Monday mornings because they do not yet express our encounters with God, anchored into the life of any day. So on Monday we have to operate, ready or not, on a series of "weekday beliefs" evocative of other encounters or other "gods." "Nice guys finish last" and "Be liked, and you will never want"[2] are two of them.

So here is another way we are amphibious creatures: we are moving between the kingdom of our officially accepted beliefs—the God of Sundays—and the kingdom of the weekday "gods" and their dogmas and symbol systems, no matter how sincerely we try to pledge our Christian allegiance.

Often people leading amphibious lives feel insecure, hypocritical, or otherwise guilty about it—unnecessarily, perhaps. Maybe the struggle to bridge the gap between Sunday and weekday worships is the sincerest thing about us. But the struggle does present another level for meditation. To a greater or lesser extent our existence and acts seem real, while God's seem less so. This means we need to lean on those Sunday beliefs, working with them and their symbols to test whether God could work in them, and become real for us in our turn.

Letting Experience Touch Us

The image of the mountain and its bedrock can be useful here once more. Suppose we decide to climb a mountain, like the green-covered old mountains of the Apppalachians or the Adirondacks. For most of the way we can walk easily up through the pines and white birches because the bedrock is hidden well below the surface. Sometimes life is like that: faith is solid and the weekday path is smooth. Notice, though, that you are not actually in contact with the bedrock but only make use of it in the trust that it is there.

Further up the trail, the rock may have emerged and

the path is broken up. Now you are conscious of the rocks and you need to test each one. You may find it smooth or slippery, stable or wobbly as you scramble carefully across, aware of its contours and stability. Life can be like that, too: you scramble across its propositions, testing them with your hands and the weight of your spirits. These rocks—these beliefs—have emerged and are concretely there.

But there is a third way to continue the ascent. This is the way of mountain climbing: together with your companions you cast a rope ahead of you to secure it around a rock which you have not yet touched. Perhaps in the mists you have not even seen it. Nonetheless you fling your future ahead of you, trusting the rocks ahead to hold while you pull yourself up.

Our state of faith sometimes resembles this third, most hazardous way. We may not have seen, nor yet experienced, the propositions of Christian faith. If so, then "grace" "atonement," "Christ in you, the hope of glory" are not yet felt realities. Perhaps others have tested them and assured us they are trustworthy; for us, though, they are still untested hope.[3]

Belief and Symbol Coming Alive

What do we do? Three things.

First, we need each other's experience and weight. It is part of the mountain-climbing method that climbers are roped together. In one sense *Christian community* is where meditation is taking place anyway, because meditation relies on the Scriptures and they, in turn, are the fruit of the community's meditation on its basic experience. We never really read the Scriptures alone: already we are surrounded by "clouds of witnesses." But we also need those Christian communities which are meeting in our day to reexperience God, to supply training methods, and to gain nourishment and mutual enrichment for the journey. We cannot get these by ourselves.

*Second,*we need to be well nourished. Since we are trying to grow and move forward, we have even more need than before to find the food we need and sit down to let God give it to us: the Scriptures, to be sure, but also the *sacraments.*We need bread to build us up and wine to turn us into lovers. In this sense community, too, with its songs and its friendships, is a sign of the covenant we hope to forge with the God who takes us in.

Third, we keep going, working with the propositions of Christian faith—the expressions in Scriptures and traditions—to pull ourselves toward our future. We will encounter them in the process of seeing whether they will bear our weight, still hidden from sight, still described to us by others. *Meditation* starts that testing process by opening up our lives, prayerfully and systematically, to the basic Christian experience. It discloses bad news, and then good news. In it we meet what we already know: that we have great needs, and are heading toward death. This is the story of our sinfulness. We also meet the God who can meet our needs and draw us toward life: this is the story of our redemption. Since both these stories lie all around us, meditation can and should enter life to bring them to life. Meditation 16, for example, focuses on this particular problem of faith, that is, on the need for spiritual sensitivity to discern God's presence in circumstances which blunt or obscure it. To a greater or lesser extent we are all blunted people. So this meditation, like all meditations, begins amidst those circumstances we find ourselves in. Throwing a rope across a chasm of silence toward a God who seems far ahead or even cut off from us, we pledge allegiance to the rock that is Christ,[4] in the trust that it will bear our weight. Will it hold or should we choose another? We will know only as we test it from below.

Obviously, the image of rock and mountain breaks

down; we are not (we hope) tackling an indifferent something, a mute challenge, but instead we are letting ourselves be atttracted toward a God, a dazzling light, an immense Someone who has been nourishing hope all along. For better or worse: none of us knows much, and none knows God well. What we are really doing is clinging together, feeding together, sharing stories, journeying onward.

These stories wait to be grasped; and because they can help us encounter our own histories, sharing in them is the next business at hand.

IV
Our Histories and God's History

("What am I doing here?")

Scriptures in hand, we turn to the record of thirty-four hundred years of Judaeo-Christian family history. It discloses two main findings:

(a) that God lives;
(b) that God has entered human history.

If these assertions are true, they bring with them a shift in the way we too must understand our whole environment, to live in it successfully.

Meeting God as the Depth of our Life

If this God *does* live, then Yahweh is "a primary objective datum of consciousness," not just a feeling or a subjective experience, and not reducible to anything else.[1] So a third finding must immediately be added to the first two:

(c) that our environment includes God amidst the rest, and this presence cannot be explained by anything else.

Further, we have to understand ourselves differently within this changed environment.

(d) The question we ask, "What am I doing here?" is at the same time the question, "What is God doing here with me?"

So far, all this seems simple, even obvious. What follows from it, though?

1. We Cannot Know Our Lives Adequately Until We Recognize God's Life with Us

Earlier we noted some facts about us: that we are designed as "amphibious beings," at home in the environments of the human and the Holy. At the same time we had to acknowledge those substitutes, the "weekday gods," or idols, to whom we may have pledged some allegiance. For the most part, those idols—typically—seem to be inert. Now, though, if God lives, the life of the Holy is impinging on my existence in an active way.

2. The Scriptures Convey How God Lives with Us

The Scriptures are the history of the human community acting with, and responding to, its living God.[2] They are a way of remembering; and the way they have been built determines how we are to use them:

First, if God is truly a living God, then the writers must be true to the nature of their material—a living God—and let God live, evoking "that which was from the beginning, which we have heard, which we have seen with our eyes, which we have looked upon and touched

33

with our hands,"[3] so that we can use them to experience this God in our turn.

Second, Scriptures are a record of different levels of truth. Any discipline evolves in interplay with its special material. It follows that what makes the Scriptures the medium of the encounter with God is not their ability to analyze, but their ability to wrestle continually with what it means to live in the same world God lives in. Scriptures still sing, gasp, praise, shout warnings, and tell stories: "This is the story of our community coming to understand our experience of God among us"; "This is the history of God as we know it in the one man, Jesus." They use words the same way poets and lovers do, sometimes in narrative ("Let me tell you what happened between us"), sometimes in babblings of wonder and praise. Instead of attempting to be truthful in the sense of conveying the indescribable, Scriptures are truthful in the sense of disclosing depths of truth coexisting with the surface and beneath it. As we read them, it helps to remember this.

The Way of Remembering Discloses Concrete Events and the Depths of God's Life Within Them

The supreme embodiment of the way of remembering is the story of Jesus' last hours and death. It shows how Jesus—and God in Jesus—used the ordinary, concrete realities we humans live with, in order to reunite them with their potential depths and fullness. From one point of view, the record tells how a human being—in every way tempted as we are—entered into a specific experience. Fearing the worst, dreading it, he longed to scuttle away to safety as we have longed to, and have done, so very often. We see Jesus alone in the dust and the yelling, moving toward the agony and the degradation; surely there was nothing conceptual or abstract, not to mention elegant or "holy," in these dismal events. Yet such visible, surface happenings as these were only part of the story the Gospels present. What appeared to the eyes of the spectators on that Good Friday, and the concrete events as the community has recorded them, did not and do not exhaust what they really meant: that Jesus the rabbi from Nazareth was at the same time moving toward the glorification of his Father and toward our salvation and that of the men and women watching him from the side of the road.

The History of Jesus Discloses the Presence of the Human and the Holy in Every History

Looking back, of course, we have seen that the first generation of Christians followed much the same procedure we need to follow now. They, too, came together, experiencing life and asking questions. How could they express what the life and death of this man had come to mean for their lives and deaths? So in company they wrestled with what God had been doing there, finding ways to interpret experience and put it into words. Today we, too, have already seen that human life has its mysterious extensions beyond and beneath our visible, day-to-day buzz of life. Like Ben Gant or Dr. Frankl, most of us have already glimpsed how wonderful and how mysterious we really are. On our small scale we already know something about the bedrock beneath our feet, or else we are aware that it is down there, needing investigation. So, as we try to focus on who we are and what we are doing here and what God is doing here with us, meditating on the Gospels helps us search for the patterns which may mirror how God is already working in our histories. As if God had only one story!

Ever since the encounter with God in Jesus was interpreted and set into words, the Christian family has used Scriptures in this way (the many quotations in this book let only a few of them speak). Today in our turn we use Scriptures to reenter the river of experience, to plunge again into its depths and let them wash over us so that we can discern God's presence and be changed.

Using Scriptures to Meet the Living God

Placing our own histories systematically against the pattern of God's actions, as Christians down the centuries have placed theirs, we can begin to see for ourselves that God is also here, with us, in our histories. "He extends His personality to include every one of us who are united to Him by faith,"[4] reported Thomas Merton, a twentieth century American Christian. Augustine, a North African Christian from the end of the Roman Empire, went even further. "Let us congratulate ourselves," he cried, "let us break forth into thanksgiving. We have been made not only Christians, but Christ."[5] His statement might be startling to sight, but not to insight. Any of our daily realities might be the very word with which Christ is calling us; it is now our part to listen. Any commonplace situation might contain within it a holy place; it is now our business to explore it to see whether God is dwelling there.

This means that each of us can hope to find God for himself or herself in the midst of the pressure and the hubbub, right where we need help the most. It also means that, just as Sts. Peter, Paul, John and the rest found Jesus the Christ active in their lives long before they coined the words we repeat so brightly on Sundays, so for us, too, the splendid Sunday abstractions we sing about and call by such names as "resurrection," "grace," "eternal home," and so on can embody themselves in our own, homely, daily foregrounds. We can experience them in our own turn, drawing on our experience on Mondays with our own joy and conviction.

Things on the surface of existence may not have visibly changed, but, at least potentially, the mystery of existence has become God's mystery, too. In the depths the mysteries are fitting together, while on the surface things grow livable.

How Should We Use Scriptures as the Unique Record They Are?

When we turn to the Scriptures one modern problem presents itself. It needs to be dealt with honestly or our prayer life will be built on intellectual avoidance. It is this: we know that the story of Jesus—and all Scriptures—emerged into human discourse at certain points in history. Since this means—it has to mean—that God enters specific environments, allowing the writers to make use of their particular world-views, their language, their needs, and their questions, so this fact must also mean that Scriptures have been shaped and flavored by environments and world-views which have been changed since the writing. Originating in the shock of experience, Scriptures were compiled, over a considerable period of time, within the musing, reflecting communities, thus shaped and preserved according to the needs of those cultures, not of ours.[6]

Obviously, then, we must make intelligent use of what are called "critical" studies of the Scriptures, for example regarding Jesus' words and deeds. We will be helped by knowing the context in which they were written down and the purposes for which they have been preserved.

But once we have recognized the uniqueness of the record, can we still hope that Scriptures can become "the word of God" for us, the channel for God to meet us? Why does Christian tradition teach this about the Gospels, for example, and not about other, equally remote histories like those of Josephus, Suetonius, or Pliny? Because it avers that Scriptures gain their authority from their reflection of God's ongoing authority, and their reality and power as reflections of God's present reality and power.

The Scriptures as Both Problem and Mystery

Of course, some critical understanding of why and how the books of Scripture were written is essential for intellectual honesty. But the need is for balance, as between problem and mystery. Considered as fascinating intellectual problems, critical quests can send the Scripture scholar back very quickly to the problem end of the continuum. Once safely back there, he or she can do with this problem what Westerners have learned to do with problems in general: solve them. Entering into mystery— the meeting with the Holy—is set to one side during all this concentration, sometimes forever.

As we look into what Scriptures are made up of, though, let us always continue to search for what they deeply are. Using the search for empirical knowledge as the foundation for our search for God, we can let the religious language function for the time being as we let poetry function. Released from "the finite horizon of its authors and its first audience,"[7] Scriptures can serve as medium for the depths of the mystery to express themselves through human history.

So far, so good: however, the fact that Scriptures could mediate a different world for us ought to encourage us even more. We would be forced to recognize that the writers of the several Scriptures have met God in the particularities of their own time and culture: so, perhaps, could we. In addition we are forced to remember that the community claimed to have received the Spirit of God to

38

guide it then, as its members wrestled with truth. In faith they responded to the Holy in their experience, depths that were there below their surface incidents. As one well-known example we can follow the development of Paul as he wrestled with table-fellowship, life in prison, and responding to his critics. But suppose—just suppose—that the Spirit which worked on Paul then, in his culture, might be working still? This would mean that the situation out of which Scriptures were originally summoned forth could be made present to us in our own, particular culture. Paul wrote to the Galatians, "It is no longer I who live, but Christ who lives in me; and the life I now live in the flesh I live by faith in the Son of God, who loved me and gave himself for me."[8] Today we can hope to share Paul's experience of the Son of God, finding his words to be our own.

Do you share this hope? If so, you will want a means to find this Jesus of Nazareth, now Jesus the Christ, wherever he is. Not only that, you will want a means to open yourself to whatever such a relationship might mean. This opening is the next business at hand.

V
Object and Subject

("My prayer seems so stiff and artificial!")

Systematic meditation on events in the Scriptures lets us continue—on a deeper level and with a better-trained eye—the business of discerning the pattern which lies within the apparent randomness of our own histories.

To work through the problems of daily life we already meditate at random and to a fairly superficial degree. Now, though, because life evidently extends on a deeper and wider range than we have been attending to, we need a better means to sit down before its problems and mysteries, both life at the breakfast table and the life in Christ which Paul promises us. To develop such a tool requires regular practice and the adoption of some guidelines.

Up to now meditation may have led to an encounter with a problem at hand: giving money, spending time, choosing friends, and so on. We are attending to an object, or "thing," as unable to respond to us as it is unable to come to life. Such an objective relationship is suited to dealing with the "gods" or idols to which allegiance may have been pledged, because idols, by definition, do not re-

40

spond to subjective approaches. We might as well talk to ourselves or the kitchen chair. Meeting with a living God, though, is gloriously different. Whenever we meditate on the history of that God, our encounter with a "thing"— with problem, history, allegiance, or nagging emotion— can melt into a meeting with the Living God in one man, Jesus Christ. Unlike objective relationships, subjective ones generate meetings—and, with meetings, conversations.

Meditation, the Medium for Sharing Life

In the first chapter meditation was defined as the mode of praying which develops organically out of the circumstances which the meditator and God have been sharing together. This book teaches one way of meditating termed "Benedictine" or "Discursive" meditation. Since the fourth century we hear of this method, transmitted from one Christian to another to teach us to reflect on an event, like a scene from the Gospels, or a truth, like our sinfulness and need of help, or an issue, like the way we use possessions. We learn to weave responses of insight and action according to our needs, our experience, and the material at hand. Not only can the meditator confront and integrate events, truths, and personal issues, but he or she is opened to a possible meeting with the Holy, from which conversation and friendship may flow. The prayer-conversation is the goal of the reflection period, which comes before it and exists for it.[1] This chapter will give an overview of the process before a final chapter, containing some practical instructions, will launch the actual business of meditating.

As Always, Developing a Friendship Takes Time

To feel unnatural or artificial while praying in this new way is only to be expected until we grow more skilled in recognizing where, and how much, our daily lives are God's environment, too. We are hoping that, as God grows more real, the overflow of confrontation into conversation will become more natural, too.

At a later stage still, the dialogue between Jesus the Christ and our own choosing, acting selves can become a simpler, wordless, almost unconscious companionship as we learn to move through the day-to-day world together with him. But this kind of close friendship is generally what we have to look forward to, not what we can enjoy at once. We have to develop it together, over a lifetime of companionship and trust.

An Opening to the Whole Mystery of This Person, Jesus Christ

Just as Jesus' contemporaries needed to develop certain skills of the heart to recognize who he really was, so we need to develop certain skills of intuition and emotion. It is vital to think logically, clearly, and often, using what are termed "left-brain" thinking skills, but we need to ease into some "right-brain" patterns as well. Because Jesus wanted to reach beyond the boundaries of rational analysis and common sense, he needed what he still needs: the gifts of trust, companionship, love, and time. With them we see him lead his friends from the surface observation of Jesus, the compelling, "natural" man, to the insight they ultimately achieved into his real nature and what he was really doing there with them.

Now, most of Jesus' contemporaries seem to have missed recognizing what *was* going on, judging him to be merely another difficult fellow and refusing to budge from their surface, empirical world of legalistic refinements, good order, and business as usual. Since the challenge Jesus made to his contemporaries was too obtrusive to be avoided, and too threatening to be tolerated for long, they dealt with him and his challenge together, crucifying him for an answer. Today we still blunt the impact of the meeting with him and his Gospel, avoiding the astringency of challenge and demand or rationalizing the mysteries away. But, like Jesus' contemporaries, we are only trying to avoid a meeting with our own mysteries and idolatries in order to stay safely within the orderly, practical, rational, and measurable world we are accustomed to. And all of us need to be confronted and challenged by the whole Christ of the Gospels, both the man Jesus who presents himself to reason and analysis and the Christ who draws us beyond them.[2]

Reliving the Story

A good place to begin is where the first Christians began: with the story of Jesus of Nazareth's passion, death, and resurrection. In the second, practice section of this book, Jesus' story has been divided into forty meditations. In each of them we can see Jesus engaged in an event, sometimes a very small fraction of an event. Conversely, we can see the actors, men and women very like ourselves, with whom he was engaged. It has been said that such scenes can be compared to the image which the camera captures in an instant of time: an impression is made and fixed, once for all, against which the prints can be multiplied forever afterward in the reverse reaction. So with such scenes as these: we see a glimpse of Jesus' mind and heart which have led him to do the things we see him doing, together with the reactions of the people around him, recorded forever in the Gospel in an historical instant of time. Today we return to the Gospel image to re-produce it afresh in our own way.

After reading the event, then, we begin by asking Jesus the Christ what the incident meant to him. In each scene, of course, we must look beyond or within the surface facts in order to confront the depths of the issue which Christ is presenting, not only to his onlookers, but to us. Those onlookers are often shown unable to recognize what the issue really was. We will want to do better than they did.

Reliving Our Own Story

Once we have received a tentative impression of events and their inner meanings, we proceed to extend the issue into the community of the Christian family and the world of today to which we are united. What, then, does this event mean to the community of God? to my next door neighbor? or to consumerism, world hunger, or voting in November? So we try to keep in mind the "world of the newspapers" and our own, intimate world in order to learn to recognize more and more of the living links between these worlds within us, the worlds around us, and the God who calls us to reproduce Christ's life and work in all of them.

The final task is to draw our own lives into the scene, then. What does the incident mean about me, and what does it point to, on any level of my life? For example, in some of the scenes we may see ourselves implicated in what we find: thus we might recognize ourselves denying Jesus just as Peter did (Meditation 9). Should this assessment of our record seem on target, we can then ask what the denial worked in Peter (on any level) and what ours could work in us. Or, to take another example, we might find ourselves called on to share, with Jesus, in his out-pouring for others, in a few of the particulars of our daily lives (Meditations 10, 14, 19, 20, 23, 24, etc.). Or, again, we might discover Jesus the Christ already among us, nourishing us in the Christian family meal or in other places just as unexpected as those his disciples found (Meditations 38, 39).

Thinking Together

As part of the attempt to fathom the issues presented by Christ, the world of our neighbor, and ourselves, we should also attempt to share in the thoughts of Christ and neighbor. One example should prove it for most of us: our treatment of minority groups, which displays a wide range of insensitivity or downright injustice which needs to be cured in each of us. It is fatally easy to combine a quest for the Holy with a horror of the obvious.

In addition to sharing the thoughts of the neighbor and our own thoughts, we must study humbly to share those of God whose thoughts are not, as yet, our thoughts, any more than God's ways are, as yet, our ways.

Talking Together

Not only should we try to share their thoughts; it is also helpful to speak with the words of Scripture and the Christian community as well. Our attempts to share in their worlds begin on the level of allegiance and choice. Now, just as with poetry, their words can serve to make the deepest levels (up to now implicit for the most part) even more explicit and hence even more consciously chosen and lived in. Many of the meditations use this device, a reminder of the clouds of witness with which (we trust) we are surrounded.

On the one hand the Christian family can teach us to say what we want our allegiance and our actions to say, just as any family can introduce its infants to the words which express the surrounding shapes and activities infants are beginning to notice. On the other hand, "we dare to say 'Our Father'" as we walk with Christ, though stumblingly; we should continue to use his words throughout our participation in his history, making them our own, too, though haltingly. Spoken, of course, together with our own plain speech; we hope that Jesus the Christ is waiting to hear what we have to say for ourselves just as any friend wants to hear a friend's own mind and heart expressed in the honest accent and plain words which are becoming dear and familiar. As we walk with Jesus the Christ, and our lives progress in his life, we are hoping that our language, too, will resonate more and more as an echo of his.

The section after each of the meditations, labeled "Prayer," is intended to foster the normal overflow of reflection into a conversation with Christ. Of course, since human problems and approaches are all different, so the prayers will often be quite different—or at least they ought to be—from those of the outlines.

Learning To Share Our Own Worlds

At its outset, of course, our allegiance to the Other we are seeking out will be a new, and fragile, and hopeful allegiance. Thus it will come to its first expression in a new, fragile, hopeful mode. Often our actions will be tentative, awkward, half-hearted; often, too, unable to say anything at prayer which seems either relevant or honest, we will find our minds wandering off. Perhaps we will find ourselves stammering things just as silly as some of the responses in the Gospels. No matter; the will to worship is a gift already, just as the words, "Lord, how I wish I could pray better"—or even, "pray at all!"—are, in themselves, fulfillment of what they ask for. "You would not be seeking me if you had not already found me."[3] Trust can tell us that we have reached the borders of that country we seek, although they may not be marked out for us we trudge down the next hillside. Now we trust that Christ is leading us further into it.

Any mistakes or clumsinesses we make along the way are quite unimportant; we will certainly make plenty of them, just as we do whenever we fall in love. Flexibility, and the courage to keep going, are the keys to any kind of progress, whether we are learning to skate or how to meet and live with God. I have found, too, that worship—through words and works—will become adequate only as God makes my life adequate, and only as slowly as that. The same trust is needed for both. Meanwhile all we really need is that deep and flexibile desire to fathom the depths of God's life today in Scriptures, our neighbors, and ourselves. Some practical directions to make the desire come true are offered in the next, final chapter of the introduction.

VI
Feeding

("What do I do next?")

From its beginning this book has described spiritual growth as a series of progressions linking one end of a continuum with its other: outer surface behavior with inner allegiance, the sense of my reality with a sense of God's reality, the discernment of God's history alongside and within personal history, and a change in relationship from one with God as object to one with God as conversing, loving subject.

In order to allow growth to happen, then, we obviously need to open ourselves to the possibility by means of a sustained dedication of time and effort. Next, to open ourselves, we turn from our own daily foregrounds and priorities to God's priorities as the community has experienced and expressed them over 3,400 years or so of recorded history. On his part the Christ of the Gospels keeps us questioning our lives, summoning each of us to draw life together, to turn around, to follow him. On our part, meditation is the way to hear his challenge once we have decided to risk making his acquaintance. Before launching out, here are some practical suggestions:

48

Place: Jesus did not say "*if* you pray"; he said, "*when* you pray,"[1] recommending that you go to your room and shut the door. This is still the best policy; but in some households where the mother is quite unable to fence off fifteen minutes uninterrupted for weeks at a time, perhaps some other arrangement would prove more practical: in a church, for example, during shopping trips when the children are with a sitter or a day care center. Nothing would give the rector more of a pleasant surprise. Another strategy might be a resolve, for Lent, to get up earlier in the morning (staying up later at night reduces many people to the tag-end of the day when they are at their lowest ebb mentally). Some can practice meditation amid the filing cabinets at the office; for most of us, the fear of interruption would impair concentration. In the same way, although strap-hanging in the subway or driving a car reinforces the sense of community in which and for which you are praying, either would be helpful for intercessions but not for meditations.

You need privacy, then, insofar as your life permits it, and regularity. Every day during Lent, at the same time, for the same number of minutes, you have an important appointment. Just as in undertaking to form any other important habit—forty days of jogging, speed reading, exercises, and so on—you will be reinforcing yourself more easily.

Duration: The question of "where" leads to the question of "for how long." How long is practical? It is more sensible to decide on a number of minutes that can be set apart every day without dislocating the rest of your duties, than to decide on something heroically penitential but in fact unattainable. During forty days there will perhaps be emergencies in which the appointment could have to give way in the interests of duty or charity—in the modern world this is unavoidable—but breaks ought to be kept to an honest minimum. So perhaps ten minutes would be a good allotment for each of the forty days, or maybe fifteen or more, or maybe less. Your own feelings and duties must decide the length as well as the location. Should you decide to expand your allotment, I have always found that the Holy Spirit makes good use of any additional moments we can give. Time yourself with clock or watch, so that the length becomes more automatic still (forming the habit, again); if the phone rings incessantly, take it off the hook without scruple. Meeting God is just as important as lots of other things.

These matters should be decided on at the beginning. At the same time, be sure you have a Bible in whatever translation is comfortable. This book uses the Revised Standard translation for all quotations except the Psalms, which are those of the Book of Common Prayer.[2]

Now, down to work. The suggestions which follow describe the stages of the meditations as they are outlined in each meditation, and on pp. 61–62 where you will find a summary of the whole process.

1. **Preparation,** the first of the four steps, includes within itself three stages to get the meditator "tuned up":

a. **Opening Prayer:** we are working in the trust that God is within us, and we already within God, in the sense that we are in his[3] power, amid his community, and in his sight. You should begin by lifting up this trust—in body and in mind—to yourself and to God.

Psychologically it is well recognized that changing bodily position reinforces concentration. In choosing the best position in which to "lift things up," there is a wide variety from which to select the most helpful. Some kneel; some sit in rocking chairs, or lie on their backs like crusading knights on their tombs. Yoga positions help others (though they are a separate study in themselves). This choice, too, ought to be a matter for personal experiment (another reason to pray in private is the greater freedom

50

it permits. God is much harder to annoy than our fellow humans).

The only requirement is that the position you choose will foster relaxation and concentration on the business at hand.

After settling down, then, recollect that God is, in fact, here with you;[4] in that case, tell him you are glad of it. You should also ask for assistance in the meditation and worship to come, asking especially for help in attempting to fathom the riches of the subject at hand. This opening prayer can be as short or as long as it needs to be. Some like to use the words of the Psalmist:

> Let the words of my mouth and the meditation of my heart
> be acceptable in your sight,
> O Lord, my strength and my redeemer.[5]

or the words of Elijah the prophet:

> The Lord lives in whose sight I stand![6]

or those of the collect at the opening of the Eucharist:

> Almighty God, to you all hearts are open, all desires known, and from you no secrets are hid: cleanse the thoughts of our hearts by the inspiration of your Holy Spirit, that we may perfectly love you, and worthily magnify your holy Name; through Christ our Lord . . .[7]

or something more spontaneous or personal. Here is a sample of this type of "prayer of recollection":

> God, thank you for giving me the desire to pray to you . . . Today I am going to pray to you about . . . I am going to do the best I honestly can. But I know saints and scholars have wrestled with this issue before you,

51

and I admit I feel very shallow and divided in myself. Luckily for me, you know everything: you know that I want to love you . . . Please help me today, through Christ, our truth and our way to you. Amen.

b. **Reading:** Next, in God's sight and assured of his help, read the selection for the day as objectively as you can, skipping over nothing that makes you uneasy. Instead, let the events and persons presented by the Gospels think, speak, and act for themselves. It may help to read it once slowly, pausing for a moment to let the scene sink in, and then repeat the reading and its moment of pause several times over. Some people find it helpful to picture the scene as though they were standing by the side of a road in first century Jerusalem, or as though it were taking place on the main street of their own city or community amid the accessories of modern times. The attempt is to absorb the scene, or better, to let it absorb you.

c. **The Issue:** The passage will probably suggest at least one issue to center on. To focus *subjectively,* you might want to listen to your feelings as you read the passage: have you felt pity? joy? guilt? peace and support? repulsion? union with Jesus' suffering? If you are aware of any feeling, positive or negative, this may be the issue you need to focus on, to spread it out before God and work with it in the presence of Jesus' work and his feelings. Or, to focus *objectively,* there may be some parallels in your life, or the world's life, that have disclosed themselves. Out of many possibilities I have chosen one to center on, and the meditation which follows will develop the passage out of that central focus.

Now, the need to choose a focus is subtle but central. Even with short passages we should not look for everything, and we should not try for everything. It is not important at all to wring every ounce of juice from it! And this is lucky for us, because in any case we human beings cannot find everything out in a lifetime, let alone in a fifteen minute meditation. Now is the time to remember again that we trust ourselves to the Spirit of God. We hope that God will disclose something, a learning we can take in.

Prayer before, during, and after is a good plan while contemplating a passage, and our lives, to find an interface between them: "God, what am I ready to learn? What do you want to disclose? God, send your Spirit upon me so I may learn it."

2. *Meditation:* Out of the printed page Jesus the Christ will make some contact with you, through reminiscences, analogies with similar events, issues you have faced or avoided, and so on. You may feel more contentment, pleasure, anger, boredom, or distress: as your emotional responses continue to color your meditation, receive them as data on how directly, or how strongly, your underlying spirit is whatever you supposed it to be. Go on saving them for prayer, as you sense where the scene moves or pinches you. Occasionally, very occasionally, a more direct impression is received: "We understand not merely the literal meanings of the words, but also that which lies behind them, even when they are harsh and angry."[8]

Section I: Jesus' history. In whatever form the contact has been received, begin by standing back as humbly and truthfully as you can, trying to listen with his ears, enter into his thoughts, let him speak to you for himself. What did the scene mean to him as he lived it then, or what does it mean to Jesus, living on as Jesus the Christ, extending it now?

Section II: The world's story. Now you should broaden out a little, developing some of the implications of that first Gospel image (but not, of course, distorting or obscuring it). What light does this passage, and Jesus' story, throw on God's relationship with his world, or on the life of my neighbor, or on the community around us? How was Jesus sharing the world's life then and how is Jesus the Christ sharing it today?

Section III: Confrontation (your own story). Now you apply everything you have seen to yourself. How is Jesus Christ sharing his existence with you, and how are you responding?

As you open yourself to whatever the Jesus of the Gospels is doing or saying, several meanings—perhaps a density of meanings—will probably emerge, from which you must make more selections as you go on. So, if the scene suggests something to which you feel drawn, to the exclusion of other things, you should rest in that one and not search further. Perhaps you can develop some of the others next year.

3. *Prayer Itself:* Your meditation, if all has gone well, should have suggested plenty of material to pray about. Now is the time to be as alert, honest, specific, and trusting as possible, holding up the resurrected Jesus, the neighbor, and yourself as you have found them in today's scene.

You may want to voice adoration; thanks for gifts to you or to others; sorrow for past failures; all sorts of petitions about your neighbor, your fears, your hopes, your plans for the future . . .

As you have seen inadequacies, sins and failures unroll themselves before you and before the God who—you trust—can heal them, you will want to ask for help and should do just that. "Lord, let me receive my sight!"⁹ You will also want to make any strengths you have uncovered more available than before. Christ wants to share in everything we can offer, good or bad, to celebrate, use, or heal it.

At this point we need to remember that whatever we ask for will be given us in order that we can give it away again: "He who has God, has all things, after the fashion in which He who made them has them."[10] Thus resurrection, growth, goodness, and so on are never to be sought for themselves, as some sort of pleasing pious decoration. Instead, they are always—and only—tools for God's work through us as we come to embody him more fully.

As said earlier, you need to express yourself through your own plain words, with no inappropriate tinkering in pursuit of sophistication or elegance. You could also make use of Jesus' words in earnest of your hope to express him later in your heart, mind and hands. And you can make use of the words of the world around you too, echoing the Christian family and the human situation in which you are carrying your neighbor and are being carried along yourself.

4. *Conclusions:* Now that the main business of mental prayer is over, some practical conclusions and a brief review need to be made.

a. **Concrete incarnation:** Looking back, decide—still, of course, with God's help—on something concrete which you can do *today* to incarnate what he has just taught you.

Suppose, for example, you have just met Jesus struggling to pray while his disciples sleep; in the first Meditation, the issue selected (out of many possible issues) has been "alertness leading to trust." It would be too vague to decide that "I really must try to be more alert and more trusting" and leave it at that. No; something more specific should be evoked. Suppose further, to give another sample out of many possibilities, that you have been avoiding a disagreeable decision: well, why not make it today? Or perhaps something unpleasant you must deal with, perhaps something trivial, suggests itself: one of those pin-pricks which stand in the way of your liberty of spirit and efficiency of love. "God requires a faithful fulfillment of the merest trifle given us to do, rather than the most ardent aspirations for things to which we are not called."[11] So, for instance, someone in your office might irritate you with sarcastic or threatening remarks; to give another example, perhaps the children have been especially nerve-wracking today. How could you incarnate Jesus Christ here?

In the office situation, you could plan on something especially soothing or accepting for the irritating colleague (or, as the case might be, you ought to accept her or him more lovingly than before, since seeing yourself accepted by Christ; and then ask your colleague, kindly, to stop being a pest. Following Christ does not mean following the line of least resistance). To pursue the second example, you might try to channel the children's ebullience with a clever piece of planning or decide on some firm and kindly piece of discipline.

To return to the observation of Chapter II: our actions, on the outward and visible level, ratify or contradict the allegiances we have pledged on a deeper level. For this reason, an increasing (as we hope) worship of Christ, and him alone, needs to be embodied by an increasing choice of the things he chooses, and a liking for the things he likes. "Instead of asking yourself whether you believe or not, ask yourself whether you have this day done one thing because he said, *do it,* or once abstained because He said, *do not do it.* It is simply absurd to say you believe, or even want to believe, if you do not do anything He tells you."[12]

Of course, you must resolve to carry out your particular resolution as though God were staying close beside you in the office or the kitchen for the rest of the day. In fact, you are hoping that you can grow in trust and knowledge that God really is.

b. Review, thanksgiving: Finally, it is time to take two moments or so—no longer—and look back over the meditation and prayer. How did things go between you and God? Did you notice yourself putting any obstacles in his way, or creating any patterns which helped things unroll smoothly and deeply?

In any case, God has given you the desire and means to pray today: many people lack that desire and that commitment. As they say, you have "hit the ground running," whether or not the race seems (from your perspective) to have been run on an Olympic level. You have not gone back to bed or turned on the television set. In actual fact, you have been letting the Spirit of God teach you to pray. For whatever degree of honesty and learning have been afforded by the past few moments, give thanks. Tomorrow you can both go further.

In addition, offer yourself to Jesus Christ once again, pledging allegiance to be used until tomorrow as he chooses. You are venturing in trust that he is yours—that he always has been—and you are trying to become his; as best you are able, you have renewed your allegiance. Then rise to your feet, open the door, and return, fortified, to the remainder of the day.

Such is the process of discursive Meditation. As a process it can be learned in a week; as a way of living its effects carry us beyond life. It is, in short, a way to enter the mystery of Jesus Christ and let God make it our mystery. Although an "objective" observer of surface fact might have to believe that Jesus of Nazareth and his provincial world are 2,000 years vanished, silted over by all the erosions of history, we Christians hope for better, and rejoice.

Because the bedrock of our earth came from the sun once, from our own star, there still is star within it; and whenever it wells up to build a new islet or a mountain range it reveals itself again as melting hot, alive, changing and rebuilding everything around it. The oldest hills we climb today, no matter how worn or homely now, were glowing once. In the same way we humans have been built on God's life, the Bedrock which is the stuff of stars. Oh, we hide it: sometimes almost everything is worn away and we have only silt to show for it, grey and cold. But we too can be warmed into a glow and changed, from stone back to star. Found in our hearts, embodied in our outward, daily patterns of life, God can perhaps use us, too, to renew the face of the earth.

Meditations

Here begin the forty meditations, added to the theory section to work the theories through. They lead through the events of Thursday, Friday and Saturday in the hope that those who use them will reexperience them and be realigned by them, as the community has been realigned and renewed by them since they were recorded. They have been planned as a personal Lent, to launch the meditator on a personal Easter of faith and life.

As said earlier, Benedictine meditation is really an expansion of the way ordinary people think. After a few days of practice, its four steps will become second nature. This is the only guarantee that can be given: this book can teach the externals of a centuries-old method of meditation and prayer in forty days or less. What happens after that depends, of course, on various things: whether it happens to be the method best suited to the user's needs; whether other methods should be added to it; above all, what you and the Holy Spirit do with it together.

Of course, these are skeleton examples, so that each can make use of them in her or his own way. As the business of meditation and prayer becomes easier and more specific to the meditator, the written suggestions will come to be of less and less use. It will be a sign of real progress when they have been outgrown. In the same way, the many quotations have been added to allow other members of the Christian family, who have worked with these same issues, a living voice. No doubt each of us can remember other voices, other wisdom. Whomever we bring with us, we remember them to gain insight and to understand that we do not wrestle alone.

Summary of Benedictine Meditation

1. **PREPARATION**

   a. *Opening Prayer:* Open yourself to God's dimension by a short prayer which will focus the way you are feeling, an expression of the faith you are hoping for, and anything else you need to lift up.

   b. *Reading:* Read the passage slowly until it absorbs you.

   c. *The Issue:* Let the scene suggest a focus to share with God, around which the coming meditation can be centered. Ask for help in learning what the passage has to teach today.

2. **MEDITATION**

   Section I: Jesus' story. What did the scene mean to Jesus as he lived it then, or what does it mean to the resurrected Jesus Christ as he lives it now?

61

Section II: The world's story. What does the scene show about how Jesus Christ lived in the world, and lives in the world you and he share today?

Section III: Your story (confrontation). How is Jesus Christ sharing his existence with you, or how might he be extending his existence in you?

3. **PRAYER ITSELF:** Talk with God about his life then and now, your own life, and the life of the world, as the mirror of Scripture holds these up to you.

4. **CONCLUSIONS**

   a. Decide on a concrete act to incarnate today what God has shared today.

   b. Review, thanksgiving, recommitment.

1. Ash Wednesday: *Gethsemane*

PREPARATION

Opening Prayer
Reading: Mark 14:32-42
The Issue: openness leading to alertness and trust

MEDITATION

I. OUR LORD

1. He went, as was his custom, i.e., he had done this kind of thing before
2. Troubled, greatly distressed (14:33)
3. Sorrowful, even to death (14:34)

II. THE TRUSTED FRIENDS

1. Peter had said: "I will never fall away!" (Matthew 26:33)
2. James and John: "Can you drink of the cup?" "We are able!" (Mark 10:38–39)
3. Yet sleeping, three times.

III. IF ONLY I COULD BE THERE!

1. By my openness: "What does it mean, to discuss a problem with God? Disclose yourself to him who knows you, so that he may disclose himself to you who have not known him." (Augustine, North African, 354–430)
2. By my honesty: "Talk to God when you are alone; you cannot talk too much then, for it will be to God that you will tell your weaknesses,

your wants and your longings." (Fénelon, French, seventeenth century)

3. By my alertness: "Jesus will be in agony even to the end of the world. We must not sleep during that time." (Blaise Pascal, French, seventeenth century)

PRAYER (using the words of the Gospels)

1. Lord, teach us to pray (Luke 11:1)
2. Lord, increase our faith (Luke 17:5)
3. Lord, lead us not into temptation (Matthew 6:13)

CONCLUSIONS

2. Thursday: *The Agony in the Garden*

PREPARATION

Opening Prayer
Readings: Matthew 26:39–46; Luke 22:41–46
The issue: courage, obedience, like his

MEDITATION

I. THE PRAYER

1. As urgent as one of my own: his sweat
2. Repeating his urgent appeals for relief
3. Repeating his struggles to surrender

II. THE SCENE

1. Alone
2. The pressures of the world, waiting around him
3. The struggle to move outward into them

III. THE BOND BETWEEN US

1. Our part: "We often do not give God what he asks from us; it is precisely what we are least willing to give, and we dread his asking it. He wants to have all." (Fénelon)
2. His part: "If Christ is not really my brother with all my sorrows, with all my burdens on his shoulder and all my poverty and sadness in his heart, then there has been no redemption. Then what happened on the Cross was only magic." (Thomas Merton, American, 1915–1968).

PRAYER: using his words

1. Father, if thou art willing, remove my cup from me
2. Nevertheless, thy will be done
3. Instead of my own will

CONCLUSIONS

3. Friday: *Judas*

PREPARATION

Opening Prayer
Reading: Matthew 26:47–50, Luke 22:47–48
The issue: freedom can also lead to tragedy: alertness, trust, perseverance

MEDITATION

I. JUDAS

1. "Rabbi!" (literally "master," "teacher"): the pupil
2. "He who has dipped his hand in the dish with me" (Matthew 26:23): the trusted companion
3. Judas had just received Communion at the Last Supper

II. OUR LORD'S UNDERSTANDING OF JUDAS

1. "Friend, why are you here?" the sadness for both
2. "Would you betray the Son of Man with a kiss?" not brotherly, but alien
3. "It would have been better for that man if he had not been born" (Matthew 26:24): our Lord's own calamity not even considered

III. GOD CANNOT FORCE US TO LOVE HIM

1. It was impossible to deceive myself any longer: deliberate disobedience, systematic lies, impure imaginings: such conduct could hardly be de-

scribed as innocent . . . I knew then that nothing would make me give up earthly joys . . . I had always thought that the world was a small price to pay for eternity; but it was worth more than that, because I loved the world, and it was suddenly God whose price was small. (Simone de Beauvoir, French, 1959).

2. Like the bee, we distil poison from the honey for our self-defense—what happens to the bee if it uses its sting is well known (Dag Hammarskjold, Swedish diplomat, 1950's)

PRAYER: recognition of part of myself; petition

1. Lord, forgive us our trespasses
2. Lord, lead us not into temptation
3. "Lord, look after me or today I will betray you" (St. Francis Borgia, Spanish, sixteenth century)

CONCLUSIONS

4. Saturday: *The Crowd*

PREPARATION

Opening Prayer
Reading: Matthew 26:50–56
The issue: the loneliness in any crowd: independence, compassion

MEDITATION

I. SEEING THEM WITH HIS EYES

1. With swords and clubs, as against a robber: what were they afraid of?
2. They laid hands on Jesus and seized him
3. "O Jerusalem, Jerusalem—how often would I have gathered your children together as a hen gathers her brood under her wing—and you would not let me!" (Matthew 23:37)—their foolish blindness

II. THEY HAD RECOGNIZED HIM, AND YET . . .

1. "A great prophet has arisen among us!" (Luke 7:16)—his words valued
2. "He has done all things well!" (Mark 7:37)—his works valued
3. "Hosanna to the son of David!" (Matthew 21:9)—his kingship recognized

III. KEEPING INTEGRITY, IN SPITE OF EVERYTHING

The tone of fortitude shown by the tortured is very different when they think of themselves only as poor, or brave, lonely wretches and when they think of themselves as members of the mystical body of Christ . . . And therefore it is vital for you to feel and know beyond all possible doubt that, notwithstanding all the tormentor's devices, there is, and always will remain, within you something that is built on rock. That this something cannot be torn out of you or severed from the rock, because it is the core of your personality and one with the rock it is built on. Being both of you and of the rock and not being anywhere outside of you and of the rock, it cannot be uprooted. Besides, being of eternity, the more it is laid bare, the brighter it shines. (Iulia de Beausobre, prisoner in Russia, 1930's)

PRAYER: petition to become like him

1. For independence, like yours
2. For compassion, like yours
3. For steadfastness, like yours

CONCLUSIONS

5. Monday: *The Arrest*

PREPARATION

Opening Prayer
Reading: Matthew 26:50–56
The issue: confronting evil; the strategies and tactics of gentleness

MEDITATION

I. THE FACT: "I WILL STRIKE THE SHEPHERD" (Matthew 26:31)

1. One of the disciples had a sword; a riot could have started
2. Scripture makes it clear Jesus could have summoned supernatural help
3. But the Scriptures must be fulfilled

II. "LEARN OF ME FOR I AM GENTLE AND LOWLY IN HEART" (Matthew 11:29)—HIS ATTITUDE

1. "Blessed are the meek, for they shall inherit the earth" (Matthew 5:5)
2. "Love your enemies and pray for those who persecute you" (Matthew 5:44)
3. "Do not resist one who is evil" (Matthew 5:39)

III. "BEHOLD, I SEND YOU SHEEP" (Matthew 10:16): FOR US

1. "When you start on your way, show yourselves as gentle sheep, although you prepare to meet

with wolves, not simply approaching them but going right into the midst of wolves. For by this I shall reveal my power more visibly, that wolves shall be overcome by sheep, whereas the sheep, though exposed to the fangs of the wolves and bleeding with innumerable wounds, shall not only not perish but even change the wolves into their own nature. Surely it is greater and more wonderful to win the soul of the foe, to turn his mind into its opposite, than to kill him . . . So long as we are sheep, we shall conquer . . . Yet if we become wolves ourselves, we shall be conquered." (St. John Chrysostom, Greek, fourth century)

2. "As my sufferings mounted I soon realized that there were two ways that I could respond to my situation: either to react with bitterness or seek to transform the suffering into a creative force . . . I have lived these last few years with the conviction that unearned suffering is redemptive." (Martin Luther King, Jr., 1960)

PRAYER: for meekness

1. To be confident enough
2. To be strong enough
3. To be committed enough

CONCLUSIONS

6. Tuesday: *The Disciples*

PREPARATION

Opening Prayer
Reading: Matthew 26:55–56
The issue: following, like a disciple

MEDITATION

I. HIS PROMISES

1. "You have not chosen me, but I have chosen you" (John 15:16): the free gift to them
2. "I will make you fishers of men" (Matthew 4:19): the entrustment
3. "Fear not, little flock: it is the Father's good pleasure to give you the kingdom" (Luke 12:32): sharing, with affection

II. HIS DISCIPLES

1. They forsook him
2. And fled
3. All of them

III. HIS DISCIPLES: STILL?

1. God does not need us. Indeed, if He were not God, He would be ashamed of us. We, at any rate, cannot be ashamed of Him (Karl Barth, Swiss, 1918).
2. It is one thing to see the land of peace from a wooded mountain top, and quite another to

walk the way which leads there (Augustine, North African, *The Confessions,* 397–398).

PRAYER: to persist; perhaps alone, like him

My Lord God, I have no idea where I am going, I do not see the road ahead of me, I cannot know for certain where it will end. Nor do I really know myself, and the fact that I think I am following your will does not mean that I am actually doing so. But I believe that the desire to please you does in fact please you. And I hope I have that desire in all that I am doing. I hope that I will never do anything apart from that desire. And I know that if I do this you will lead me by the right road, though I may know nothing about it. Therefore I will trust you always though I may seem to be lost and in the shadow of death. I will not fear, for you are ever with me, and you will never leave me to face my perils alone. (Thomas Merton, American, 1958)

CONCLUSIONS

PREPARATION

Opening Prayer
Reading: Matthew 26:57–66
The issue: uninvolvement, more or less deliberate
("sins of omission"): the need for openness, commitment

MEDITATION

I. THE PRISONER

1. Alone, forsaken by his own, condemned already, etc.
2. Silent: why?
3. "Hereafter you will see the Son of man"; the truth, the challenge in it

II. EVASIONS

1. Caiaphas: "It is expedient that one man die for the people, so that the whole nation should not perish" (John 11:50)—so close to the truth!
2. The false witnesses, who had obviously been with Jesus
3. The decision: "No man can love two masters: for either he will hate the one and love the other, or he will be devoted to the one and despise the other. You cannot serve God and Mammon." (Matthew 6:24)

III. "NOW IS THE JUDGMENT OF THIS WORLD": THE TRIAL

1. On an ordinary scale: "Without scheming to do wrong, or to make others unhappy, there may be error, and there may be misery. Thoughtlessness, want of attention to other people's feelings, and want of resolution, will do the business." (Jane Austen, English novelist, 1813)
2. On the scale of Caiaphas: Today it seems to me that I was trying to compartmentalize my mind. On the one hand there was the vulgar business of carrying out a policy proclaimed in the anti-Semitic slogans printed on streamers over the entrances to towns. On the other hand there was my idealized picture of Hitler. I wanted to keep these two apart . . . But in the last analysis I myself determined the degree of my isolation, the extremity of my evasions, and the extent of my ignorance . . . of the persecution, the deportation, and the annihilation of the Jews. (Albert Speer, Nazi armaments minister, 1940's)

PRAYER: for self-knowledge, contrition, courage, etc.

1. We have done these things which we ought not to have done
2. We have left undone those things which we ought to have done
3. Those areas I avoid in my own life, which I ought to see: acknowledgment
4. Forgive us, we know what we do

CONCLUSIONS

8. Thursday: *The Mocking*

PREPARATION

Opening Prayer
Reading: Mark 14:65; Luke 22:63–65
The issue: prejudice and oppression: knowledge of him, of human nature, of ourselves

MEDITATION

I. THE PRISONER

1. "The world has hated me before it hated you" (John 15:18)—but why?
2. "The spirit of the Lord is upon me because he has anointed me,
   he has sent me to preach good news to the poor.
   He has sent me to proclaim release to the captives
   and recovering of sight to the blind,
   to set at liberty those who are oppressed,
   to proclaim the acceptable year of the Lord."
   (Luke 4:18–19, Isaiah 61:1–2; Jesus announces his ministry)

II. THE CROWD

1. "Do not wonder if the world hate you" (1 John 3:13)
2. There are two things that can unite men: common ideals, common scoundrelism. (Adolph Hitler, German, 1923)
3. The struggle for the oppressed is God's struggle. (James Cone, black American theologian, 1975)

III. OURSELVES

1. They say we are the Lawd's children, I don't say that ain't true,
   They say we are the Lawd's children, I don't say that ain't true,
   But if we are the same like each other, Ooh, Lawd, Lawd,
   Well, why do they treat me like they do? (spiritual)
2. Blush with shame, people, blush with shame. For by your sins you deprive yourself of so much good, and must make yourselves deserving of so much evil. (Catherine of Siena, Italian, fourteenth century)

PRAYER: for alertness, strength, change

1. Shame: it is true, etc.
2. O eternal Trinity, mad with love, of what use to you was our redemption? None at all, for you have no need of us, you who are our God. For whose good was it? Only humanity's. (Catherine of Siena)
3. What shall I do?

CONCLUSIONS

9. Friday: *Peter*

PREPARATION

Opening Prayer
Reading: Luke 22:54–62
The issue: grief, love, rededication like Peter's

MEDITATION

I. PETER

1. Peter followed "at a distance"
2. "I know not the man!"—again and again!
3. His boast: "Even though they all fall away, I will not!" (Mark 14:29)

II. OUR LORD AND PETER

1. "Simon, Simon"—Peter's old name, not his nickname
2. "I have prayed for you, that your faith may not fail" (Luke 22:32)
3. The Lord turned and looked at Peter

III. THE PENITENT

1. He went out, and wept bitterly
2. "Lord, you know everything: you know that I love you!" (John 21:17)
3. We have been born anew to a living hope! (1 Peter 1:3)
4. All our natural evil ceases to be our own evil as soon as our will turns from it; it then changes its nature, loses all its poison and death, and

only becomes our holy cross on which we happily die from self and into the Kingdom of Heaven (William Law, English, eighteenth century)

PRAYER

1. Lord, you know everything
2. You know that I love you
3. "Lord, I don't love you at all" (St. Philip Neri, Italian, sixteenth century)

CONCLUSIONS

10. Saturday: *The Night, the Prison*

PREPARATION

Opening Prayer
Reading: Luke 22:66 (inferred)
The issues: sharing with Christ our frustration, darkness, imprisonment, etc.

MEDITATION

I. THE PRISONER

1. "I am the way" (John 14:6)—but imprisoned
2. "I am the Light" (John 8:12)—but in darkness
3. "Come unto me" (Matthew 11:28)—but all alone

II. THE TRUTH WILL MAKE YOU FREE (John 8:32)

1. "You are slaves of the one you obey, either of sin, which leads to death, or of obedience, which leads to righteousness" (Romans 6:16)
2. "Who will liberate me from this body of death?" (Romans 7:24)
3. "The glorious liberty of the children of God" (Romans 8:21)
4. "I called to the Lord from my narrow prison and He answered me in the freedom of space." (Viktor Frankl, Viennese psychiatrist in Auschwitz, 1945)

III. THE WAY OUT

1. He has put himself in our hands!
2. His patience with us
3. Our companionship, our joy in each other

PRAYER

1. Trust, obedience, blind offering, as best I can
2. "Free at last!
   Free at last!
   Thank God almighty, I'm free at last!" (Martin Luther King Jr., 1968)

CONCLUSIONS

11. Monday: *Pilate*

PREPARATION

Opening Prayer
Reading: John 18:28–38
The issue: ambition vs. the Kingdom: whose citizen
am I?

MEDITATION

I. THE PUBLIC OFFICIAL

1. "What accusation?"
2. "If this man were not a malefactor": already condemned, of course
3. "Judge him by your own law": rejected by everyone

II. THE GENTLEMAN OF CULTURE

1. "Are you the king of the Jews?"
2. "Am *I* a Jew? What have you done?"
3. "So you *are* a king?"
4. "What is truth?"
5. "I find no crime in him."

III. THE KING

1. If we are to say that religion cannot be concerned with politics then we are really saying that there is a substantial part of human life in which God's writ does not run. If it is not God's then whose is it? Who is in charge if not the God and Father of our Lord Jesus Christ? (Desmond

Tutu, contemporary South African churchman and black resistance leader)
2. The Gospel is not a truth among truths. Rather, it sets a question against all truths. (Karl Barth)
3. To love is to bring one's whole life under discipline. (Alan Paton, white South African author and resistance leader, 1968)

PRAYER: a renewed pledge of allegiance

Here I am entirely at your service, great King and Lord of the Universe. I put myself at your service by your leave and, indeed, with your help, and with no claim that this privilege is due me for any personal worth or merit of my own. Myself and all that is mine I put before you; do with me what you wish. (St. Ignatius of Loyola, Spanish, sixteenth century)

CONCLUSIONS

12. Tuesday: *Herod*

PREPARATION

Opening Prayer
Reading: Luke 23:6–12
The issue: flippancy, heartless superficiality: silence, love like Jesus'

MEDITATION

I. HEROD

1. Our Lord had called him "that fox" (Luke 13:32)
2. Herod had long desired to see Jesus: a diversion!
3. So—he questioned him at some length—a curiosity!
4. Treated him with contempt and mocked him—a laughingstock!
5. Sent him back to Pilate and became friends with Pilate—a good joke!

II. OUR LORD

1. His strength—whence?
2. His silence—why?

III. IT STILL HAPPENS

A man who knows death is near has his mind made up, but he is also silent. Wordlessly, and even, if it must be, misunderstood and alone, he does what is necessary and right, he offers his sacrifice. . . . Let us learn for a while to do the right thing without talking about it (Dietrich Bonhoffer, German resistance hero and martyr, 1945).

PRAYER: petition

1. Courage to speak out
2. Courage to be silent
3. Courage to go on loving

CONCLUSIONS

13. Wednesday: *Barabbas*

PREPARATION

Opening Prayer
Reading: Matthew 27:15–26
The issue: choosing between the good and the best

MEDITATION

I. THE CHOICE THAT DAY

1. "Which of the two?"—the deep-rooted weakness
2. "Barabbas!"—the deep-rooted antipathy
3. "See to it yourselves!"—"Not to decide is to decide"

II. "YOU HAVE NOT CHOSEN ME, BUT I HAVE CHOSEN YOU" (John 15:16)

1. "God so loved the world"—the strength of that love
2. "That he gave his only Son"—the cost to him (John 3:16)
3. The Father's choices

III. THE CHOICE OF BARABBAS

1. What was Barabbas perhaps thinking, hoping, praying?
2. Suppose Barabbas' family were in the crowd?
3. My everyday choices

PRAYER

1. Lord, we have not chosen you
2. But you have chosen us
3. Gratitude, self-offering

CONCLUSIONS

14. Thursday: *The Scourging*

PREPARATION

Opening Prayer
Reading: Luke 23:22; Mark 15:15
The issue: traditionally the scene where we offer Jesus our own physical pain, effort, fatigue, compulsion, etc. in companionship with him, imitation of him

MEDITATION

I. "I GAVE MY BACK TO THE SMITERS" (Isaiah 50:6)

1. Pilate: "I have found no crime in him: I will therefore chastize him and release him"—the injustice
2. Jesus delivered to be scourged: his helplessness

II. THE EFFECTS

1. "By his stripes we are healed" (Isaiah 53:5)
2. "As we share abundantly in Christ's sufferings, so we share abundantly in his comfort, too" (2 Corinthians 1:5)
3. The suffering around us; our own suffering: its value?

III. HAVE I SOMETHING I NEED TO OFFER HIM?

1. My own weakness, troubles, sufferings?
2. The mystery of sharing: "O dear friends who are

reading this, holiness will not cost you anything extra: go on doing whatever you are doing now, suffer whatever you are suffering now. Nothing needs to be changed but your hearts" (J.-P. de Caussade, French, eighteenth century)

3. Or ought I to work for a remedy?

PRAYER: The prayer of St. Richard of Chichester, English, thirteenth century:

> Day by Day,
> Dear Lord, of thee three things I pray:
>> To see thee more clearly,
>> Love thee more dearly,
>> Follow thee more nearly,
> Day by day . . .

CONCLUSIONS

PREPARATION

Opening Prayer
Reading: Mark 15:16–20
The issue: recognition, allegiance, trust

MEDITATION

I. THE HONORS

1. They began to salute him
2. "Hail, king of the Jews!"
3. They struck his head with a reed, and spat on him
4. They knelt down in homage to him

II. "HE WAS DESPISED AND REJECTED BY MEN" (Isaiah 53:3–6)

1. The purple robe, the reed, the crown: the humiliation
2. Before the whole battalion: the brutal humiliation
3. "Extreme affliction: physical pain, distress of soul, and social degradation" (Simone Weil, French, 1941)

III. THE KINGSHIP

1. The king extremely afflicted: what must I be worth, then, for God to have risked so much for me?
2. "Once you were no people, but now you are a

people: a royal priesthood, a chosen nation, God's own people" (1 Peter 2:9)

3. "Jesus does not want to become an earthly king. This is why he came: to transform us, to live in us, so that we become like him, so that we are not just cowering servants, performing the Law, but a free people, freed by the Spirit, transformed by Him and in Him" (Jean Vanier, Canadian contemporary)

PRAYER

1. Praise: "You are the king of glory, O Christ!"
2. Thanksgiving for his trust in me
3. Resolve to go on struggling

CONCLUSIONS

PREPARATION

Opening Prayer
Reading: John 19:4–5
The issue: alertness, sensitivity: recognizing Christ around us

MEDITATION

I. "BEHOLD THE HUMAN CONDITION"

1. Behold this mob
2. Behold Pilate himself
3. Behold Jesus, our Lord: if only they had really seen Him!

II. "SEEING, THEY DO NOT SEE, AND HEARING, THEY DO NOT HEAR" (Matthew 13:13): THE UNEXPECTED APPEARANCE

1. "He had no form or comeliness, that we should look on him, and no beauty, that we should desire him . . .
2. "He was despised, and we esteemed him not . . .
3. "We have turned, every one, to his own way: and the Lord has laid on him the iniquity of us all" (Isaiah 53:2–6)

III. "THE SON OF MAN IS COMING AT AN HOUR YOU DO NOT EXPECT" (Luke 12:40): THE UNLOOKED-FOR ARRIVAL

1. The needy: "Lord, that I may see!" "Lord, that I may hear!" "Lord, if you want to, you can make me clean!"

2. The comfortable: "This is the heir: let us kill him, that the inheritance may be ours" (Luke 20:14)
3. The disciples in Emmaus: "He was known to them in the breaking of bread" (Luke 24:35)

PRAYER: petition

1. "Now that I've seen what I have seen, I know that I belong here whether I want to or not. This business is everybody's business." (Albert Camus, French, *The Plague,* 1947)
2. Love immeasurable, in yourself you show us the world's need. (Catherine of Siena)

CONCLUSIONS

PREPARATION

Opening Prayer
Reading: Matthew 27:20–25; John 19:6–16
The issue: external pressure: independence, compassion like his

MEDITATION

I. HIS OWN RECEIVED HIM NOT (John 1:11)

1. "Which of the two?" "Barabbas!"
2. "Then what should I do?" "Crucify him!"
3. "What evil?" "Crucify him!"
4. "We have a law!"

II. THE SNARES

1. The chief priests and elders persuaded the crowd—pressure from the leaders
2. Pilate: "the more afraid"—why?
3. An autonomous person of today must work constantly to free himself from shadowy entanglements. (David Riesman, American: *The Lonely Crowd,* 1950)

III. IT STILL HAPPENS

1. That is the great thing about our movement . . . that these men have outwardly become a unit, that actually these members are uniform not only in ideas, but that even the facial expression is almost the same. Look at these laughing eyes,

this fanatical enthusiasm, and you will discover how in these faces the same expression has formed, how a hundred thousand men in a movement become a single type. (Adolph Hitler describes the Nazi rally in Nuremberg, 1936)

2. "I do not pray that thou shouldst take them out of the world but that thou shouldst keep them from evil." (John 17:15)

3. "Be of good cheer, I have overcome the world." (John 16:33)

PRAYER

1. Lord, help me to overcome my own weakness
2. And the malice of my enemies
3. And the dear entanglements of my own world

CONCLUSIONS

PREPARATION

Opening Prayer
Reading: John 19:12–16; Matthew 27:24–26
The issue: Christ in my neighbor: recognition leading to identification, justice, service

MEDITATION

I. THE FINAL REJECTION

1. "You are not Caesar's friend": the appeal to fear
2. "Here is your king!" the appeal to compassion
3. "Away with him!"—again and again
4. "Shall I crucify your king?" "We have no king but Caesar!"
5. "His blood be upon us and on our children"

II. "A STRANGER TO MY OWN KINDRED" (Psalm 69:9): BEFORE, AND SINCE

1. "I looked for sympathy, but there was none,
2. "For comforters, but I could find no one" (Psalm 69:22)
3. "His own received him not" (John 1:11)—we are "his own"!

III. "AND WHO IS MY NEIGHBOR?" (Luke 10:29)

We *are* the world . . . Through our senses and our minds, our loves, needs, and desires, we are implicated, without possibility of evasion, in this world of matters and of men, of things and of persons, which not only affect us and change our lives but are also affected and changed by us. From the moment we sit down at the table and put a piece of bread into our mouths, we see that we are in the world and cannot be otherwise than in it, until the day we die. The question, then, is not to speculate about how we are to contact the world—as if we were somehow in outer space—but how to validate our relationship, give it a fully honest and human significance, and make it truly productive and worthwhile for our world. (Thomas Merton)

PRAYER: identification

1. The prayer of the unseeing: "Lord, when did we see thee . . . and did not minister unto thee?" (Matthew 25:44)
2. For the social framework through which we see the world
3. For the insight to recognize Christ
4. For the strength to choose Christ

CONCLUSIONS

19. Wednesday: *The Cross*

PREPARATION

Opening Prayer
Reading: John 19:17
The issue: the opportunity which is sometimes hidden in suffering: alertness, recognition of it, offering

MEDITATION

I. "THE WAY LEADING TO LIFE" (Matthew 7:14)

1. "If any man would come after me
2. "Let him deny himself
3. "And take up his cross daily, and follow me" (Matthew 16:24)

II. THE CROSS, TO ST. PAUL (Colossians 1:24)

1. "I rejoice in my sufferings for your sake;
2. "In my flesh I complete what is lacking in Christ's afflictions
3. "For the sake of his body, that is, the Church"

III. "THE GATE IS NARROW AND THE WAY HARD" (Matthew 7:14)

1. "The cross is God's truth about us, and therefore it is the only power which can make us truthful. When we know the cross we are no longer afraid." (Dietrich Bonhoffer, German resistance hero and martyr, 1930's)
2. "We would prefer a saviour who would make us

excellent by assuring us of our excellence and who reinforced all our most flattering opinions of our own intelligence. Instead, God has given us a Saviour who upsets our values and leads us naked to an infamous Cross with Him. O Jesus, there the world abandons Thee! We need not carry things so far, we say; that would exaggerate Christian verities and make them distasteful ... Without the Cross, religion has no reality." (Fénelon)

PRAYER (Collect, Monday in Holy Week):

1. Almighty God, whose most dear Son went not up to joy but first he suffered pain, and entered not into glory before he was crucified:
2. Mercifully grant that we, walking in the way of the cross,
3. May find it none other than the way of life and peace.

CONCLUSIONS

20. Thursday: *Simon*

PREPARATION

Opening Prayer
Reading: Mark 15:21
The issue: service, though unwilling, like Simon's

MEDITATION

I. THE SERVANT

1. Simon, of Cyrene (a foreigner, perhaps a black man)
2. A passerby, coming in from the country—preoccupied?
3. Compelled

II. THE SERVICE

1. Jesus helped with his cross
2. "Not everyone who says 'Lord, Lord' shall enter the Kingdom of Heaven, but he who does the will of my Father who is in Heaven" (Matthew 7:21)
3. "Draw near to God and he will draw near to you" (James 4:8)

III. THE COMPANIONSHIP

1. The true man trusts in a strength which is not his, and which he does not feel, does not always desire (George MacDonald)
2. "But how can God bring this about in me?" Let

him do it and perhaps you will know (George MacDonald)
3. How foolish we are! We admire and bless this divine action in the writings which tell us its history, and then when it is ready to continue writing its history on our own hearts, we keep tight hold of the paper (de Caussade).

PRAYER

1. Recognition: my burdens
2. Self-acceptance: I am unwilling, etc.
3. Ratification, as best I can: "Dear God, I give you all, willingly . . . The best is to remain quiet. Because though I may not know how to give, You know how to take. Yet I would have wished to be, once, just once, magnificently generous to You!" (George Bernanos, French, *Diary of a Country Priest,* 1930's)

CONCLUSIONS

21. Friday: *The Women*

PREPARATION

Opening Prayer
Reading: Luke 23:27–31
The issue: perseverance, love, in spite of everything

MEDITATION

I. THE WOMEN

1. Jesus' understanding of women, unique in his culture
2. Women now bewailing and lamenting him
3. Amid the hostility of the mob

II. THE CONVERSATION

1. "Do not weep for me"
2. "Weep for yourselves and for your children"— the impending fall of Jerusalem
3. "What will happen when it is dry?"

III. THE EFFECTS: FOR HIM, FOR US

1. "See: He is only waiting for us to look at Him!" (St.Teresa of Avila, Spanish, sixteenth century)
2. "Rieux thought it too: that a loveless world is a dead world, and always there comes an hour when one is weary of the pressures of one's work, of devotion to duty, and all one craves for is a loved face, the warmth and wonder of a loving heart . . . and what filled his breast was the passionate indignation we all feel when con-

fronted with the anguish all men share" (Albert Camus, *The Plague,* French, twentieth century)

PRAYER

1. For recognition, compassion, courage, like theirs
2. For recognition, self-forgetfulness, like his
3. His eyes on me: Lord, what do you want me to do?

CONCLUSIONS

PREPARATION

Opening Prayer
Reading: Mark 15:22
The issue: following Jesus Christ, no matter where
or how far

MEDITATION

I. "CUT OUT OF THE LAND OF THE LIVING" (Isaiah 53:8)

1. The place: notorious from its very name
2. Outside the holy city: an accursed place
3. Banished from his fellow human beings, like all those we condemn

II. "THE LONGEST JOURNEY IS THE JOURNEY INWARD" (Dag Hammarskjold)

1. "The first step places the disciple in the situation where faith is possible. If he refuses to follow and stays behind, he does not learn how to believe. He who is called must go out of his situation, in which he cannot believe, into the situation in which, first and foremost, faith is possible . . . So long as Levi sits at the receipt of custom, and Peter at his nets, they could both pursue their trade honestly and dutifully, and they might both enjoy religious experiences, old and new. But if they want to believe in God, the only way is to follow his incarnate Son." (Dietrich Bonhoffer, German, 1939).

2. "The heart of Jesus is the heart of a lover. When He calls people forth, it is not because He has something for them to do as workers, but because He loves them. When He calls people to become followers, it's not just the mission that He has for them, but something much deeper. It is the call of a person who loves and says, "Walk with me for I love you. You are precious in my eyes. Fear not." (Jean Vanier)

III. OUR PART: OFFERING, WITH NO LIMITS (Hebrews 13:13)

1. "Let us go forth to him"
2. "Outside the camp," i.e., outside man-made definitions or boundaries
3. "And bear the abuse he endured"

PRAYER: sharing the confession of Fénelon:

1. "O God, I talk grandly of the cross, but I want it in name only"
2. "I welcome the cross from afar, but when it is near I want to draw back."

CONCLUSIONS

PREPARATION

Opening Prayer
Reading: John 19:23–24
The issue: traditionally the scene where we offer
him any "coverings" which stand between him and
us

MEDITATION

I. THE SCENE: THE FACT

1. His clothing stripped off: the indignity, the defenselessness
2. Intended as another degradation
3. His garments diced for: the squalor

II. THE ISSUE: FOR US

1. "Our Lord Jesus Christ, though he was rich, yet for your sakes he became poor so that by his poverty you might become rich" (2 Corinthians 8:9)
2. "Whoever of you does not renounce all he has, cannot be my disciple" (Luke 14:33)
3. "Blessed are the pure in heart (or "clean in heart", or single-hearted"), for they shall see God" (Matthew 5:8)

III. THE OFFERING: REMEMBER, YOU CANNOT GIVE YOUR SELF TO GOD UNLESS YOU OWN IT FIRST

1. "Jesus, I have no pretensions, I have no preconceived plans, I am trying to strip myself of all

107

that is self, I am no longer my own. My soul is open before You, like a blank sheet of paper. Write on it what You will, O Lord: I am Yours." (Pope John XXIII at twenty-one years old, *Journal of a Soul,* 1903).

2. "I don't know Who—or what—put the question, I don't know when it was put. I don't even remember answering. But at some moment I did answer *Yes* to Someone—or Something—and from that hour I was certain that existence is meaningful and that, therefore, my life, in self-surrender, had a goal. From that moment I have known what it means 'not to look back,' and 'to take no thought for the morrow.' " (Dag Hammarskjold, 1961).

PRAYER

1. My priorities: it is true, etc.
2. Petition: for insight to recognize them, realign them, etc.
3. "Create in me a clean heart, O God, and renew a right spirit within me" (Psalm 51:11)

CONCLUSIONS

24. Tuesday: *The Nailing*

PREPARATION

Opening Prayer
Reading: Mark 15:23–24
The issue: traditionally the scene where we ask to be united with Jesus by whatever special "nails" he has chosen for us

MEDITATION

I. THE LAMB LED TO THE SLAUGHTER (Isaiah 53)

1. Declining the drugged wine—still desiring to be alert
2. The brutal words and handling
3. The three nails: the physical pain

II. THE COMPANIONSHIP: THE FACT

1. "All those who belong to Christ Jesus have crucified 'the flesh' with all its affections and desires" (Galatians 5:24)
2. "For until I am substantially united to him, I may never have full rest, nor very bliss; that is to say, until I be fastened to him so that there be right naught that is made, between my God and me" (Juliana of Norwich, English, fourteenth century)

III. THE COMPANIONSHIP: SOME MEANS FOR GAINING IT

1. By fidelity, like his
2. By fortitude, like his

3. By humility and patience, like his: or should I work for a remedy?

PRAYER: offering

1. Those painful "nails" which are created by my special circumstances
2. My desire to share them effectively with you
3. My reliance on your creative ingenuity and love

CONCLUSIONS

PREPARATION

Opening Prayer
Reading: Luke 23:33 (use a crucifix if you have one)
The issues: Love, union with him

MEDITATION

I. THE FIGURE ON THE CROSS

1. The weight: the pain of it
2. The helplessness: sweat, dust, flies
3. The isolation

II. "WERE YOU THERE WHEN THEY CRUCIFIED MY LORD?" MY PRESENCE

1. The figure: so familiar, yet so shocking
2. Wanting to look and yet not to look
3. The pain in watching another's pain: mine, his Father's

III. "LOVE ONE ANOTHER AS I HAVE LOVED YOU" (John 15:12)

1. "Christ's whole body groans in pain ... and each of us is a part of his cry in that whole body. You cried out in your own day, and your day has passed away; another succeeded you, and cried out in his day. You here, he there, and another there. The body of Christ cries out all the day long, one member replacing the other whose cry has died away. Therefore there is only one man

111

who reaches unto the end of time, and those who cry out are always Christ's members." (Augustine)

2. The world's need, my need
3. The response

PRAYER

1. Love
2. Silence
3. Self-offering

CONCLUSIONS

26. Thursday: *The Inscription*

PREPARATION

Opening Prayer
Reading: John 19:19–22
The issue: recognition, allegiance, self-offering

MEDITATION

I. THE WRITING

1. In Latin, Greek and Hebrew: for everyone to read
2. "Jesus of Nazareth"—the country bumpkin
3. "The King of the Jews!"—the irony; yet the truth

II. THE LAMB IS LORD OF LORDS AND KING OF KINGS (Revelation 17:14)

1. "My kingship is not of this world" (John 18:36)
2. "The kingdom is within you" (Luke 17:21)
3. "I, when I am lifted up from the earth, will draw all men to myself" (John 12:32)

III. THE LAMB IN THE MIDST OF HIS THRONE (Revelation 7:17)

1. King of grief, and pain, and rejection
2. The Lord seeks hearts filled with love for God and their neighbor. This is the throne on which he loves to sit and on which he will appear in the fulness of his heavenly glory. (St. Seraphim of Sarov, Russian, nineteenth century)

3. The Beloved is of that nature, that He will admit of no rival, but will have thy heart alone, and sit on His own throne as King (Thomas a Kempis, Dutch, fourteenth century).

PRAYER

1. Thine is the kingdom, the power, the glory!
2. Thy kingdom come, using me

CONCLUSIONS

27. Friday: *The Thieves*

PREPARATION

Opening Prayer
Reading: Mark 15:27, 32b
The issue: recognition: humility, leading to knowledge of ourselves and of him

MEDITATION

I. THE COMPANIONS

1. Two thieves, or brigands, or guerrillas
2. One on either side, our Lord between them
3. Also reviling him: his aloneness

II. NUMBERED WITH THE TRANSGRESSORS (Isaiah 53)

1. "I came, not to call the righteous, but sinners" (Matthew 9:13)
2. Jesus' usual choice of companions: publicans and sinners
3. His choice of me

III. THE COMPANIONSHIP: THE FUTURE

He cometh down to us in the lowest part of our need. For he hath no despite of that He made, nor hath He no disdaine to serve us at the simplest office that to our body longeth in kind, for love of the soul that he made to His own likeness. (Juliana of Norwich)

PRAYER: two petitions:

1. The words of St. Augustine: Let me know Thee, O Thou who knowest me; Let me know Thee as I am known.
2. The words of Huub Oosterhuis, a Dutch contemporary:

   > May your name
   > 'I will be there'
   > direct us to peace

CONCLUSIONS

PREPARATION

Opening Prayer
Reading: Matthew 27:39–44
The issue: trusting inner truth despite surface evidence

MEDITATION

I. SEEING THOSE HE HAD TRIED TO SERVE

1. The ordinary people: those who passed by
2. The chief priests, with the scribes and elders: the leaders of Israel
3. And the thieves on each side: his fellow-sufferers

II. BUT WHAT WAS THE REAL TRUTH?

1. The truth in their crimes: "If you are the Son of God . . ." "He saved others, but . . ." "He is the King of Israel . . ." "Let God deliver him, if He desires him!"
2. The Messiah of prophecy: They pierce my hands and my feet; I can count all my bones; they stare and gloat over me (Psalm 22:16, 17)
3. The Suffering Servant: We esteemed him stricken, smitten by God and afflicted. But he was wounded for our transgressions, and by his stripes we are healed (Isaiah 53:4–5)

III. THE RESPONSE (1 Corinthians 1:22–24)

1. Christ crucified: a stumbling block to the Jews (because they still demand tangible signs of God's power)
2. Folly to the Gentiles (because they still rely on human cleverness)
3. But to those who are called, both Jews and Gentiles: the power of God and the wisdom of God

PRAYER: expressing the basic choice
for faith and trust

In the words of Dostoevsky (Russian novelist, nineteenth century)

1. Stavrogin and Shatov in *The Possessed:* "Do you believe in God, yourself?" ... Shatov looked passionately and defiantly on Stavrogin ... "I haven't told you that I don't believe!"
2. Ivan in *The Brothers Karamazov:* "I must have justice ... I want to be there when everyone suddenly understands what it has all been for!"

CONCLUSIONS

29. Monday: *"Father, Forgive"*

PREPARATION

Opening Prayer
Reading: Luke 23:34
The issue: love, self-forgetfulness, like his

MEDITATION

I. THE APPEAL

1. "Father"—the appeal to affection
2. "Forgive them"—Jesus had already forgiven them himself
3. "They know not what they do"—the consequences to them

II. HIS WAY WITH ENEMIES

1. "Love your enemies; pray for them that persecute you; so that you may be sons of your Father who is in Heaven." (Matthew 5:44–45)
2. "Greatly daring, I would venture this interpretation: if you do not forgive those who have wronged you then your heavenly Father will not be able to forgive you, for you will never be able to recognize forgiveness so long as you have not forgiven those others . . . The nearer one is to the Divine the more one is able to love one's enemies, and I myself am far from it, though I wish to be nearer." (Alan Paton)

III. OUR WAY OF IMITATION

"Good Friday came (in the death camp on the River Kwai). In my contemplation I recognized that it was no easy thing to call that figure on the cross 'Lord.' I heard his words: 'Father, forgive them, for they know not what they do.' This he had said for his enemies. But what was I to say for mine? I could not say what he had said, for he was innocent whereas I was not. Humbly I had to ask, 'Forgive me *and* mine enemies, for we do not know what we do.'

"(After victory) the incoming liberators were so infuriated by what they saw that they wanted to shoot the Japanese guards on the spot. Only the intervention of the victims prevented them. Captors were spared by their captives. 'Not an eye for an eye, a limb for a limb this time,' said these exhausted but forgiving men" (Ernest Gordon, Scottish, *Through the Valley of the Kwai,* 1940's)

PRAYER: petition

1.   Father—our Father
2.   Forgive us *and* our enemies
3.   We do not know what we do

CONCLUSIONS

30. Tuesday: *"Today You Shall Be with Me"*

PREPARATION

Opening Prayer
Reading: Luke 23:39–43
The Issue: why did one thief change? humility, trust

MEDITATION

I. THE CONVERSION

1. "Do you not fear God?"
2. "We, too, are condemned to death"
3. "Justly condemned, because of our deeds"
4. "This man has done nothing wrong"
5. "Jesus, remember me"

II. THE FEAR OF GOD IS THE BEGINNING OF WISDOM (Psalm 111:10)

1. The "fear of God"—here, appreciation of God's just demands
2. Knowledge of ourselves; of him
3. "Leave and give yourself to be helped by the mercy of God. And thus, be your state what it will, you will always have the full benefit of this short and sure way of resigning up yourself to God." (William Law, English, eighteenth century)

III. THE REWARD

1. "In Paradise"
2. "Today"
3. "With me"

PRAYER

1. Lord, we too are condemned to death
2. And, indeed, justly
3. Jesus, remember us

CONCLUSIONS

PREPARATION

Opening Prayer
Reading: John 19:25–27
The issue: loving God by loving others

MEDITATION

I. THE LITTLE GROUP

1. The middle-aged woman
2. The young man whom Jesus loved
3. The son himself: the cause of their agony

II. THE REQUEST

1. "Woman"—a term of respect
2. "Behold your son"—someone for her to love and care for
3. "Behold your mother"—a new son to love and care for her

III. THEIR FUTURE LIFE TOGETHER

1. The mutual love, and grief, and support
2. The mutual joy: Easter, Pentecost
3. "I have always thought that the best way to love God was to love many things" (Vincent Van Gogh, Dutch artist, 1880's)

PRAYER: petition

1. To become sensitive to you and to others
2. To become more vulnerable to my own
3. To become more available

CONCLUSIONS

32. Thursday: *"Why Hast Thou Deserted Me?"*

PREPARATION

Opening Prayer
Reading: Mark 15:33–36
The issue: union with Christ in darkness: trust

MEDITATION

I. THE LOUD CRY

1. "God, my God"
2. "Thou hast deserted me"
3. "Why?"

II. THE CHOICE OF THE QUOTATION (Psalm 22:1)

1. Triumphant: remembering a Psalm about the Messiah
2. Agonized: remembering a Psalm of suffering and darkness

III. THE TERROR OF DEEP DARKNESS (Job 23:16–17)

1. Job: "He has torn me in his wrath, and hated me: he has gnashed his teeth at me: God has given me up to the ungodly, and cast me into the hands of the wicked . . . He crushes me in a tempest, and multiplies my wounds without a cause" (Job 16:9; 9:17)
2. Jeremiah: "O God, Thou has deceived me, and I was deceived" (Jeremiah 20:7)

124

3. Abraham Lincoln, 1841: "I am now the most miserable man living. If what I feel were equally distributed to the whole human family, there would not be one cheerful face left."

PRAYER: to the God who has known it himself (Psalm 23:1, 4)

1. The Lord is my shepherd; I shall not be in want
2. Though I walk through the valley of the shadow of death, I shall fear no evil
3. For you are with me

CONCLUSIONS

PREPARATION

Opening Prayer
Reading: John 19:28–29
The issue: sharing in his thirst, sharing in his love

MEDITATION

I. THE WORDS

1. The physical meaning of the words
2. The vinegar: meant as refreshment
3. The bitterness of taste: "They gave me gall to eat, and when I was thirsty, they gave me vinegar to drink" (Psalm 69:23, a Messianic Psalm)

II. "MY SOUL IS ATHIRST FOR GOD" (Psalm 42:2): OUR THIRST

1. "Blessed are they who hunger and thirst after righteousness, for they shall be satisfied" (Matthew 5:6)
2. "Whoever drinks out of the water that I shall give him shall never thirst; the water that I shall give him will become in him a spring of water welling up to eternal life" (John 4:14)

III. THE DRINK: GOD'S, MINE

1. "I am the vessel. The draught is God's. And God is the thirsty one." (Dag Hammarskjold)
2. " 'Oh,' the priest said, 'that's another thing altogether—God *is* love. I don't say the heart doesn't feel a taste of it, but what a taste. The smallest glass of love mixed with a pint pot of ditch-water. We wouldn't recognize *that* love. It might even look like hate. It would be enough to scare us—God's love. It set fire to a bush in the desert, didn't it, and smashed open graves and set the dead walking in the dark? Oh, a man like me would run a mile to get away if he felt that love around.' " (Graham Greene, English, *The Power and the Glory*, 1949)

PRAYER

1. Recognition: I am reluctant, etc.
2. Offering: my opportunities
3. Resolve, petition, gratitude, etc.

CONCLUSIONS

PREPARATION

Opening Prayer
Reading: John 19:30
The issue: union with him, perseverance, to the end,
like his

MEDITATION

I. THE WORDS: "IT IS FINISHED"

1. The earthly life is finished
2. The ordeal of his passion is ended
3. The Father's work is completed

II. THE WORK ANTICIPATED

1. To his disciples: "I came to cast fire upon the earth, and would that it were already kindled! I have a baptism to be baptized with, and how I am constrained until it is accomplished" (Luke 12:49–50)
2. To his Father: "I have accomplished the work which Thou gavest me to do" (John 17:4)
3. "Now is the Son of Man glorified, and in him God is glorified" (John 13:31)

III. THE WORK COMPLETED

1. At the Creation: "God saw everything that he had made, and behold, it was very good" (Genesis 1:31)
2. At the Redemption: "God so loved the world that

he gave his only Son, that whoever believes in him should not perish, but have eternal life" (John 3:16)

3. At my own death:

"Depart, O Christian soul, out of this world;
In the name of God the Father Almighty who
created you;
In the name of Jesus Christ who redeemed you;
In the name of the Holy Spirit who sanctifies
you.
May your rest be this day in peace,
and your dwelling place in the Paradise of God."

PRAYER: "Anima Christi" (medieval German or English prayer on the passion)

1. Soul of Christ, sanctify me
2. Body of Christ, save me
3. Water from the side of Christ, wash me
4. Blood of Christ, refresh me
5. Passion of Christ, strengthen me

CONCLUSIONS

35. Monday: *"Father, Into Thy Hands"*

PREPARATION

Opening Prayer
Reading: Luke 23:46
The issue: faith, trust, commitment like his

MEDITATION

I. THE COMMENDATION

1. "Father"—the affectionate reliance
2. "My spirit"—the human and divine
3. "I commit into Thy hands"—the total surrender

II. THE FATHER AND HIS SON

1. "Thou art my well-beloved Son; with thee I am well pleased" (Luke 3:22)
2. "My Father and your Father, my God and your God" (John 20:17)

III. INTO HIS HANDS

1. For life:
   "Behold the handmaid of the Lord; let it be done to me according to your word" (Luke 1:38: Mary at the annunciation)

   "I shall be what the Lord wants me to be . . . O loving Jesus, I kneel at Your feet, sure as I am that You will bring about what I cannot even imagine" (Pope John XXIII at the age of 22, *Journal of a Soul,* 1903)

2. For death:

> "Father, if Thou art willing, remove this cup from me: nevertheless, not my will, but thine, be done" (Luke 22:42: Jesus at Gethsemane)

> "I notice in my body the beginnings of some trouble that must be natural for an old man. I bear it with resignation, even if it is sometimes rather tiresome and also makes me afraid it will get worse. It is not too pleasant to think too much about this; but once more, I feel prepared for anything . . . So let us continue moving slowly towards Jesus, as if He stood waiting with outstretched arms" (*Journal of a Soul,* 1961; Pope John is referring to the diagnosis of his terminal illness, cancer)

PRAYER: offering

1. "Father"—and all that he means
2. My spirit, my life, my death
3. I commit into thy hands

CONCLUSIONS

PREPARATION

Opening Prayer
Reading: John 19:30–37
The issue: traditionally the scene where we offer our
lives to him, unconditionally

MEDITATION

I. THE DEATH

1. "He gave up his spirit"
2. A Roman soldier, in the course of his duty, pierced his side with a spear
3. Intended to prove that Jesus was unquestionably dead

II. CHRIST OUR PASSOVER IS SACRIFICED FOR US (1 Corinthians 5:7)

1. "Unless a grain of wheat falls into the earth and dies, it remains alone; but if it dies, it bears much fruit" (John 12:24)
2. "The Old Man of the Earth stooped over the floor of the cave, raised a huge stone, and left it leaning. It disclosed a great hole that went plumb down. 'That is the way', he said. 'But there are no stairs.' 'You must throw yourself in. There is no other way.' " (George MacDonald, *The Golden Key*)

III. THE GIFT

1. "If we die with him, we shall also live with him;
"If we endure, we shall also reign with him;

"If we deny him, he also will deny us;
"If we are faithless, he remains faithful—
　　"For he cannot deny himself" (ancient Christian poem, 2 Timothy 2:11–12)
2.　"This is our Lord's will, that our prayer and our trust be alike large" (Juliana of Norwich)

PRAYER: can I give any less?

1.　The past we share: his death for me, what I have done, etc.
2.　The future we shall share: my death to self, my life in him, etc.

CONCLUSIONS

PREPARATION

Opening Prayer
Reading: Matthew 27:45, 51–54
The issue: recognition, adoration, witness to him in
everything

MEDITATION

I. THE AFTERMATH

1. The torn curtain: the barrier to the Holy of Holies is removed
2. The eclipse, the earthquake: all of creation responds
3. The opened tombs: this act affects even the dead
4. "Truly, this was the Son of God!"

II. GOD IS AT WORK: WITNESSES FROM THE GROUND AND FROM THE SKIES

1. Love and dread are brethren. The dread that makest us hastily to flee from all that is not good, and fall into our Lord's breast, as the child into the mother's arms . . . that dread it is kind and gracious and good and true. (Juliana of Norwich)
2. "See I am God: See I am in all things: See I never left My hands of My works, nor never shall without end: See I lead all thing to the end I ordain it to, from without beginning, by the same might, wisdom and love that I made it with.

How should anything be amiss?" (Juliana of
Norwich)

III. CHRIST IN YOU, THE HOPE OF GLORY (Colossians 1:27)

1. Lord of my whole universe, all of it: the atomic particle to the cosmos
2. Lord of my whole worship: my own identity, values, meaning
3. Lord of life and death: what is eternal life? When do I enter into it?

PRAYER: a prayer of St. Francis of Assisi

1. Almighty, most holy, high and supreme God, highest good, wholly good, who alone art good:
2. To thee we render all praise, all glory, all thanks, all honor, all blessing
3. And to thee we ascribe all good for ever and ever

CONCLUSIONS

38. Maundy Thursday: *The Deposition from the Cross*

PREPARATION

Opening Prayer
Reading: Mark 15:42–45
The issue: Holy Communion: to him, to his Church, to me

MEDITATION

I. "WITH A RICH MAN IN HIS DEATH" (Isaiah 53:9)

1. Joseph of Arimathea, "also looking for the kingdom of God"
2. He took courage, and went to Pilate, and asked for the body
3. Pilate gave it to Joseph: now useless to anyone

II. "THIS IS MY BODY, WHICH IS GIVEN FOR YOU" (1 Corinthians 11:24)

1. The Body of Christ: our fellowship
2. The Body of Christ: the bread which gives us strength
3. The Body of Christ: made up of its members: I in him, and he in me, and they in me
4. The cost in love

III. "AS OFTEN AS YOU EAT THIS BREAD AND DRINK THE CUP, YOU PROCLAIM THE LORD'S DEATH UNTIL HE COMES" (1 Corinthians 11:26)

1. "The Body of Christ, the Bread of Heaven"
2. "How shall I repay the Lord for all the good things he has done for me?
3. "I will lift up the cup of salvation and call on the name of the Lord." (Psalm 116:10–11)

PRAYER: praise, offering, desire

1. "Lord, give us this bread always" (John 6:34)
2. "Lay me down like a stone, O God, and raise me up like a loaf" (Tolstoy, *War and Peace:* prayer of Platón Karatáev)

CONCLUSIONS

PREPARATION

Opening Prayer
Reading: John 19:39–42
The issue: our welcome for Jesus Christ, like
Joseph's

MEDITATION

I. THE SCENE

1. Carefully and thoroughly wrapped
2. With costly spices, to postpone decay as long as possible
3. Laid in the unused tomb: meant as a final honor

II. "THAT WE MIGHT DIE TO SIN AND LIVE TO RIGHTEOUSNESS" (1 Peter 2:24): THREE VIEWS

1. "We were buried with Him by baptism into death, so that, as Christ was raised from the dead by the glory of the Father, we too might walk in newness of life" (Romans 6:4)
2. "It is not like a child that I believe in God and confess Him. My Hosanna has come forth from the crucible of doubt" (Feodor Dostoevsky, Russian, *Diary,* 1881)
3. "The resurrection is the calling forth of the Spirit inside me—God calling me forth from the grave of my own being." (Jean Vanier)

III. BURIED ALIVE?

1.   His life, shared with ours?
2.   His commandments to love God and neighbor?
3.   His constant appeals?

PRAYER: The advice of St. Basil, Asia Minor, fourth century:

"Begin to say humbly, 'I am a sinner; I give you thanks, Lord, for having patiently borne with me' . . . Then ask for the reign of God and then for respectable things, and do not cease until you have attained them."

CONCLUSIONS

40. Saturday before Easter: *The Day of Waiting*

PREPARATION

Opening Prayer
Reading: Matthew 27:62–66
The issue: sharing his trust, anticipation, joy

MEDITATION

I. THE END OF HIS WORK ON EARTH

1. A threat, even when dead and buried!
2. Secured against fraud, as professionally as possible
3. "I have glorified thee on earth, having accomplished the work which thou gavest me to do; and now, Father, glorify thou me in thy own presence with the glory which I had with thee before the world was made." (John 17:5)

II. HIS WORK IN US: JESUS SPEAKS

1. "You will have sorrow now
2. "But I will see you again
3. "And your hearts will rejoice
4. "And no one will take your joy from you." (John 16:22)

III. "I CALLED TO THE LORD FROM MY NARROW PRISON" (Viktor Frankl)

As far as we can see, our hands are empty: we resemble the grass growing on the summit of some steep ravine where no other vegetation can live. Be-

low in the valleys rise the mighty oaks, whose roots are buried in the rich soil. We, however, are weak and tiny plants, hardly visible, unprotected from wind and storm, almost withered away, almost without roots. But yet, whilst the topmost branches of the oak trees lie still wrapt in darkness, the light catches us in the early morning, and we see what none other can see: we see the sun of the coming day, and we cry out our welcome—"Come, Lord!" (Karl Barth)

PRAYER

1. You are rising from the dead, You are ascending to heaven! You are beyond suffering, You will never suffer again. You are happy, and will be

happy forever . . . My God, if I really love You, how happy I must be! Whatever happens, I am happy because of Your blessedness! (Charles de Foucauld, French explorer and hermit, twentieth century)

2. All shall be well, all shall be well; all manner of thing shall be well. (Juliana of Norwich)

CONCLUSIONS

Notes

I. Beginnings

1. William Wordsworth: "Ode. Intimations of Immortality from Recollections of Early Childhood," *The Complete Poetical Works of Wordsworth* (Boston: Houghton Mifflin Co., n.d.), p. 355.

2. Genesis 12:1.

3. Matthew Fox has defined prayer as "a radical response to life" in his *On Becoming a Musical, Mystical Bear* (New York: Paulist Press, 1976), pp. 49–76. Among many helpful insights he offers one which is less helpful: that "to respond to life is to respond to Providence" (p. 63), citing Tolstoy that "God *is* life." This book considers prayer from a perspective closer to the main Judaeo-Christian tradition: that God is a personal, not an impersonal, God, with passionate likes and dislikes. To be sure, God is Lord over all of life, but this is not the same thing as saying that God *is* all of life. "Life" is made up of various things, some good and some radically evil, some of which God in some sense created, some of which are problematical. What do we mean by "Creator" or "Providence"? In what sense, for example, did God create the

earthquake, the cancer cell, or the warlike side of human nature? When we love God, do we also love these?

No, Fr. Fox's term "Life" is too global, no matter what he says; better, it is too impersonal to stand in for the Christian God who is shown to be Love, not life (1 John 4:8). This shift of identity will make quite a difference to the shape and flavor and content of prayer, as we pray from the midst of our own life to a God who dwells within life and beyond it as healing and judgment.

4. Clement of Alexandria: "Stromateis No. VII," *Clemantis Alexandrini Opera,* Vol. 9 of *Patrologiae Graecae,* ed. J.-P. Migne (Turnholt, Brepols, n.d.), book 7, col. 451.

5. Augustine, "Confessions." *Aurelii Augustini Opera,* Vol. 32 of *Patrologiae Latinae,* ed. J.-P. Migne (Turnholt: Brepols, n.d.), book 7, col. 742. All of us begin with a very immature, tentative idea of who God is or what to expect. After all, God's very name—"Yahweh"—means in some sense a boundless creativity, Being without end. Just as God can never be burned out, like a bush in the desert, so God can never be fully comprehended: "I will be whatever I will be" (Exodus 4:14).

6. Mark 9:24.

II. Outer to Inner

1. Hans Küng: *Does God Exist?* (Garden City: Doubleday, 1980), pp. 445–451.

2. Andrew M. Greeley: *Life for a Wanderer* (Garden City: Doubleday, 1971), p. 81.

3. Viktor E. Frankl: *Man's Search for Meaning* (New York: Simon & Schuster, 1969), pp. 63–64, 142.

4. Martin Luther: "Deutsch Catechismus 1529," Vol. 30, Part I of *Werke,* ed. Hermann Bölaus, Weimar, 1910 (rpt. Graz: Akademischen Druck, 1964), pp. 132–133. Many since Luther have written on the source, nature and function of these deepest allegiances. Further readings might include Paul Tillich, on the nature of our

"God" or "idols" as preliminary or ultimate concerns, in Vol. I of *Systematic Theology* (Chicago: University of Chicago Press, 1951), pp. 11–13, or Regis Duffy on dialogue between faith and praxis in *Real Presence* (San Francisco: Harper & Row, 1982), pp. 17–19.

5. Thomas Wolfe: *Look Homeward, Angel* (New York: Charles Scribner's Sons, 1952), pp. 376–377.

6. Luther, p. 133.

7. For example, in Romans 12:1–2.

8. It also has to be meditation on a thinking level, at least at the beginning. Popular, more holistic ways abound with which to encounter oneself; it is much more immediately rewarding, for instance, to soak in hot tubs or take shoes off and run barefoot in the wet grass, and much easier to do. But we now need a place for hard, systematic thinking: left and right brain thinking, to be sure, but a focused quality of attention by which our allegiances, and their surface symptoms, can be encountered and then named.

III. My Reality and God's Reality

1. Langdon Gilkey: *Naming the Whirlwind: The Renewal of God-Language* (Indianapolis: The Bobbs-Merrill Company, Inc., 1969), pp. 416–420.

2. Arthur Miller: *Death of a Salesman* (New York: The Viking Press, 1949), p. 133. Notice, too, that we have symbols for these "weekday beliefs." Television advertisements are powerful precisely because they manipulate our everyday, American symbols so well.

3. This chapter has touched on some of the problems related to using the words, or symbol systems, of Christianity. The dynamics of reexperiencing the basic Christian experience itself will be discussed more fully in Chapter IV.

4. I Corinthians 10:4.

IV. Our Histories and God's History

1. Rudolph Otto: *The Experience of the Holy,* trans. John W. Harvey (Oxford: Humphrey Milford, 1924), pp. 8–11, 39.

2. In writing this chapter I have found especially helpful the insights of Paul J. Achtemeier, *The Inspiration of Scripture* (Philadelphia: Westminster Press, 1980), Chapter 6; Volney P. Gay: "Public rituals versus private treatment: psychodynamics of prayer," *Journal of Religion and Health,* Vol. 17, No. 4 (1978), pp. 244–260; and Paul Ricoeur, *Essays on Biblical Interpretation* (Philadelphia: Fortress Press, 1980), pp. 98–103.

3. 1 John 1:1.

4. Thomas Merton: *The New Man* (New York: The New American Library [Mentor-Omega Books], 1961), p. 99.

5. Augustine: "Tractatus in Johannis Evangelium No. 22," *Aurelii Augustini Opera,* Vol. 36 of *Corpus Christianorum,* ed. Radbodus Willems (Turnholt: Brepols, 1954), p. 216.

6. Everyone who takes the incarnation seriously understands its implications. God became *this* carpenter's baby, in *that* small town, during *that unique* period of history. God evidently made—and still makes—use of specific situations precisely because God seeks to enter specific worlds. They are redeemed from their sinfulness while their uniqueness is preserved: *that* first century outlook, *this* post-industrial culture.

7. Ricoeur, p. 103.

8. Galatians 2:20.

V. Object and Subject

1. A standard work on Benedictine Prayer is Dom Eugene Boylan's *Difficulties in Mental Prayer* (Westminster, Maryland: Newman Press, 1965).

2. Christian writers generally use the name "Jesus" or "Jesus of Nazareth" to refer to the historical, first-century man, and the name "Christ" or "Messiah" to refer to the resurrected person of faith. Notice what this usage implies: that Jesus the man, dead around 30 A.D., is still available for us, living in Jesus the Christ. The Christian doctrines of resurrection and ascension are promising specific advantages here, teaching as they do that the human limitations of one man in one time and place no longer apply to the historical man Jesus. His activity, they teach, is now universally extended, including every generation and every individual within it. This belief is part of what may need to be tested out: that we can expect to find him waiting for us, too, in many places and in many ways.

As a believing Christian I will use "Jesus" for the historical man and "Christ" for the resurrected and ascended and living person who has promised that he will work on us in our generation, too.

3. Blaise Pascal: *Pensées,* No. 553 (Paris: Garnier Frères, n.d.), p. 212.

VI. Feeding

1. Matthew 6:6.

2. *The Book of Common Prayer* (Kingsport: Kingsport Press, 1977).

3. What gender is God? This question seems rather like the question "What race is God?" or "What language does God speak?" I have chosen to use the conventional, masculine form because it is the one most Christians start with. But of course we know that to call God "male" or "female" is to miss the breadth of God. Through Scripture and Christian spirituality we know it: that God has disclosed the divine life under the forms of father, and mother, and all ages, and every nation.

If all goes well, then, meditation ought to put us more

and more at the disposal of God, who can then freely come with whatever form the meditator needs. For example, God might well choose to meet us as the one "in whom we live, and move, and have our being" (Acts 17:28), that is, with the female face of God. At that moment words like "she," "her," "Mother," are the appropriate response. Or meditators of either sex might want to begin using feminine forms as their expression of obedience: God is in charge, not we ourselves. We hope to grow larger, to meet a larger God than the one we know; and we will discover—in God's good time—what form, or forms, God wills to take for us.

4. During the whole period of prayer and meditation you will be making an attempt to "suspend disbelief" in the sense advocated in Chapter I. God, of course, is just as aware as you are that your belief is not adequate; he is also aware that nobody's is. Most people find the best attitude is one of openness and hopefulness, not of forcing an attitude of certainty that is out of character. "Lord, I believe: help my unbelief!"

5. Psalm 19:14, *The Book of Common Prayer,* p. 607.

6. 1 Kings 17:1.

7. "The Holy Eucharist: Rite Two," *The Book of Common Prayer,* p. 355.

8. Paul Tillich: *The Shaking of the Foundations* (New York: Charles Scribner's Sons, 1948), p. 162.

9. Luke 18:41.

10. C.S. Lewis: *George MacDonald: An Anthology* (New York: The Macmillan Co., 1947), no. 43.

11. François de Sales: *Introduction to the Devout Life* (Garden City: Doubleday and Co., Inc., 1955, p. 407.

12. Lewis, 1947, no. 167.

Notes for Meditations
(by number)

1. Aurelius Augustinus, "Enarrationes in Psalmos No. 103," *Aurelii Augustini Opera,* Vol. 37 of *Patrologiae Latinae,* ed. J.-P. Migne (Turnholt: Brepols, n.d.), column 1389.

François Fénelon, *Spiritual Letters to Women,* trans. the author of Spiritual Letters of St. Francis de Sales (New Canaan: Keats Publishing Co., 1980), p. 32.

Pascal, No. 553, p. 210.

2. Fénelon, *Letters,* trans. John McEwen (London: Harville Press, 1964), p. 206.

Thomas Merton, *Conjectures of a Guilty Bystander* (London: Sheldon Press, 1977), p. 139.

3. Simone de Beauvoir, *Memoirs of a Dutiful Daughter,* trans. James Kirkup (Cleveland: The World Publishing Company, 1959), pp. 144–145.

Dag Hammarskjold, *Markings,* trans. Leif Sjoberg and W. H. Auden (London: Faber and Faber, 1964), p. 58.

4. Iulia de Beausobre, *Creative Suffering* (Westminster: Dacre Press, 1940), pp. 42–43.

5. John Chrysostom, "In Matthaeum Homilia No. 33", *Johanni Chrysostomi Opera,* Vol. 57 of *Patrologiae Graecae,* ed. J.-P. Migne (Paris: Petit-Montrouge, 1862), column 389.

Martin Luther King, Jr., "Suffering and Faith," *Christian Century,* Vol. 77 (1960), p. 510.

6. Karl Barth, *The Epistle to the Romans,* trans. Edwyn C. Hoskyns (Oxford: University Press, 1968), p. 35.

Augustine, *Confessions,* VII, 21.

Thomas Merton, *Thoughts in Solitude* (New York: Farrar, Strauss & Cudahy, 1958), p. 81.

7. Jane Austen, *Pride and Prejudice,* Vol. 2 of *The Novels of Jane Austen,* ed. R.W. Chapman (Oxford: Clarendon Press, 1946), p. 136.

Albert Speer, *Inside the Third Reich,* trans. Richard

and Clara Winston (New York: The Macmillan Co., 1970), pp. 112, 115.

8. Joachim Fest, *Hitler,* trans. Richard and Clara Winston (New York: Harcourt Brace Jovanovich Inc., 1974), p.146.

James H. Cone, *God of the Oppressed* (New York: Seabury Press [Crossroad], 1975), p. 100.

Catherine of Siena, *The Prayers of Catherine of Siena,* ed. Suzanne Noffke (New York: Paulist Press, 1983), pp. 152, 78.

9. William Law, *Selected Mystical Writings,* ed. Stephen Hobhouse (New York: Harper and Brothers Publishers, 1948), p. 213.

10. Frankl, p. 142.

King, "Speech for the March on Washington," quoted in David Levering Lewis, *King, a Biography* (Urbana: Univ. of Illinois Press, 1979), p. 229.

11. Desmond Mpilo Tutu, *Hope and Suffering* (Grand Rapids: William B. Eerdmans Publishing Company, 1984), p. 170.

Barth, p. 35.

Alan Paton, *Instrument of Thy Peace* (New York: The Seabury Press, 1968), p. 63.

Ignatius of Loyola, *Spiritual Exercises of St. Ignatius of Loyola,* trans. Lewis Delmage (New York: Joseph F. Wagner, Inc., 1968), p. 56.

12. Eberhard Bethge, *Dietrich Bonhoffer,* trans. Erik Mosbacher *et al.,* ed. Edwin Robertson (London: Collins, 1970), p. 734.

14. Jean-Pierre de Caussade, S.J., *Abandon à la Providence divine* (Paris: Périsse Frères, 1874), p. 21.

15. Simone Weil, "The love of God and affliction," *Waiting on God,* trans. Emma Craufurd (Glasgow: Collins [Fontana Books], 1959), p. 93.

Jean Vanier, *Be Not Afraid* (Toronto: Griffin House, 1975), pp. 52–53.

16. Albert Camus, *The Plague,* trans. Stuart Gilbert

(New York: Random House [The Modern Library], 1948 (Copyright by Stuart Gilbert), p. 194.

Catherine of Siena, p. 103.

17. David Riesman, *The Lonely Crowd* (Garden City: Doubleday & Co. [Anchor Books], 1953), p. 294.

Louis L. Snyder, *Hitler and Nazism* (New York: Franklin Watts Inc., 1961), p. 71.

18. Thomas Merton, *Geography of Holiness,* ed. Deba Prasad Patnaik (New York: The Pilgrim Press, 1980), p. 21.

19. Dietrich Bonhoffer, *The Cost of Discipleship,* trans. R. H. Fuller (New York: The Macmillan Co., 1958), p. 120.

Fénelon, *Meditations and Devotions,* trans. Elizabeth C. Fenn (Morehouse-Gorham Co., 1952), pp. 96, 141.

Book of Common Prayer, p. 220.

20. C. S. Lewis, *George MacDonald: An Anthology* (Garden City: Doubleday & Co., 1955), Nos. 136, 233.

de Caussade, p. 142.

Georges Bernanos, *The Diary of a Country Priest,* trans. Pamela Morris (Garden City: Doubleday & Co., Inc. [Image Books], 1959), p. 217.

21. Teresa of Avila, *The Way of Perfection,* ed. F. Benedict Zimmerman (London: Thomas Baker, 1935), pp. 151–152.

Camus, p. 243.

22. Hammarskjold, p. 65.

Bonhoeffer, pp. 54–55

Vanier, p. 48.

Fénelon, *Meditations and Devotions,* pp. 72–73.

23. John XXIII, *Journal of a Soul,* trans. Dorothy White (New York: McGraw Hill Book Co. [Signet], 1965), p. 193.

Hammarskjold, p. 169.

24. *Juliana of Norwich,* ed. Franklin Chambers (New York: Harper & Bros., n.d.), p. 113.

25. Augustine, No. 85, column 1085.

26. Serafim of Sarov quoted in Paul Evdokimov, *The Struggle with God,* trans. Sr. Gertrude, S.P. (Glen Rock: Paulist Press, 1966), p. 116.

Thomas a Kempis, *The Imitation of Christ,* trans. Ronald Knox and Michael Oakley (New York: Sheed & Ward, n.d.), p. 69 (Translation copyright Evelyn Waugh and Michael Oakley, 1959).

27. Juliana of Norwich, p. 13.

Augustine, "Confessionum," *Aurelii Augustini Opera,* Vol. 32 of *Patrologiae Latinae,* ed. J-P. Migne (Turnholt: Brepols, n.d.), col. 779.

Huub Oosterhuis, *Times of Life* (New York: Paulist Press, 1979), p. 15.

28. Feodor Dostoevsky, *The Possessed,* trans. Constance Garnett (New York: The Modern Library, 1936), p. 256.

Dostoevsky, *The Brothers Karamazov,* trans. Constance Garnett (New York: The Modern Library, n.d.), p. 253.

29. Paton, p. 106.

Ernest Gordon, *Through the Valley of the Kwai* (New York: Harper & Row [Jubilee Edition], 1975), pp. 214, 230.

30. William Law, *A Serious Call to a Devout and Holy Life* (New York: Paulist Press, 1978), p. 492.

31. "Vincent Van Gogh," *The Protestant Mystics,* ed. Anne Fremantle (New York: The New American Library [Mentor Books], 1964) (Copyright W.H. Auden and Anne Fremantle).

32. Albert J. Beveridge, *Abraham Lincoln* (Boston: Houghton Mifflin Co., 1928), I, 316.

33. Hammarskjold, p. 88.

Graham Greene: *The Power and the Glory* (New York: Viking Press [Bantam Books], 1967), p. 189.

34. *Book of Common Prayer,* p. 464.

35. John XXIII, pp. 207, 210.

36. C. S. Lewis, No. 39.

Juliana of Norwich, p. 127.

37. Juliana of Norwich, p. 28.

38. Leo Tolstoy, *War and Peace,* trans. Louis and Aylmer Maude (New York: Simon and Schuster, 1942), p. 1076.

39. Feodor Dostoevsky, "Note Book XI," trans. Arlene Boyer, Vol III of *The Unpublished Dostoevsky,* ed. Carl R. Proffer (Ann Arbor: Ardis, 1976), p. 175.

Vanier, p. 113.

St. Basil quoted in Evdokimov, p. 180.

Frankl, p. 142.

40. Barth, p. 150.

A Little Brother of Charles de Foucauld, *Silent Pilgrimage to God,* trans. Jeremy Moiser (London: Darton, Longman and Todd, 1974), p. 36.

Juliana of Norwich, p. 57.

Bibliography

Achtemeier, Paul J. *The Inspiration of Scripture*. Philadelphia: The Westminster Press, 1980.

Augustine. "Confessionum." *Aurelii Augustini Opera*. Vol. 32 of *Patrologiae Latinae*. Ed. J.-P. Migne. Turnholt: Brepols, n.d.

————. "Enarrationes in psalmos." *Aurelii Augustini Opera*. Vol. 37 of *Patrologiae Latinae*. Ed. J.-P. Migne. Turnholt: Brepols, n.d.

————. "Tractatus in Johannis Evangelium No. 22." *Aurelii Augustini Opera*. Vol. 36 of *Corpus Christianorum*. Ed. Radbodus Willems. Turnholt: Brepols, 1954.

Austen, Jane. *Pride and Prejudice*. Vol. 2 of *The Novels of Jane Austen*. Ed. R. W. Chapman. Oxford: Clarendon Press, 1946.

Barth, Karl. *The Epistle to the Romans*. Trans. Edwyn C. Hoskyns. Oxford: University Press, 1968.

Bethge, Eberhard. *Dietrich Bonhoffer*. Trans. Erik Mosbacher *et al.* Ed. Edwin Robertson. London: Collins, 1970.

Bernanos, Georges. *The Diary of a Country Priest*. Trans.

Pamela Morris. Garden City: Doubleday & Co., Inc. (Image Books), 1959.

Beveridge, Albert J. *Abraham Lincoln*. Boston: Houghton Mifflin Co., 1928.

Bonhoffer, Dietrich. *The Cost of Discipleship*. Trans. R. H. Fuller. New York: The Macmillan Co., 1958.

The Book of Common Prayer. Kingsport: Kingsport Press, 1977.

Boylan, Dom Eugene. *Difficulties in Mental Prayer*. Westminster, Maryland: Newman Press, 1965.

de Beausobre, Iulia. *Creative Suffering*. Westminster: Dacre Press, 1940.

de Beauvoir, Simone. *Memoirs of a Dutiful Daughter*. Trans. James Kirkup. Cleveland: The World Publishing Company, 1959.

Camus, Albert. *The Plague*. Trans. Stuart Gilbert. New York: Random House (The Modern Library), 1948 (Copyright by Stuart Gilbert).

Catherine of Siena, *The Prayers of Catherine of Siena*. Ed. Suzanne Noffke. New York: Paulist Press, 1983.

de Caussade, Jean-Pierre, S. J. *Abandon à la Providence divine*. Paris: Périsse Frères, 1874.

Chrysostom, John. "In Matthaeum homilia no. 33." *Johanni Chrysostomi Opera*. Vol. 57 of *Patrologiae Graecae*. Ed. J.-P. Migne. Paris: Petit-Moutrouge, 1862.

Clement of Alexandria. "Stromateis No. VII." *Clemantis Alexandrini Opera*. Vol. 9 of *Patrologiae Graecae*. Ed. J.-P. Migne. Turnholt: Brepols, n.d.

Cone, James H. *God of the Oppressed*. New York: Seabury Press (Crossroad), 1975.

Dostoevsky, Feodor. *The Brothers Karamazov*. Trans. Constance Garnett. New York: The Modern Library, n.d.

———. "Note Book XI." Trans. Arlene Boyer. Vol. III of *The Unpublished Dostoevsky*. Ed. Carl R. Proffer. Ann Arbor: Ardis, 1976.

————. *The Possessed.* Trans. Constance Garnett. New York: The Modern Library, 1936.

Duffy, Regis. *Real Presence.* San Francisco: Harper and Row, 1982.

Evdokimov, Paul. *The Struggle with God.* Trans. Sr. Gertrude, S.P. Glen Rock: Paulist Press, 1966.

Fénelon, François. *Letters.* Trans. John McEwen. London: Harville Press, 1964.

————. *Meditations and Devotions.* Trans. Elizabeth C. Fenn. Wilton, Connecticut: Morehouse-Gorham Co., 1952.

————. *Spiritual Letters to Women.* Trans. the author of Spiritual Letters of St. Francis de Sales. New Canaan: Keats Publishing Co., 1980.

Fest, Joachim. *Hitler.* Trans. Richard and Clara Winston. New York: Harcourt Brace Jovanovich Inc., 1974.

Fox, Matthew. *On Becoming a Musical, Mystical Bear.* New York: Paulist Press, 1976.

Frankl, Viktor E. *Man's Search for Meaning.* New York: Simon & Schuster, Inc., 1969.

Gay, Volney P. "Public rituals versus private treatment: psychodynamics of prayer." *Journal of Religion and Health,* Vol. 17, No. 4 (1978).

Gilkey, Langdon. *Naming the Whirlwind: The Renewal of God-Language.* Indianapolis: The Bobbs-Merrill Company, Inc., 1969.

Gordon, Ernest. *Through the Valley of the Kwai.* New York: Harper & Row (Jubilee Edition), 1975.

Greeley, Andrew M. *Life for a Wanderer.* Garden City: Doubleday and Co., 1971.

Greene, Graham. *The Power and the Glory.* New York: Viking Press (Bantam Books), 1967.

Hammarskjold, Dag. *Markings.* Trans. Leif Sjoberg and W. H. Auden. New York: Alfred A. Knopf, 1977.

Ignatius of Loyola. *Spiritual Exercises of St. Ignatius of Loyola.* Trans. Lewis Delmage. New York: Joseph F. Wagner, Inc., 1968.

John XXIII. *Journal of a Soul.* Trans. Dorothy White. New York: McGraw Hill Book Co. (Signet), 1965.

Juliana of Norwich. Ed. Franklin Chambers. New York: Harper & Bros., n.d.

King, Martin Luther, Jr. "Suffering and Faith." *Christian Century,* Vol. 77 (1960).

Küng, Hans. *Does God Exist?* Garden City: Doubleday & Company, Inc., 1980.

Law, William. *Selected Mystical Writings.* Ed. Stephen Hobhouse. New York: Harper and Brothers Publishers, 1948.

———. *A Serious Call to a Devout and Holy Life.* New York: Paulist Press, 1978.

Lewis, David Levering. *King, a Biography.* Urbana: Univ. of Illinois Press, 1979.

Lewis, C. S. *George MacDonald: An Anthology.* Garden City: Doubleday & Co., 1947.

A Little Brother of Charles de Foucauld. *Silent Pilgrimage to God.* Trans. Jeremy Moiser. London: Darton, Longman and Todd, 1974.

Luther, Martin. "Deutsch Catechismus 1529." Vol. 30, Part I of *Werke.* Ed. Hermann Bölaus. Weimar, 1910 (rpt. Graz: Akademischen Druck, 1964).

Merton, Thomas. *Conjectures of a Guilty Bystander.* Garden City: Doubleday & Co., 1966.

———. *Geography of Holiness.* Ed. Deba Prasad Patnaik. New York: The Pilgrim Press, 1980.

———. *The New Man.* New York: The New American Library (Mentor-Omega Books), 1961.

———. *Thoughts in Solitude.* New York: Farrar, Strauss & Cudahy, 1958.

Miller, Arthur. *Death of a Salesman.* New York: The Viking Press, 1949.

Oosterhuis, Huub. *Times of Life.* Trans. N. D. Smith. New York: Paulist Press, 1979.

Otto, Rudolph. *The Experience of the Holy.* Trans. John W. Harvey. Oxford: Humphrey Milford, 1924.

Pascal, Blaise. *Pensées.* Paris: Garnier Frères, n.d.

Paton, Alan. *Instrument of Thy Peace.* New York: The Seabury Press, 1968.

The Protestant Mystics. Ed. Anne Fremantle. New York: New American Library (Mentor Books), 1964 (Copyright W. H. Auden and Anne Fremantle).

Ricoeur, Paul. *Essays on Biblical Interpretation.* Philadelphia: Fortress Press, 1980.

Riesman, David. *The Lonely Crowd.* Garden City: Doubleday & Co. (Anchor Books), 1953.

de Sales, François. *Introduction to the Devout Life.* Garden City: Doubleday & Co. (Image Books), 1955.

Snyder, Louis L. *Hitler and Nazism.* New York: Franklin Watts, Inc., 1961.

Speer, Albert. *Inside the Third Reich.* Trans. Richard and Clara Winston. New York: Harcourt Brace Jovanovich Inc., 1974.

Teresa of Avila. *The Way of Perfection.* Ed. F. Benedict Zimmerman. London: Thomas Baker, 1935.

Tillich, Paul. *The Shaking of the Foundations.* New York: Charles Scribner's Sons, 1948.

————. *Systematic Theology.* Vol. I. Chicago: Univ. of Chicago Press, 1951.

Thomas a Kempis. *The Imitation of Christ.* Trans. Ronald Knox and Michael Oakley. New York: Sheed & Ward, n.d. (Translation copyright Evelyn Waugh and Michael Oakley, 1959).

Tolstoy, Leo. *War and Peace.* Trans. Louise and Aylmer Maude. New York: Simon and Schuster, 1942.

Tutu, Desmond Mpilo. *Hope and Suffering.* Grand Rapids: William B. Eerdmans Publishing Company, 1984.

Vanier, Jean. *Be Not Afraid.* Toronto: Griffin House, 1975.

Weil, Simone. "The love of God and affliction." *Waiting on God.* Trans. Emma Craufurd. Glasgow: Collins (Fontana Books), 1959.

Wolfe, Thomas. *Look Homeward, Angel*. New York: Charles Scribner's Sons, 1952.

Wordsworth, William. "Ode. Intimations of immortality from recollections of early childhood." *The Complete Poetical Works of Wordsworth*. Boston: Houghton Mifflin Co. (Riverside Edition), n.d.

EDDIE BETTS

THE BOY FROM BOOMERANG CRESCENT

EDDIE BETTS

THE BOY FROM BOOMERANG CRESCENT

RESEARCH & INTERVIEWS
Ali Clarke

CULTURAL EDIT
Jack Latimore

**SIMON &
SCHUSTER**

London · New York · Sydney · Toronto · New Delhi

THE BOY FROM BOOMERANG CRESCENT
First published in Australia in 2022 by
Simon & Schuster (Australia) Pty Limited
Suite 19A, Level 1, Building C, 450 Miller Street, Cammeray, NSW 2062

10 9 8 7 6 5 4 3 2 1

Sydney New York London Toronto New Delhi
Visit our website at www.simonandschuster.com.au

A catalogue record for this book is available from the National Library of Australia

ISBN: 9781761102394

Jacket design: Meng Koach
Front and back jacket images: Kristina Wild
Endpaper images: Lawrence Furzey
Illustration: Debra Nangala McDonald
Author photo: Cameron Spencer / Getty Images via AFL Photos
Typeset by Midland Typesetters, Australia
Printed and bound in Australia by Griffin Press

For my mob.
It takes a village and without that village
I would never be where I am today.
Thank you for the sacrifices you made for me.

CONTENTS

Foreword by Leon Egan   ix

Chapter One	1	Chapter Thirteen	139
Chapter Two	13	Chapter Fourteen	147
Chapter Three	27	Chapter Fifteen	161
Chapter Four	39	Chapter Sixteen	167
Chapter Five	49	Chapter Seventeen	187
Chapter Six	59	Chapter Eighteen	211
Chapter Seven	73	Chapter Nineteen	221
Chapter Eight	83	Chapter Twenty	233
Chapter Nine	91	Chapter Twenty One	243
Chapter Ten	99	Chapter Twenty Two	265
Chapter Eleven	111	Chapter Twenty Three	273
Chapter Twelve	123		

Final Word   287

A Note on the Illustrations   289

FOREWORD

I first met Eddie Betts in person whilst I was working as the Indigenous Program Manager at AFL Victoria in 2010. Our offices were based at Optus Oval, the home ground and training venue for Carlton Football Club.

It was a chance introduction. I was walking around the outside of the ground with my father, who is a lifetime-devoted Carlton supporter – he was just thrilled to be at the home of his beloved Blues. As we were walking along, just chatting, we noticed Eddie walking along by himself just outside of the gate where the players enter the venue. When Eddie saw us, other Aboriginal people, he stopped and waited.

I introduced myself and I also had to introduce my father as I thought that he was going to be too awe struck to speak.

My father eventually mentioned that he was a lifelong supporter of the Blues and of Eddie.

For the next 10 minutes Eddie Betts made my father feel like he was the most important person in the world. The respect that Eddie showed, the genuine interest in who my father was and where he was from, was amazing to witness. I took a few ripping photos of Dad and Eddie together, one of which still holds pride of place in his home today.

As we were saying our goodbyes and best wishes, Dad and Eddie shook hands like only us Aboriginal community do and they shared a cuddle that meant the world to my Dad (and I suspect to Eddie too).

As we were walking away, I looked at my father and noticed a smile from ear to ear and a real bounce in his step. His moment of pure joy had just happened. Following this meeting, I always had a special interest in following the career of Eddie Betts because I knew that he was a genuinely respectful young man.

In February of 2018, I was working as the Indigenous Relationship Manager at the AFL Players Association, and we were gathered at the Bi-Annual AFL Indigenous All-Stars Camp in Adelaide where all Indigenous players come together for a week-long camp of football, Culture and connectedness.

At this camp I witnessed a moment in time that has changed the landscape of sport in our country forever, with regard to how racism is now dealt with. This is the time that Eddie

Betts took the opportunity at our hotel venue to speak to all his Indigenous peers as a group. He stood, and then paced, whilst commanding the attention of all within the room, and he implored all his brothaboys – 'From today onwards when we hear racism, we all call it out or nothing is going to change.'

Eddie challenged the room multiple times to better gain an understanding of who was with him and whether he had their full support. In the end, the decision was made unanimously by all attending Indigenous players, along with full support from the AFL Players Association and the AFL. Eddie Betts is the one person responsible for creating positive cultural change by taking the responsibility to bravely challenge his peers to no longer accept racism.

I truly admire Eddie as a person and a father, for his strong leadership capacity, resilience and desire to make our country better for all.

Leon Egan

ONE

ONE

We used to play spot the eagles as we flew across the Nullarbor in our little two-door Magna. We'd spot them circling over the highway and count them sitting on the dead kangaroos by the side of the road. Mum always had the trip mapped out and planned ahead. Sometimes we'd do the drive non-stop. We'd stock up on music cassettes at the servo – country music mainly, like Alan Jackson, a bit of Creedence, John Fogerty. Then we'd play the cassettes on repeat for two days. Other times we'd pull up and get a motel room in Border Village, home of the Big Roo on the South Australia – Western Australia border. What I remember most is the long, flat drive, the eagles, sometimes a camel out on the plains or some emus, the kangaroos along the road, and the trucks that wouldn't stop for anything.

I loved those trips. They'd take a couple of days. We used to pull the seats out of the back of the Magna, put a mattress in the boot and away we'd go. It'd be Mum, me and my two sisters, Sarah and Lucy, shuttling across the Nullarbor between Kalgoorlie and Port Lincoln. We'd always get somebody to come along with us to share the driving with Mum. We were always squeezing people in.

During the long drive we'd play games to break up the time. Car cricket was popular – I remember red trucks were an 'out', and the blue cars were 'fours'. I'd also take my mind off things by playing with a couple of little teddy bears. I would lay-up on the mattress and pretend they were playing footy, taking 'screamers' and 'hangers'. Before I knew it five hours would have passed. My imagination took me onto an Aussie Rules ground, thinking of my family, being like my Uncles playing in the Blackfulla carnival.

I'm not the first Eddie Betts. I'm not even the second. I'm also not the first to play football. I might not even be the best footballer to have carried the name. Edward Frederick Betts, my grandfather, was born on South Australia's west coast and lived there most of his life before he died on the floor of a Port Lincoln prison cell.

He came into the world at the Koonibba Mission on 10 March 1938 and lived in the children's home there. Back then, they called it a 'native home'. It was supposed to develop the next lot of workers for the area. My grandfather and the rest of the kids were westernised, taught to be 'reliable Christians'. Eventually, his dad – my great-grandfather – moved the family to Cummins, a little wheatbelt town on the Eyre Peninsula. He made money by doing all sorts of different things there, including moving wheat along the railway line.

They reckon wheat lumping was tough. Once the grain was sewn into jute bags, the lumpers had to throw the bags up on their shoulders – some of them were as heavy as 90 kilos – and get them in and out of the storage terminals. Lumping was so important to the history of the area that there's a bronze statue of a lumper in Cummins now. Eddie followed in his dad's footsteps and became a lumper, too, in nearby Ceduna.

He also played a bit of footy for the Rovers there, which is how he met his wife, Veda. They married in 1959.

Whenever you talk to people who can remember my granddad, they all mention how brilliant he was at football. He won the Mail Medal in 1958, given to the 'fairest and most brilliant' player in the entire country association. He and Veda had two children while they were living in Ceduna.

When the North Whyalla Football Club asked Eddie to come and play for them, he packed up the family and headed east on a bus. Unfortunately for North Whyalla, their rivals, the West Whyalla Dragons, got wind of the trip and sent a group of players some 150 kilometres to intercept the bus at Kimba, about halfway between Ceduna to Whyalla – and by the time they reached Whyalla, Eddie was signed to be a Dragon and had the promise of a better job at BHP.

He played with West Whyalla for a few years, and during that time another one of my Aunties was born. But pretty soon the family was off to Port Lincoln, after Eddie was chased by the Tasman Football Club, where he got to play with his brother George Burgoyne. I only mention that because in most of the teams he played for, Eddie was the only Black-fulla on the team. He only played until 1968, because at the end of that season he was sent to hospital feeling unwell. He ended up being diagnosed with high blood pressure. He must have been gutted to have to stop playing footy, but he was left with no choice and forced to retire. By then, he was generally seen as one of the best Rovers the Far West Football League had seen.

Some people ask me why my granddad never went to Adelaide to play with one of the two SANFL clubs there that had tried to get him. The reason that was never going to happen is that he and my grandma knew Port Lincoln was the best place for their family, and by that stage there were six kids knocking around – including my dad, Edward Robert Betts.

Around the time my granddad retired, the wheat lumping jobs were drying up because Port Lincoln had finally gotten silos. By then, he was drinking heavily. Later on, the coroner, in a report on his death, wondered if he'd been driven to drink by the combination of having no job, not being able to play footy anymore and being 'dumped' by the white people who had previously loved and cheered him for his game. I kind of think he ended up drinking just because there was nothing else.

Eddie had been arrested a few times while he was playing footy: three times for being drunk in public, once for having a 'ferocious dog at large'. He even got pinged a couple of times just for being an Aboriginal person drinking liquor. Back then, you didn't even have to be drunk or out in public to get in trouble for it. Towards the end of 1968, he was admitted to the hospital at Port Lincoln suffering from acute alcoholism. Veda reckoned it all went downhill pretty quickly once he knew he couldn't play footy anymore.

By the time I arrived, in 1986, at the Port Lincoln hospital, my dad had grown up and moved around a bit and was playing footy, too. My grandfather died in October of the next year, so I don't remember anything that happened. It was only when I moved to Adelaide to play with the Crows that I started looking into what had gone on.

Mum was with Dad on the beach when they got a call informing them that my grandfather had died in a police cell. Mum says Dad fell to his knees, howling. They jumped in the car, dropped me off and kept going to Nanna Veda's house, which turned out to be surrounded by cameras and reporters. It was all a mess.

Many years later, when I started to ask people what had happened in that hospital and that prison cell, a lot of my cousins on my grandfather's side started to open up to me about it. I also sat down and read the coroner's report for the first time with my partner, Anna. I never knew the forensic details of my grandfather's death until we both read that report. I knew he died in the cells, but I didn't know about so much that happened in the lead up. It made me wild to think that, while the police and doctors were all cleared of responsibility for his death, his life leading up to that point was scarred by the structural racism that denied him the opportunities that would have allowed him to thrive.

*

So what happened to the first Eddie Betts in October of 1987?

The coroner's report said my grandfather was in an 'off-the-bottle' period. Only four of the kids were still living at home. Dad had moved to Western Australia where some other family of ours come from. One weekend, Nanna Veda was busy helping my Uncle move to a new house; no one is quite sure, but we think that's when my granddad started drinking again. Certainly by the Monday it was noticed that he was shaky and unwell.

In the early hours of the Tuesday morning, he woke my Aunties and told them to call an ambulance. They dialled triple-zero from the public phone box across the street and he was taken to the Port Lincoln hospital. He told them he'd had too much to drink over the weekend. According to the coroner's report, however, the doctor's notes included the lines 'patient much too well known', 'domestic violence (mutual)', 'may well be swinging the lead' and 'does nothing to help himself'. The notes finished with the phrase, 'Admission to maintain the peace.' The coroner's inquiry and the Royal Commission both cleared the doctor of any negligence, however the coroner confirmed that Eddie was sober.

Eddie checked himself out around 10.30 am. When he left the hospital, he headed to a meeting place for Aboriginal people in town called the Red Shed, but he called a cab soon after and went home. By lunchtime, he was so unwell that he had to go back to the hospital again, and one of his daughters called the ambulance. When asked by the paramedics, he said that the only drink he'd had since leaving hospital that morning was a soft drink. Later on, when the investigation happened, everyone who'd seen him that morning said they didn't think he'd been drinking.

He walked into the hospital unaided. But while he was waiting, and again while he was being seen by staff, he got increasingly agitated. He was complaining of a pain in his stomach. The doctor kept telling him to calm down – which he'd do for a bit, but then he'd start up again, waving his arms around and asking for tablets or injections for the pain.

Finally, the police were called and my grandfather was removed from the hospital under the *Public Intoxication Act 1984*. This time around, while the coroner found no causative connection between the doctor's attitude and my grandfather's subsequent death, the doctor's notes included the lines 'do not believe he has a primary medical problem', 'his presentation is an insult' and 'this is purposeful and deliberate behaviour'.

By 2 pm, however, he was dead in the police cell.

I think I wasn't ready to deal with that story earlier in my life. But now, the more I think about it, the angrier I get. My grandfather's blood alcohol reading from his autopsy showed that he wasn't intoxicated when he passed away – and that he was, in fact, very sick.

He died of heart failure.

I could have grown up with him. I could have had another grandfather, but all I was left with were memories and stories told by my cousin-uncle David, who was in the cell next to him. He told us that he listened to my granddad shout in pain as he called for help. Davo said that he also called out asking for someone to come and help, but that no one heard him. There is no suggestion at all in either the coroner's report or the report of the Royal Commission that Eddie was neglected, but for many years afterwards Davo said he could still hear my grandfather yelling out.

The fact that nothing came of it – that all the evidence pointed away from any individual being responsible or accountable – hurts, and still causes trauma for our entire family.

People often look to me for answers, wondering what I can do to stop deaths like my grandfather's from happening – and I feel a sense of pressure to be able to do that. My profile can help to highlight what is going on, but I often don't have the solutions.

That's mainly because there is no easy solution. There are so many issues facing my people and sometimes this burden of needing to make things better is all too much for me. I want to be able to prevent Aboriginal deaths in custody, we all do, but pulling apart a system that isn't set up for us is incredibly hard. To make positive changes, we need to collaborate and we need to respect Indigenous community leadership on what is best for our People.

I know that playing footy has given me a platform and if I can use it to educate people about what it's like growing up in an environment where it's seen as normal for the police to take people away, then it might help.

I inherited my grandfather's name, and I was lucky to inherit his sporting skills, too. I was even luckier to be born in a time and place where I was able to make the most of the opportunities that I was given and earned. Poppa Eddie wasn't so lucky.

You needed to know about my grandfather's life – and his death – to understand who I am and who I've become. That was his story – and this is mine.

TWO

TWO

Each of Mum's four brothers played footy and even now she says she always wanted to marry a footy player – and that she was only ever going to get the best one. She often tells the story of how she was watching a local game one day, saw that Dad was the best on ground, and decided then and there that he'd be the one.

My dad was Wirangu and Kokatha, and came from Port Lincoln. He played in the same footy team as my mum's brothers. He was good enough to get called up to the Mallee Park A-Grade side, where he played a full season. Then they dropped him for the grand final because he was one of the younger boys. But Mum's brother, Trevor, as well as Byron Pickett's dad, Normie, and Daniel Wells' dad, Leonard, said, 'If Eddie Betts doesn't play, *we* don't play.' So, the club had no choice. He got a game and the Mallee Park Peckers went on to win the flag. Once, I asked Mum how Dad went that day and she just said, '*Deadly*. He always played deadly.'

Mum and Dad got married not long after Poppa Eddie died. There wasn't really a proposal or anything, but because Nan and Pop were Christian, they did what the church told them to and decided to get married in the local chapel.

I was born on Dad's Country in Port Lincoln. Mum had Nanna beside her when I was delivered at 8.20 am on a Wednesday morning. She reckons I was 'snow-white and bald'. Mum always says I was the perfect kid. You might think otherwise when you hear about some of the things I got up to, running amok with the older boys at school. I think she means I was 'perfect' because I didn't get sick and I'd just get on with things. She also reckons I never complained, so when I finally *did* get sick, they'd all know I was really ill. Then Nanna and Pop would make their bush medicine for me and, depending on what it was, I'd either drink it down or rub it on my body. It tasted pretty gross, but it seemed to work. We would always use bush medicine when we'd spend time out bush with Pop and the family in Kalgoorlie. One day, I jumped on a tree, it snapped in half and I impaled myself on it. I had a huge hole at the base of my back where my brothers pulled me off the broken bit. The bush medicine fixed that up – though I still have a huge scar on my back.

That wasn't the only time my love of adventure and speed got me in trouble. Mum says I got concussed three times as a kid. Once, I was riding a motorbike and fell off and hit my head. Another time, Dad and I were on the bumpy-cars at the show and got hit so hard that I was knocked out cold – my family were very panicked! And the third time . . . well, I can't remember.

Mum reckons I had no patience and that everything I did had to be flat-out. She always laughs out loud remembering the time I went roller skating – she reckons it was the funniest thing she ever saw. I'd never been on roller skates before, but that didn't stop me from going at top speed from the start. I'd go at a million miles an hour until I ran out of room, and then, since I didn't know how to stop, I'd just crash into the barrier. Then I'd turn around, go a million miles an hour in the other direction until I crashed again.

Early life for me was in Kalgoorlie, living in a rented three-bedroom house in Cavalier Crescent, just up the road from Nanna and Pop's. We spent most of our time at their place, since there were always plenty of people around and lots of fun to be had there.

Nanna had so many grandkids, and she used to offer up a 50-dollar prize to whichever one of us went to school the most in a year. I was obviously competitive from an early age and really wanted to win. One morning, I woke up at 5am, got dressed, jumped on my bike and rode in the dark to Nanna and Pop's place to tell them I was ready for school. I'm not sure they were too impressed that I was waking them up so early with the news, so they told me to jump in bed with them and I went back to sleep. I did win the $50 that year – but I'm probably lucky the bet wasn't laid for my high school years. By then, I hated going to school, and even cash wouldn't have changed my mind.

I only ever ate Weet-Bix. I'd have three for breakfast, three for lunch and three more for dinner, all with powdered milk and sugar. Pop used to make his tin cup of tea with powdered milk and when he was finished I'd take the powder and milk it up with warm water, then pour it over the cereal, sprinkle on some sugar and top it all off with more powdered milk. It sounds pretty gross now, but I remember it tasting great when I was a kid. To this day, I usually eat Weet-Bix for breakfast before every training session and game.

When I got a bit older we used to get to Nanna and Pop's by 7.30am every school morning and Nanna would have a massive pot of porridge cooked for all 16 of us cousins. We'd eat that while our parents headed off to work and then we'd get going to school. The house was perfectly located in between the primary school and the high school.

It's funny remembering all these stories from my childhood. I remember growing up with my family was deadly; we were free to play and there were always people around to comfort us when we needed it. The 'nuclear' idea doesn't apply to our family. My family isn't just my mother and father and siblings – it's also my Aunties and Uncles, my cousin-uncles, my cousins, my cousins' cousins, my friends, my friends' cousins, and on and on. I always had someone to sleep in the same bed with and we would share everything – money, food, thoughts, stories, laughter.

Most of my life in Kalgoorlie revolved around my Pop's place at 12 Boomerang Crescent. There was an alleyway next to his house that went down to 27 Starlight Street, my Aunty Tessa's house, who was basically my other mum. All my male cousins lived there too, and that front yard was our playing field, our training track, our basketball court and our tackling chute. We used to chase and play with each other up and down there, back and forth between the two houses, until it was too dark to see. Our goal posts were shoes and socks and the basketball hoop at Pop's was an old milk crate with the bottom cut out of it, nailed to a tree.

We also used to play this game called 'Boondies' where we'd make forts in the backyard. We'd dig up holes and the dirt was so hard that it'd come up in rocks – the game was chucking these clumps of dirt and rocks at each other.

My biggest influence growing up were my brothers – or my cousins, to use the whitefulla term. I idolised my Dad and Uncles, but it was my older cousins who I wanted to be like the most. I grew up mimicking them – and they were mimicking their fathers. Every year, they'd play footy at the Blackfulla Carnival and I was their water-boy from the age of seven.

I had a few cousin-brothers who were younger than me – Kevin, Donald, Richard – and we wanted to compete against the older boys. The ones who were a few years older than me – Victor, Tim and Andrew Champion, Russell 'Rusty' Carbine – well, there's no other way to say it than that I wanted to be just like them. I wanted to be with them and to be a part of their pack. We'd play full-contact games of footy and, of course, I'd lose most of the time – but that always pushed me to get better. I hated losing. Sometimes I'd even cry. There were times when they weren't interested in me hanging around, but I was always ready to play whenever they were.

We would go bush heaps and spend whole days out there hunting, shooting and mucking around. There were plenty of old mines in and around Kalgoorlie, and we used to go looking for them and find the ones that had water in the bottom. They were our swimming holes. We'd make water slides out of the clay or just jump off rocks into them. We also had 'the Tree', which we tied a rope to and would swing off into the water all day. I vaguely remember jumping off the big cliff at the place we called 'Open Cut' – but I'm pretty sure a few others *fell* off it. Mum didn't like us going to that place. She thought it was too dangerous.

When I ask Mum what she remembers about me growing up, the first thing that comes to mind for her are the times I had brushes with the *monarch* (the WA police) or *wulja* (the SA police), although I reckon you could argue that the law was brushing against me more than it needed to.

One time, when I was in primary school at Kalgoorlie, one of my cousins ran down to tell Mum the police had 'got me'. Mum skittled off to the police station and asked to see me, but they told her I wasn't there. Mum was left standing in front of the station, asking whoever would listen, 'Where the hell is he? You arrested him and now you can't *find* him?' She demanded that they ring around all the hospitals to see where I was. When they still couldn't locate me, she rushed over to my Aunty's house – to find me sitting there watching videos on the couch.

What had happened was that a few of us had been wandering around the Kalgoorlie streets near dark, and the cops put their 'spotties' on us and lined us all up against a fence. Then they asked for our names, which we gave them. I remember one of the coppers saying, 'Well, the winner is Mr Betts: you're staying with us. We've got a warrant for you.' And then they cuffed me. I told them I hadn't done anything wrong and that they *couldn't* have a warrant for me, but they put me in the back of the police car. The rest of my brothers scattered – including Tim, who took off and ran straight to our house. He was the one who told Mum the cops got me. Mum went barrelling off to the police station, but I was still being held in the back of the car. Around then the coppers finally worked out that the warrant they had was in fact for my dad – also Eddie Betts. They asked me if I knew where he was, and I told them I had no idea (even though I knew he was just around the corner).

Eventually they let me out of the car but by then it was dark. I was eight or nine at the time, but already old enough to realise that it could be dangerous for somebody like me to be outside by myself after dark in the streets of Kalgoorlie. The coppers knew that too. Whenever you saw headlights coming in your direction you understood there were two threats: it was either the coppers that were going to pull you up or a civilian car that you were going to get chased by.

Another time, the cops chucked me in the back of a paddy wagon after I had been riding a motorbike up and down the street next to Kalgoorlie high school, which was at the end of Pop's street, after school had finished for the day. Mum saw what was happening and barrelled up, demanding to know why I'd been arrested. The whole time, I was crying my eyes out. I had refused to give them my name and address. I was just too scared. I was scared of the cops themselves and I also thought I'd get in trouble at home. One thing's for sure, though: there were plenty of white kids riding motorbikes around that school and the coppers never picked them up.

When I was growing up, being stopped by the police was always a possibility. It was a reality hanging over us. It was an expectation. Sometimes, when something bad has consistently been a part of your life and it's caused you nothing but fear, that fear just becomes normal.

That's not to say I didn't do some things that were wrong. Mum still tells me about the day a police van pulled up out the front of the house with one of my cousins sitting in the front seat and me in the lock-up bit in the back. She guesses I was about 10 years old. We had broken into the house around the corner. I can't even remember why we did it, but Mum reckons one of us took a poster, one took a balloon and another took a cup. Apparently, I took a spoon. To this day, I have no idea why I wanted it. I do remember being the one who had to climb through the window at the house just because I was the smallest.

When I think back to my childhood, what I really recall is that it was all about family. We never went without and we were raised with a strong sense of belonging. Our family made sacrifices for each other and we learned to put others before ourselves. We were taught to respect our Elders and our traditions, and, most importantly, we were taught to have a strong sense of self-identity. I believe that these sorts of family connections not only keep us together but are the reason why our Culture has survived and thrived for so long.

Mum also reckons that even back then she used to tell people she was going to have an AFL-playing son. I certainly didn't end up playing just to make that come true, but she always did everything in her power to make sure her kids could have the opportunity to play at the highest level.

Sport was very important to me as a kid. It allowed me to feel like there was somewhere I could belong outside of my family networks. It was where I thought I could fit in best. I was good at it, and it gave me a way to break down barriers without any awkward conversations. I played footy first, basketball second and all the others a distant third – but it was soccer that got my name in the paper for the first time.

'BETTS PUTS ON ONE-MAN SHOW,' says the headline in *Goldfields Magazine* of 2 June 1994. I had booted 11 of 13 goals for the Under 7s Boulder soccer team against the YMCA Blacks. Apparently, I was the difference between the two sides. 'YMCA tried hard all game but just did not have an answer to Betts' goal scoring prowess,' the paper reported.

Growing up in the '90s in Kalgoorlie wasn't easy for my family. The ongoing impact of colonisation and accompanying trauma was felt throughout the community, and my family certainly wasn't immune to the intergenerational side effects of this. It was only one generation above me that some of my family were stolen; some came back, some never returned, but the impact of children being taken away was etched into our minds and, it's been proven, in changes to our genetics forever.

We experienced family and domestic violence so regularly when I was young, and it was usually related to alcohol misuse. Sometimes the pain of the past, or even the present, became be too much and family members would drink alcohol to get by, or basically to numb themselves.

Us cousins had to learn how to care for each other during repeated episodes.

Aunty Tessa's daughter, my sister Ella Smith, and I learnt strategies together to support the young cousins if something was going down. Ella and I were the middle-ordered cousins and therefore, while the older brothers were out of the house, we were generally home looking out for the smaller kids. We became experts on managing situations, reading people, diffusing tension and even sheltering the younger cousins.

Ella and I have always been really close. We have a strong bond that was developed through our upbringing but also continues today, being leaders in our communities, using our voices and raising our kids to be strong on Culture and identity.

There were times when the violence was too much for some of my Aunties and my mother, and occasionally they took things into their own hands. They were strong and resilient and not afraid to call it out if they saw something that wasn't right. The safest option for our family was not to phone the police; we were never sure what would happen if the cops came, so we tried to manage things ourselves internally. Calling the police was usually the very last resort.

Getting involved meant conflict and this could be full on, however, there was one thing for sure: my family members never held grudges. Usually by the next morning everyone would be friends again and it was like the day before hadn't even happened. Our family Culture is usually very peaceful, so alcohol-fuelled violence just brought out the worst.

As we all went on to get jobs and undergo further education, my whole family's approach to violence changed. My mother now works in our community with domestic violence survivors and uses Cultural healing practices to heal our people.

I sometimes wonder about the burden on her now, especially since I've had kids, and how protecting not only yourself but your children from violence must have been really tough.

THREE

Dad didn't want me to play soccer – simple as that. He had worn the blue and white of the Mines Rovers footy club in Kalgoorlie and that meant I was going to as well. Mum took me down to the club to get a game in the Under 11s, and after all that alleyway football with my cousins and brothers, I was hooked.

I vaguely remember turning up for the first training. I was still a shy kid, but that club was a little bit different for me. I felt comfortable there because I knew most of the kids through school – and because several of my family members were playing in the older grades. Even before I picked up a football, I felt like I belonged on that paddock.

My first coach was Trevor Tasker, who was one of the local firemen. His son Damien played with us, and we made it to the grand final in that first year but lost. It was all about having fun in those days and that suited me, because for years I had been playing more competitive footy in that alley with my brothers. Those games were intense. Playing for the Mines Rovers Under 11s was just about being free and chasing the ball. I was so busy having fun that I had no idea if I was any good or not. I hoped I was, because I wanted to be like my dad, my brothers and my Uncles. (I had one Uncle who was so starving for the ball, you knew not to kick it to him: Trevor 'Hungry' Sambo would never pass it off.)

I can't remember specific games from that time – not even my first match. But the overwhelming memory I have when

I think about those games of footy is running – running and chasing that ball. I think I kicked six or seven goals in my first or second game. The footy back then was so different from what it is for kids now. There weren't 'zones' or places you had to be: if you wanted the ball, you went and got it.

To get to the games, we'd ride our bikes or grab a lift with anyone we could. There were two main ovals we had to get to: Boulder City's, which had two club rooms, and Railway's. We hated Railway; they were our great and fierce rivals.

After a match, if I was lucky, Mum would give me 10 or 20 bucks and I'd be able to stay and watch my brothers and relatives play in the 17s, 18s and seniors. I used to love sitting around and watching those games.

There wasn't really a date when Mum and Dad split up. It was more that he went off to prison and took ages to come back, and they just moved apart.

I remember going there to visit him – walking through the police doors to sign in, sitting in a room with the other visitors and waiting for the man in the green uniform to come in and say hello. Dad would be happy to see us, but I can't remember saying anything to him. My mum and sisters might have different memories – I can't say. Dad was away for a long time and it was during that period when Nanna started to get sick. Nanna was gentle and loving and so important to us all, but she was diagnosed with cancer and she passed away soon after that.

Nanna was a major support for Mum and when she was gone Mum soon began to battle with depression. I was about 11 when the situation was at its hardest. Again, I have no clear memories of it, but often Mum's sisters would come and take me out of the house to stay with them for a while. Without a doubt, that was the toughest time our family has ever gone through. None of us ever saw the inside of a child welfare office though, because someone would always step up and help.

My memory is patchy with this stuff. Some people have suggested that I might have forgotten in order to protect myself. I'm glad I don't remember it all. And I don't blame my parents for anything. Not one bit.

After Dad got out, I'd head over to Port Lincoln to see him and I'd play footy there too, running out for Mallee Park. It was an all-Aboriginal club, and again, it felt like home to me. A lot of the players there were really talented – probably more talented than me. I got to play with my cousins there too. The style of footy we played was very different – every single play and move was done on instinct. I loved that. That year, I was runner up in the Under 14s Best and Fairest for the Lincoln League.

The games were easy enough, but getting people to training wasn't. I always turned up just because I wanted to kick, but on average the most we'd get to any session would be about

10 players. I never got annoyed at people for not showing, though – it was just one of those things. I was still happy to be there, even if there were only nine others playing with me.

My love of footy, combined with shuttling between Port Lincoln and Kalgoorlie, started to interfere with my schooling. To say I wasn't a massive fan of school at that time is an understatement. I enjoyed travelling and moving around, but missing a lot of school is one of the biggest regrets of my life. I spend a lot of time now talking to kids about how important education is and why life has been harder for me without it. Now, though, I also have the knowledge to understand why I didn't feel overly safe at school as a kid. The education system I was in was built for certain types of people, and I wasn't one of them. Our Indigenous perspectives are different and at times that can make things complex for a kid like me in a classroom. In the end, when I finished primary school, I still couldn't read and write. In class, I just used to hope and pray that they wouldn't ask me anything.

The best times for me were recess and lunch because I could run around and play footy. For me, footy meant an even playing field and a language we could *all* speak. Out on the field, there were no perspectives that I didn't understand.

We did have a '*Nunga*' class in Port Lincoln that was only for Blackfullas, and I loved being in there. It helped me feel okay about being at school – even if just for a while. We even had a 'Black bench' where we'd meet and eat our lunch.

That doesn't sound like much, but that bench was a safe place for us, and it's really important for minority groups to have those. It allows us to be around people who understand us and who can empathise fully when things are hard. That bench gave me a sense of security when I was feeling unsure.

It's hard to describe the feeling of being part of a minority within a population. Humans have lots of things in common across cultures – we seek love, security, shelter, and so on. Our Aboriginal Culture is so unique and our history is so long, though, and colonisation has been traumatic for us. Sometimes, even simple childhood routines like going to school are hard for us mob.

When I felt like I didn't belong, I'd start to get into trouble. I experimented with alcohol, I stole little things, I smoked. I remember stealing a bunch of chocolates from the school canteen and going home to share the box with everyone. I know now that I was just bored and uninterested, but that led me to some seriously risky behaviours. In my soul, I never intended to do anything that would hurt anyone; that's not in my nature. I was just doing silly things for a thrill or to pass the time.

Anna ran into one of my old literacy and numeracy teachers once, and the teacher remembered that I was always 'the one in class who would have all the stats from the footy on the weekend'. 'He'd sit in class and compare his stats to everyone else and to his games from previous weeks just to work out how he could get better for the next game,' the teacher told Anna.

In 2001, I went from playing in the Under 14s to the Under 17s, even though I was still eligible for the younger grades. I wasn't intimidated – I was over the moon. Finally, I'd get to play with the older cousins I'd been taking on in the alley-ways back in Kalgoorlie. In those games in the higher grade, I learned a lot and learned fast. Playing with the older guys was great for my footy – but after most games, we'd go back to one of the boys' houses, where I also learned about smoking gunja and drinking.

People could see that I was determined and focused on footy, but I still didn't have a goal. I never set out to win the awards that I won, it was just great when I got them. I didn't think past the next game or the next week.

Our main rival was the Marble Range Football Club, whose home ground was on the highway just outside Port Lincoln. We also had a great rivalry with the Boston Tigers. I kicked nine goals in one game against them – even though the game plan had been to set up my cousin Michael Burgoyne, who ended up with 21 goals.

It's hard to get good stories about that time out of people – they're all too modest. But everyone I played with and against in that comp was just as good as me. It just seemed like roadblocks started to pop up once people started getting into alcohol and smoking.

I remember hanging out one day with my clan – me, Victor, Tim Russell, Andrew, Josh Saunders – when we got a phone call to tell us the Port Lincoln Best and Fairest ceremony was on. They had rung because Victor was leading the vote count. We headed to another cousin's house, and by the time we got there the call had come through that Victor had won the thing. I had come runner-up, and third place went to Josh.

But we were already sitting around and smoking weed.

Yep: the top three placegetters were not only not at the ceremony, they were sitting around getting wasted together. It must have been an ordinary look to the other players who had actually turned up and hadn't won anything. There was nothing we could do, though; we just told them to deliver the trophies to the clubroom and that we'd pick them up later.

Now that I had won a trophy, I didn't actually *want* it, and it ended up at Dad's place. At the time, he was living in a two-bedroom flat just around the corner from the Mallee Park footy club. It was actually kind of cool when I dropped it in. He had won seven Best and Fairest awards and when I handed him my trophy, he said, 'Put it up there, son, next to mine.'

That year, I was chosen to play against Port Adelaide Country, which involved jumping on a bus and traveling 650 kilometres to Adelaide for the comp. We did pretty well and I won the Best and Fairest for that team. Then I got picked to go back and actually play for the Port Adelaide Magpies (yep, I wore the Port black and white before ever donning the Crows tri-colours). Because it was a scholarship squad, I got taken through the Crows' change rooms, which were pretty cool to see.

You'd think I would have been over the moon. On the whole, though, with only one other Aboriginal kid in the scholarship program, I felt really uncomfortable and uneasy. I also didn't bring any shorts. I just didn't pack any. I was too embarrassed to say anything, so when we had to do a beep test the first morning I was there, I rocked up in a pair of rolled-up, baggy Nike tracksuit pants. Someone gave me some shorts and I played in a trial match later that day. We went to the movies that night. I sat there the whole time just not wanting to be there. I cried afterwards and rang Mum, asked her to come and pick me up. She was staying in Adelaide and came and got me. All I wanted was to be back in my bubble with the boys in Lincoln. Mum understood, so she spoke to the people in charge and I went home – just like that. I didn't hear from anyone there again.

That's just one example of how my mum always made sure I had every opportunity to play football that she could give me – while still looking after me as I did it.

Meanwhile, the AFL was playing out on television screens around the country – and I was hardly watching any of it.

If you asked me who I barracked for in those days, it was probably the Crows – but I wasn't really into it. I maybe saw part of the 1997 and 1998 grand finals. Watching the game on TV meant I couldn't be outside playing it – so why would I do that?

FOUR

My mum's dad, Cadley Sambo, was a Gubrun man who spent his early years painted up darker than he actually was because the welfare people of the time were collecting all the little half-caste kids to send them to the Methodist Mogumber Mission north of Perth.

The journalist and writer Stuart Rintoul wrote about my grandfather in his 1993 book *The Wailing: A National Black Oral History*. In that book, my grandfather tells the story of how the mounted police would trample the camp where he lived, which destroyed the food supply. His mother would paint him up with burnt quandong to make his skin appear darker.

Poppa Cadley was around 15 when he and two of his cousins were picked up after nicking a suitcase from a farmhouse. He got sent to the mission but he only lasted there a couple of weeks. He said they were 'big bullies' who used to force people who had bleeding hands and knees to pick potatoes out of the ground while they drove the plough. So, my grandfather took off, along with three others. They headed for the trainline. Once they hit the tracks, they knew which direction to go and started walking.

My grandfather was headed for Coolgardie, five or six hundred kilometres from the mission. He split up from the others, only walking at night and ripping the clothes off his body to wrap around his bleeding feet. During that long walk, he would have had plenty of time to think about the contents of the suitcase they'd stolen. He used to laugh about that with the family later: the only things in it were pretty yellow and green dresses.

On Christmas Day he made it back to his parents' home at Southern Cross, a historic gold mining town on the eastern edge of the wheatbelt, located halfway between Perth and Coolgardie. From there, he went to a station in Coolgardie where he had an Uncle who took him under his wing. He worked there until Mr A.O. Neville, then the 'Chief Protector of Aborigines' tracked him down. Neville intended to take Poppa Cadley back to the mission, but the station's owner told Neville that my grandfather was one of the best workers he had and asked if they could 'keep' him. Poppa Cadley ended up staying on that station until he was 18.

He told Mum that he remembered his sister being five or six when she was taken from their mother, Lucy. She was another one of the many who were stolen.

Lucy, my great-grandmother, was illiterate, but that didn't stop her from going to the postmaster, the schoolmaster, the baker, the police officer, the priest, and everyone else she could think of to get them to write and ask permission for her to go and visit her daughter. That consent was never granted and they say she died from a broken heart. A letter of permission arrived the day she passed away.

As a teenager, my grandfather was allowed to see his sister for 20 minutes a month. He went on to marry and eventually

Mum's four brothers came along. They had a tough time in Kalgoorlie – a hard place for Black people to grow up at that time. That's why, when Mum was around 12 years old, they all packed up and headed over to Port Lincoln in South Australia.

Just as Mum had moved, she decided she needed to get me away from Kalgoorlie as well, and also out of Port Lincoln. Footy was going well: I was kicking goals and playing in rep teams, but Mum was getting worried about my behaviour off the field. She'd heard of a footy program that Phil Krakouer, from North Melbourne, was running out of Broadmeadows TAFE for Aboriginal players from right around the country. Mum told me and my cousins, Donald and Victor, about it and we decided that we wanted to go and join.

Joining the program obviously meant moving to Melbourne, a big change for the family. We didn't have a house there for starters. We spent our first few nights at Byron Pickett's place in Sunshine. There was me, Donald and Victor, my mum, my two sisters, Aunty Tessa and her four kids, and another cousin, Trevor. We camped on the floor in the garage. It's just what you did, we didn't complain. We got on with it. As a family we made sacrifices and hard choices to seal opportunities for each other. I was always around big family groups anyway, so I was used to the idea of living with everyone like that.

The program felt like home right from the start because it was all Aboriginal people. Up until then, they were the only people I had been around, so it was exactly what I'd grown up with. All of us in that program became close and we're still close today. It's sometimes hard to explain how talking with Blackfullas is more comfortable for me. There's an immediate sense of connection and shared experience. I remember one of the younger AFL boys coming over to our house and ending up staying for a couple of hours. He wasn't from where my mob is from, but there was just that connection straight off, and we yarned for hours and became brothers.

We did school classes as part of the program, and we'd spend part of each day learning skills like metalworking and woodworking – but I was always watching the time until I could get out on the field and play footy. I loved that program and it provided me with the support and a safe environment to progress in important ways off the field.

The family found a three-bedroom home to rent in the north-west suburb of Glenroy. A whole heap of other boys who had come to Melbourne from interstate ended up in a house that the TAFE found for them. We had a big mob of mattresses on their lounge room floor and sometimes I'd stay there overnight too. We loved being together and it made it easier for all of us young fullas who had relocated to Melbourne. We all supported each other in many ways, whether it be financially or just having each others' back with TAFE work. We even shared our playing gear, like footy boots and shorts. In those days we were responsible for our own meals. Charcoal chicken on bread with chips was a popular dish, with a plastic bag in the middle to chuck the bones in (my family still does that). At that time, though, I mostly ate a Blackfulla staple of Keen's chicken curry and rice.

At this early point in my career I mainly focused on what was in front of me. And that wasn't necessarily making the AFL. In those days it was often just about living day to day. Things could be real tight financially. At different times we each had to call family back home – for me it was often my Aunty Tinker or Uncle Rock – and hit them up for whatever they could spare to help us all out with shopping or bills or whatever we were faced with. On the field, my focus was on playing my best footy for the boys that I was playing alongside. It was never about individual honours, it was about how I was contributing to the team, how we could be the best we could be. I was 15 years old and my mind was always in the moment.

In 2002, I got the opportunity to have a run in the under 18s with the Templestowe Dockers. That meant I'd be playing with older guys again, but I was used to that from the games with my older cousins. Templestowe picked up Victor and my other cousins Tim Champion and Russell Carbine who had come across from Kalgoorlie and Port Lincoln for a visit but ended up staying. We made the grand final that year and I was surprised to get runner-up in the club Best and Fairest. I'd missed about six games because of family funerals back in Kalgoorlie. I ended up winning the overall Best and Fairest for the league, but unfortunately I didn't get to go to the vote count because I was away for another funeral.

The Oakleigh Chargers got wind of the news that myself and a few more 15-year-old brothers were all playing for the Dockers and invited us to train with them. They had assumed that because we were with the Dockers that we were within the same zone of eligibility. But the three of us were living in the Glenroy catchment, therefore outside the zone for the Chargers. The Calder Cannons, which was a club located in the north-west metro zone which covered Glenroy, then expressed interest in having me trial for them. I got the nod and as it turned out I was also the only Blackfulla on the team. For me, the footy felt very different from when I was playing with the boys from the TAFE course. Despite that, I loved what I was learning at Calder and I was more than happy to be playing footy however and whenever I could.

The Cannons were based in Coburg, which was across town. This meant I couldn't jump on a train or tram and had to rely on getting a lift to the ground with Aunty Tessa. One morning, I had to get to the oval early to catch a team bus to play Gippsland in the TAC Cup. Aunty Tessa said she'd drive me, but we only made it around one corner before she realised we were pretty much out of fuel. Aunty Tessa didn't want to just leave the car in the street, but she didn't want to chance getting it to a petrol station in case it conked out on the way. So we got together all the money we had – $20 – and decided I'd go alone in a taxi. Aunty Tessa drove back home while I waited around on the street, ready to hail down the next passing cab. But with time running out, I started knocking on doors to see if someone would let me use their phone to call one to come and collect me.

I think it was the third door I knocked on that finally opened. Who knows why they let me – a complete stranger – in to use their phone, but they did. When the cabbie turned up, I had to tell him that I only had 20 bucks and to just get me 'as close as possible'.

'Okay, we'll try and get you there,' he said. Then he turned on the meter, and – bang! – $2.50 right away. I started to panic. I thought I was going to miss the bus for sure. My leg kept jiggling with nerves and I couldn't sit still as I watched the meter tick over and my cash disappear dollar by dollar until finally it was all gone. We weren't even that close to the oval – we were still a few kays away from it, actually. So I did the only thing I could do: I put my bag over my shoulder and ran hard. I reckon I got there in about 10 minutes. When I rounded the last corner and saw the bus, I finally slowed down, wandered up and casually hopped on. I actually played okay that day – I kicked five – but no one knew what I'd done to make it onto that damn bus.

FIVE

Heaps of kids in the community dream of growing up and playing AFL like the champions we grew up watching on TV. I was no different. I would watch Andrew McLeod play for the Adelaide Crows and pretend to be him while playing with my cousins, and at night I'd have dreams about playing footy. However, it wasn't until my first year at the Calder Cannons Under 18s that the conversations started to centre on potentially fulfilling those childhood dreams.

I didn't understand the elite levels of the game – how structured and organised and professional the players are. In suburban footy, you just played. In the TAC Cup, though I was still playing with my mates, it was a totally different way of going about it.

I was quite underage when I started in that competition and I remember thinking, at my first training session, 'These boys are massive.' I looked down at my skinny arms and thought, 'Fuck me. How am I going to keep up with these massive dudes?'

When I got picked for the team, I was handed the number nine jumper that David Rodan had worn and won back-to-back Best and Fairest awards for the entire competition. David's name was on my locker, too. To this day, I consider myself privileged to have worn that guernsey.

I still had no idea how big a deal the TAC Cup was. It was only when we got flown to play in Tasmania that I started to get a grasp on it. At that point, I still wasn't completely comfortable with anyone in the team, so most of the time I stayed in my room while they went shopping and sightseeing.

I still felt shame being the only Blackfulla in the team. I didn't have much money either so when we went away on trips I couldn't really do all the things everyone else was doing. My family did everything they could to support me, like paying for my fees and uniforms, but we felt the struggle a little when I needed extra money for trips away. I felt like this didn't help with my bonding with teammates and sometimes I would spend hours alone on the trips away, hiding from people so they wouldn't know I had no money.

Those barriers wore down gradually over time and I ended up getting pretty close to some of the boys on that team. Us mob see the strength in relationships and put trust before anything else. Developing strong relationships is at the core of everything we do and walking into whitefulla dominated environments can be daunting. Just striking up one trusting relationship within that workplace or team can mean so much in the long run for better outcomes all 'round.

About five rounds into the season at Calder Cannons I ended up getting selected in the state team for Victoria Metro. For those training sessions, I had to take a 45-minute train ride into the city, then another 35-minute train out to Oakleigh. Then I'd walk for another five minutes to get to the oval.

I was too self-conscious to ask anyone in the team for a lift home. At the end of training, as I was setting out on the walk back to the train station, I'd watch the other players jump in a car with their mum or dad.

I never missed a training session and was never late. I would always spend the day of training looking at the clock and working out when I would need to leave in order to get there with enough time to prepare before training. I'd factor in train delays, ticket inspectors, and whether I had enough money to get there and home again for hours before I even had to leave. The freedom I had as a child really set me up well to deal with whatever obstacles or challenges came my way. Anyway, I mostly avoided paying for the train ticket so I could keep the money for snacks. I just used to sneak out behind someone who was leaving the station.

Getting selected for Vic Metro was actually a whole family effort. All my Aunties, Uncles, sisters, brothers and cousins contributed wherever possible in order to give me the best opportunity to participate in that state team. I relied on Mum and Aunty Tessa when they could help, and often my mum's older sister Aunty Tinker would send money across from Port Lincoln to contribute. We took the journey together.

As well as playing at Calder we had to choose a local club to play at and a big mob of us Blackfullas went and played at Templestowe. It was here I met one of my closest mates and his family. The Wasons supported me a lot through my early career.

Scotty Wason, his brothers and sisters and mum and dad, Faye and Tony, were able to connect us mob with the team in a way that made us all feel comfortable. We would head off after training to his parents' place for a feed and it helped us all settle into the footy club quickly. We connected strongly with all the players on this team and I honestly think it was 'cos of the way the Wasons welcomed us like we were family. It was like being at home, the door was always open.

Having a culturally safe space for us to go and gather, like at the Wasons' house, provided me with an opportunity to be able to develop on-field as well as feeling secure off-field. This was imperative in my young years and gave me a sense of stability when moving from a small town away from community to the big city. It was huge for my confidence.

When Tony passed away later on in my career I was absolutely devastated. He went too early to cancer and I felt his loss greatly. The funeral was huge, attended by heaps of people from the footy club who he obviously meant as much to as he did to me. He was so respected and loved by everyone. We still have a roll of foil from the funeral in my cupboard that I kept when I was helping Aunty Faye pack up after the wake. I'll have to drop that back to her one day!

Around the time I started at Templestowe I signed with a manager. I'd met Tommy Petroro through the club. He used to look after all of the young fullas there. He'd do everything for us and the club, from coaching the Under 18s to taking us fullas to games. He and I already had a good relationship, so it was a really easy decision for me to sign with him. Tommy supported me to manage things I hadn't really needed to consider before that point. Prior to meeting him, us fullas basically lived pay cheque to pay cheque. I didn't really have a good understanding of saving money, or even budgeting for bills.

Robert Hyde, my coach at Calder, was also an important mentor for me. Us players had big respect for him and that respect was mutual too. It made us want to play for him. I also always felt at ease around him. That mutual respect and belief in oneself was key to making the club successful. The Cannons won a lot of premierships with 'Hydie'. We would play to our strengths, stick to our game plan, and, most importantly, we had a good club culture. As teammates, we wanted to see one another achieve more, do better, be successful. We played for each other.

In my first year, we won the grand final and I made the under 18s All-Australian team. I was also given my first ever off-season training and weights program.

I went home to community and didn't really give it much attention. My thinking was, 'Off-season training? Can't be that important.' Not only did I even struggle to read it, but I felt so happy to be back home in community with my mob that the thought of going off and actually doing it didn't even cross my mind. I hadn't seen my family for so long. We spent days out in the bush hunting and eating bush foods, getting roo, making stew and damper, sleeping under the stars. Home was away from the rigid schedules and time constraints in the city, and I needed that sense of freedom. I could spend all day on the bikes, hunting and just being around my mob.

Unfortunately, the fitness team back at the club didn't see it the same way when I eventually fronted up again a fair bit heavier than when I'd left. When I walked back in I weighed around 75 kilos – 10 or so more than before the break. The guys certainly let me know about it too.

When I started pre-season training ahead of my second year at the club, I began to get injured more than I had before. I developed osteitis pubis, which is where the lower-front part of your pelvis gets inflamed right where the pubic bones meet. All that extra weight had been putting extra pressure on my groin. My knees started playing up too, and I began to have issues with my patellar tendons. Looking back, it probably shouldn't have come as a surprise.

I had come back unfit but my commitment to the team was still strong. I showed up no matter the hurdle to get there, so I didn't feel any resentment from my teammates about how I returned from the off-season. I just kept my head down mostly and tried to get the work done at training and in games. And I still loved being out there playing footy. My fitness might have suffered because of the weight gain and the injuries, but my speed and skills remained about the same.

Because I'd been an All-Australian the previous season, I got automatic selection back into the Victoria Metro side and I played three or so games with them in that second year. We won again that year too.

A few of my teammates and coaches had spoken to me about scouts watching our games and that the opportunity to attend the AFL national draft was up for grabs, but I was more focused on what I could do in the present – and that was to play footy at my highest standard in the TAC competition, yet still enjoy myself and have fun while doing it. I wasn't overly fussed with being drafted. I just wanted to win another premiership with the Cannons.

My family have always taught me to live in the moment, to focus on doing a good job on what you are doing now. I love the game, so whatever task was at hand, I would be focusing on that. Out on the field, I felt no barriers; I could play equally like everyone else and that bought so much joy to my heart and soul. Footy was the equaliser.

SIX

SIX

I received a letter to attend the AFL draft camp. I didn't prepare for draft camp like I needed to. I don't think anyone really stressed the importance of the camp to me, how it could shape potential selection into the AFL. I knew it was a 'sounding camp' to meet clubs and show off my skills, but I didn't really consider the 'testing' element of it. I thought I'd just go there, play footy and show selectors what I could do on the field.

The camp itself was incredibly intimidating. It was in Canberra at the Australian Institute of Sport and I was blown away by all of the technology and facilities at the place. We were essentially either in our rooms, in meetings, or doing training and tests. You watched everyone else and saw how they were going and you were supposed to keep up. Once all that running, jumping and timing was done, you'd go back to your room and wait around for the next task. I was there in a pretty impressive draft year: the cohort included names like Danyle Pearce, Buddy Franklin and Jarryd Roughead.

First up for me was the beep test – and I was the first person to pull out. I just couldn't keep up.

Next was the three-kilometre time trial. Before it, I was just thinking, 'Nah – not doing that.' And I didn't: I told them my knees were sore and so I just didn't do it. I was okay to do the ball training right afterwards though. No one seemed to question me for not doing the time trial, and I didn't feel overly embarrassed by not doing it either. I just got on with things I knew I could do. I was aware of how far behind the rest of the cohort

I was physically – but I also knew that when it came to kicking the ball and playing, I'd be able to match them.

Reflecting on the draft camp now, it was a whole other level of professionalism for me and at the time I wasn't comfortable in that environment. I *was* underprepared, but I knew myself enough to realise that I had a good foundation, a team-first attitude, and wicked game instinct. All that came from my childhood of running around with my cousins, and from our mobs' belief in strong communities and working together. Individualism was not in my nature. That's why the whole draft camp experience was awkward for me.

I think the only test I did okay at was the hand-eye coordination challenge. You had to stand in front of a series of lights and when one lit up you'd hit it as quickly as you could and they'd measure your accuracy and the time it took to connect. I think I might have won that one, but it's fair to say that after not being up to scratch on any of my other test results, I wasn't expecting anyone to knock on my door with good news.

That's how it happened at the draft camp back then: you'd just wait and hope that someone would come and give you a time that a club wanted to meet with you. If they did, you'd wait for the minutes to tick down, then walk along the corridors and head into a conference-type room. In front of you would be the club's coach, the fitness and wellbeing team, and maybe a few others.

I talked to a few clubs. One particular meeting that stuck in my mind was with a coach who had a reputation for being particularly intimidating. By the time the team had called me in, I had heard a lot of stories about this coach and I was as nervous as anything. But it was pretty funny in the end.

'So, Eddie,' the coach started off, 'you know a few of the boys, right? They're your cousins, right?'

'Yep,' I nodded.

'So, Ed: we draft you, and one of your boys is going out one night and he's going to get on the piss. He asks you to come with him. What do you say?'

I didn't really have to think about it.

'Well, yeah . . . I'd probably go with him and get on the piss, too.'

The coach paused.

'So, then, Ed,' he went on, 'this mate of yours is going to get a tattoo. Do you?'

'I don't know. I might.'

He wasn't looking too impressed.

'I guess it depends on the tattoo,' I added.

I pride myself on my honesty, but sometimes it can get me into trouble and that situation possibly wasn't my best work. Afterwards I heard that the fitness staff were impressed that I didn't try to bullshit my way through the coach's questions. Then, before I knew it, the two days were up and I was flying back to Victoria.

*

It's hard to explain, but I've never been one to dwell on the past. In our Culture, we don't look back like that very often. We live in the moment, endure it, persist and we keep moving forward. So I didn't think too much more about the draft camp at the time. Most people that went probably had a thousand questions to answer from family and friends when they returned, but I didn't really talk to anybody about it at all – I just got back to living life. I had finished my TAFE course by that stage, but didn't have a clue what I was going to do next. I was thinking I could probably head back to Kalgoorlie and work in the mines if things didn't turn out with footy.

I was back in Kalgoorlie, having a drink, when I watched the draft unfold. Name after name was called out, but no 'Eddie Betts'. It finally started to sink in. By the time they got around to naming the last pick, I was thinking, 'Fuck this, I'm gonna have a proper drink.' So I went around to my cousins' and sat sipping with them and I didn't even talk about it. But it hurt, getting overlooked.

That night I went and sat on my grandmother's grave in Kalgoorlie and had a yarn with her about what I was going to do with my life now. I was disappointed that I was overlooked, but deep down I felt my background would mean I would have to work twice as hard to get noticed. I had the skills, but skills only take you so far. I was killing it on the field, I knew that I could play, but my fitness wasn't up to scratch.

My manager rang a little while later and said I should keep my chin up, since the rookie draft and the pre-season draft were still to come. But I thought, 'Yeah, whatever. If they haven't taken me now, they'll *never* want me.' As a lad, I also had a different set of social skills to the majority of the kids in the draft and some people failed to appreciate how hard it was to anticipate and make adjustments to communicate effectively with recruiters and coaching staff. That's an unfair and unjustified burden for young Blackfullas to carry in any situation, let alone a high-pressured, high-stakes scenario like the draft. Some clubs are just now starting to make the necessary reforms to have Aboriginal liaisons sit in the drafting meetings, which means young Aboriginal players are more likely to open up and therefore recruiters are able to get a better insight into where the player is at.

I had my 18th birthday to look forward to. We had a massive party planned for the Saturday, 26 November. My family, including Dad, were all coming over to Kalgoorlie from South Australia for it. However, halfway through that week, a spanner was thrown into the works.

Sarah Mulkearns was a fitness trainer with the Calder Cannons and her husband, Peter, was the podiatrist at the Carlton Football Club. Sarah and I had a good relationship and she must have said something to her husband about Carlton giving me a shot. The phone rang on the Tuesday. I picked it up and on the other end of the line was someone telling me I was going to have a chance to train with Carlton. 'How soon can you get on a flight to Melbourne?'

My first answer was, 'I don't suppose you can wait until Sunday? I'm having a few people over for my birthday.'

There was a pause, but then the response I got back was basically, 'If you want to do something with your life and play AFL footy, you need to straighten up and get on the flight that we've booked for you – *tomorrow.*'

I was gutted at the thought of not having an 18th. I'd have to be back in Melbourne – by myself and missing out on a drink with all my brothers.

'Okay,' I said. 'I'll get on that plane.'

When I told my family what had happened, they were all pumped. And, of course, they all still had a big party on the Saturday night to celebrate.

I remember rocking up to Carlton for the first time. I knew three of the boys there. A couple of them had been rookied and drafted the year before, but I had played in a premiership team with Adam Bentick and gone back-to-back with Jesse Smith and Nick Becker. Because the opportunity had presented itself so quickly, I hadn't properly organised anywhere to stay, so the club arranged for Jesse's family to welcome me into their home in Sunbury.

I was trialling with Trent Knobel, the big ruckman, and we knew we had two weeks to make an impression. It was pretty daunting. There I was on a footy field with the likes of Anthony Koutoufides and Brendan Fevola. I was way too shy to talk to them at all – but just training alongside them was enough of a buzz.

I was overweight, but I remember training pretty well that first day. At one point, I took the ball off 'Fev' in a handball game. He didn't like that too much and grabbed me and slung me. Bret Thornton came over and stuck up for me. That was the first of many laughs I'd have with Fev. By the end of each day, I'd be absolutely stuffed and would need all of my energy just to make it home for dinner. I'd literally fall into bed, but I was running around kicking a footy for the Carlton Football Club every single day.

The coach at the time was Denis Pagan and I really liked him. He was ruthless. Old school. In those first two weeks, even though he didn't say much to me, I watched him tell everyone exactly what they needed to do and exactly how things were. I liked that. Most of those early sessions went by in a blur. I didn't feel any nerves. I think the best way I can describe it is that I was *pumped*. Then at the end of the two weeks training trial, my manager rang me and said the club would pick me up on the rookie draft, as they had the first pick. I was stoked – but also pretty chilled about it. After all, I knew that being a rookie meant I couldn't actually *play* for them that season.

But that didn't matter to me too much. I was just happy to be able to train inside a professional football club.

Then the pre-season draft came around. I hadn't thought that being elevated was even a possibility for me, given big Knobel was available and everyone knew Carlton wanted *and* *needed* a ruckman. Richmond had first pick in that draft, and the Blues were up third. You can imagine that they were a little flat when the Tigers took the big man. But with Trent off the table, apparently Denis Pagan said to the recruiting team, 'Well, we just lost our ruckman – let's pick the next best thing.'

I'd got my licence by then and was out driving around in my first car, a busted up red Ford Falcon that was given to me by my Pop in Kalgoorlie. He wanted to help me get to training and I was so proud to be able to drive something that was mine. So I was out cruising around when my manager called me with the news: I was now on the club's 'senior list'. *That's* when I felt blown away. I could actually run out in the navy blue and *play*. I rang Mum as soon as my manager hung up. And she simply said, 'Well done – but I always knew you was going there.'

The news travelled fast and immediately all my mob changed their favourite team to Carlton – all except Mum's dad, Pop, who was West Coast Eagles through and through. He made a point of calling to tell me he loved me, but he wasn't changing his team for *anyone*.

*

As I was moving to Melbourne I needed to find somewhere to live full-time. Mum and Aunty Tessa came back over and moved back into a house we'd stayed at earlier on in Muriel Street, Niddrie. My sisters and my cousins came too, so very soon I had a lot of my family with me.

The first day back at the club after the Christmas break was the first time I met 'Bulldog', the club's property steward. Everyone knew Carlton had been after a big man and Bulldog found it hilarious that instead of a 'tall', in walked me, the shortest guy in the team. I remember his exact words: 'Well, this is the smallest ruckman I've ever seen.'

Denis stuck the training into us straight away – and we trained *hard*. I played in a couple of the pre-season games and we won the pre-season cup. But all of that was overshadowed by Denis telling me I'd be playing in Round 1. It was a Wednesday and we'd be playing North Melbourne that weekend. Denis just said, 'It's the hard work you've done – the way you've been training and the way you can tackle and put pressure on. You keep doing that and you'll stay in the team.'

I had a smile that went from ear to ear. It was crazy to me that I could be in that position, ready to play in Round 1. Denis made it very clear what my role was for my first game. I was to go out there, tackle, and put pressure on – we had Fev and Lance Whitnall up front. But I also recall thinking – a flash in the back of my mind – that I might just get a goal on debut.

I excitedly told Mum and we rang the news through to the rest of the family. There were lots of congratulations – and plenty of requests for tickets. The AFL organised a flight for Dad to come across from South Australia. That was pretty special.

I was nervous as anything the night before the game. The next morning, I woke up and went about life as usual. I ate breakfast and hung out with the family. That day passed like any other for me, but the butterflies in my stomach really got going again as I was getting dressed in the change room. It was a surreal feeling being in that moment with no idea of what was about to happen next, aside from the fact that I would shortly be running out to play my first AFL game.

We were called into a team meeting and Denis gave his pre-game spiel. Written on the whiteboard were a lot of notes about team structure. I looked at it and tried hard to understand what was written, but I still couldn't read. And because I couldn't read it, I was distracted and stressed. Then Denis asked me to respond to a question I hadn't heard. All the blood drained away from my face. I remember going, 'Um . . . er . . . I don't know.' All the boys laughed, but fondly. They didn't know that I couldn't read. No one at the club would know until my second year.

We headed to the race (the tunnel that leads from the change rooms to the ground) and before I knew it I was running out through the banner. Instead of looking straight out in front of me, I was spinning my head around wildly trying to look at everyone in the crowd around the ground. There weren't that many people there by AFL standards – probably 20,000 – but it was an incredible crowd to me. I remember Lance Whitnall running past me and telling me to get my head in the game.

Considering who I was matched up against, I knew I'd need everything I had. There I was, a little fella in his first big game, lining up against none other than Glenn Archer, the 'Shinboner of the Century'. Later on he was named the toughest man in AFL history: a fierce competitor. When I learned he was my matchup, I hoped it was some kind of joke they were playing on me because I was on debut. But that's where the team needed me. Out there on the field before the bounce, I was so nervous I found it difficult to even look at him. And he knew I was shitting bricks, because he deliberately didn't say a single word to me.

My first AFL goal came off a forward-50 stoppage. Whitnall grabbed me and said, 'Eddie, run through and I'll tap it to you.' Sounded simple enough. I took off. Whitnall's kick bobbled towards the boundary line. I sprinted after it, managed to collect it in the pocket and snapped it towards the sticks. And it sailed straight through the middle.

I threw my hands in the air. The crowd went crazy. Everyone in the team swamped me. It was another surreal moment. I couldn't believe I'd kicked it. But I also always *knew* I would kick it too, if that makes sense.

My second was another snap in the pocket down the other end. Unfortunately, by that stage we were losing by a large margin. That didn't stop me from doing the same kind of celebration I'd done earlier though. Whitnall pulled me up and told me to calm the celebration down a bit because we were getting beaten so badly. All I could say was, 'Sorry, mate – I'm just excited.'

Carlton didn't have the best season on the field in my first year. We picked up the wooden spoon, and of course I was disappointed that we didn't win more, but I also played 19 AFL games and kicked 19 goals wearing the number 19 jumper. I also won the Best First-Year Player award. I was so proud of getting that award.

It came with a watch that I passed over to my Pop. Nothing could repay the contributions, sacrifices and support he and so many of my family members had made to get me there, but I wanted my Pop to have that watch, as even just a small token of my gratitude.

SEVEN

I still felt that all the attention on me after that first year at Carlton wasn't warranted. I was actually kind of embarrassed that people knew who I was. I still do grapple with that concept a bit. I always feel like I'm still just a kid from Port Lincoln and Kalgoorlie.

In my second season I felt a sense of responsibility to the fans who had embraced me after that first year. Unfortunately, I let them, the club, and myself down when I came back from the off-season overweight. Once again, I'd done absolutely nothing during the break. I remember the fitness team giving me the off-season program before I left, but reading those programs was still difficult for me. I always just played footy and didn't really place much importance on preparation. In community we kinda don't follow routine like that too much. It all added up to a steep learning curve for me.

I felt embarrassed and self-conscious when I got back to pre-season training and realised everyone else was so much further in front of me in their fitness. I remember being acutely aware of the situation. I asked Bulldog for a large T-shirt to wear and in training laps I'd run with my thumb holding my jumper out from my stomach so people wouldn't see my gut. Denis would have been very disappointed in how I'd returned, but I think he realised that to get the best out of me, I didn't need to be shamed in front of the other boys. I don't recall any specific conversations with him, but I just knew in my own mind that how I came back wasn't good enough and that I'd have to work hard to shape up. I started well behind the line again that pre-season.

By this time, most of my mob had moved back to Port Lincoln or Kalgoorlie, leaving only Mum and Aunty Tessa with me in Melbourne. Denis was still coaching and, while I was enjoying being back at the club, after having gone home in the off-season, I was really missing my family. For me, the effect of my family leaving was significant. From a busy community-based environment at home, it was suddenly just me, my mum and Aunty Tessa, and they were both working a lot. It all just left me feeling like there was a huge void in my heart. During the Christmas break, I went back to Port Lincoln for two weeks to be with my mob again.

I loved being back in Port Lincoln with everyone. My nanna's Sunday roasts were the best. She would spend all day preparing them. She had about seven dogs running around and everyone would just meet at her place for a feed. We would sit out the back with a fire drum going and sing country music – mostly Uncle Alan Jackson – while having some drinks until night would come. I felt a strong sense of belonging and connection. My mind was at ease and the structure and routine of a footy club was the last place I wanted to be.

When it came time for me to head back to the club, my anxiety started to build up. I constructed a plan to lie to them that my father was unwell and that I needed to stay a few extra days – then I simply turned my phone off so no-one could contact me. After a couple of days and numerous missed calls from the club, I finally answered my phone and the footy manager, Shane O'Sullivan ('Shane-O'), was on the other end. It ended up being a pretty simple conversation, as he knew I'd lied (nothing gets past Shane-O). He said, 'Ed, if you want to save your career and come back and play footy, *get on the next plane.*'

I knew I had to take responsibility for my actions and, being an extremely loyal person, the fact that I'd lied to people sat uneasily with me – therefore I knew I had to have some difficult conversations with Denis upon my return.

Shane-O had become a strong father-figure in my life by that point. I felt I could always trust him. He took the time to build a respectful relationship with me. For Aboriginal people, relationships and connections are imperative to our being. I would say the relationship Shane-O built with me not only saved my career at certain points, but enabled me to thrive in an environment where I sometimes felt like an alien. This relationship was not a surface-level relationship – he was not just my footy manager. Shane-O gave me a safe place to go to in that footy club.

Shane-O came into the meeting I had with Denis to talk through my indiscretion. During the conversation, I was upfront and honest about why I'd lied to the club and stayed on in Port Lincoln. Denis was rightly pissed off with me. He questioned my integrity and loyalty to the club. He was disappointed on many levels, he said, and focused in particular on the fact that he had given me an opportunity when so many other clubs had overlooked me.

I copped an almighty spray regarding my lack of professional standards and was told in no uncertain terms that this type of behaviour would not be tolerated by the club. I had work to do to demonstrate my commitment and regain the respect of my teammates, coaches and staff. It was clear that I needed to repay the belief they all had in me. I set myself to do better.

I started feeling more like I belonged in my second year. I played regular footy and was contributing the best I could to the team. It was pretty depressing that we couldn't get any on-field success though. I spent a lot of time practising and developing my craft 'cos I really wanted team success.

Matty Lappin was a fabulous mentor for me too. I watched him at training and spent a lot of time reviewing his videos, paying attention to where he would position himself at the ball drop in order to be a good small forward. And it was probably because I was feeling a bit more comfortable at the club that I decided to do something about my reading.

I'd started to realise that not being able to read and write well enough wasn't exactly helping me. I'd muddled through for as long as I could and, like most people who struggle with literacy, I'd gotten pretty good at getting by. I'd started to find that being upfront about it was the best way to avoid any awkwardness. If someone wanted me to write something down, I'd just ask them how to spell it, and we'd all move on.

Around that time, the AFL Players Association (AFLPA) started a course where a couple of tutors would meet with anyone in the league who needed help with their literacy. It was open to all players from all clubs, but I only remember Aboriginal players being there.

The course was actually a lot of fun right from the get go, since all of the brothers were together. Because I enjoyed it, after our group lessons finished that year, I stayed on to do some one-on-one work for another year. That gave me the platform to keep on learning. Like my early days of training, if I was committed to something I would always show up, I wouldn't want to let my teachers down (just like my coaches) and I would plan for my arrival at the classes, like training, with an hour to spare.

I tried my hardest to get better and really appreciated the support the teachers gave me in order to learn this very important life skill. These days, I can read and write properly and my life is better for it. I'm still not the world's best speller though, so I love autocorrect and predictive text!

*

That 2006 season was a pretty long and dreary one on the field, but it *was* the year I won my first AFL 'Goal of the Year' award.

We were playing against Collingwood at the Melbourne Cricket Ground (MCG). It was late in the season and they'd been having a good year and were on track to make the finals. We were slightly ahead in the second quarter, and a punch-on was happening in the centre square after Alan Didak had elbowed Heath 'Scotto' Scotland in the face (which meant a fair few people probably only saw the goal on replay).

The umpires pushed on with play and the ball was kicked long into the pocket. Tarkyn Lockyer cleaned it up, but I smothered his handball and got possession. Then Simon Prestigiacomo tried to hunt me down hard up against the sideline. I remember looking up and seeing Fev with his hands up, asking for it – but in a split second I decided to just have a crack and threw it on the boot. It arced up and sailed through.

I can't really explain how it feels to do something like that. I just don't think about it as I do it – *at all*. I keep it simple. But it was a pretty special one. And Fev was the first person to run in and hug me. And we still stir Scotto about missing it all because he was left on his back in the middle of the ground.

The prize for Goal of the Year was a brand spanking new Toyota Aurion – but by the time I won, the rule was that you could only keep it for a year. I still considered myself lucky though – I loved driving that car.

One day while behind the wheel, I pulled it into a pub parking lot in Moonee Ponds to eat a sandwich I'd just bought when some cops pulled in behind me. I registered them but just put my head down to take a bite of my sandwich. Before I even had time to take that bite, both cops were standing either side of the car's front doors. The cop on the driver's side directed me to get out. He asked me where I'd got the vehicle and if it was mine. All I could think to say was that I'd won it. They kept asking me the same question and I kept saying the same thing over and over too, hoping they'd start to believe me. They didn't.

They checked the registration – which, of course, was linked to a Toyota dealership, and not to me.

I told them, again, 'I won it for Goal of the Year in the AFL. I play for the Carlton Football Club.'

Finally, one of them checked all my details and after that they arrogantly got back in their own car and left. I probably could have gotten more upset and indignant about that incident at the time – but for any Blackfulla sitting in a shiny, expensive new car, sadly that scenario is all too common.

EIGHT

My cousin Richard Sambo, myself in the middle and my youngest sister, Lucy, taken at the back of Aunty Tessa's house in Kalgoorlie.

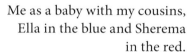

Me as a baby with my cousins, Ella in the blue and Sherema in the red.

Playing for the Mines Rovers Football Club Under 12s team.

Playing for Victoria Metro in 2003. (Photo by GSP Images via AFL Photos)

Calder Cannons Grand Final in 2004.

In 2005, I debuted for
Carlton Football Club
and was awarded the
Best First-Year Player.
(Photo by GSP Images
via AFL Photos)

Receiving a kiss from Mum after Carlton won the 2007 pre-season cup.
(Photo by Michael Willson via AFL Photos)

My brothers.

Anna, Pop (back) and Mikaela (my niece).

With Anna, and Lewis in a Crows jersey, announcing my move to play for Adelaide in 2014. (Photo by Michael Willson/AFL Media)

Anna and Billy at the Adelaide Oval for one of the international series games I played in for Australia.

Brett 'Ratts' Ratten at my house in Adelaide after my 200th game in 2014.

A moment's silence for Phil Walsh with the West Coast boys in 2015. We all broke down and ended up walking off in tears.

(Photo by Paul Kane/Getty Images via AFL Photos)

The following year, I lost another important person in my life: my Pop. Here I am with all my brothers out the front of 12 Boomerang Crescent for Poppa Cadley's funeral in 2016.

Aunty Tessa and my mother.

In 2007, Carlton drafted Aboriginal players Joe Anderson from Darwin and Clinton Benjamin from Broome. We immediately hit it off as is usual with Blackfullas coming into a footy club. Pretty soon after they arrived, we all moved in together which helped with my development as much as theirs. We became like one little family and, after seeing how settled I was, my mother, Aunty Tessa, and my cousins began to drift back towards Kalgoorlie. Before moving in with brothers 'Benji' and 'Joey', I'd spent the previous year living with a couple of my *wadjala* teammates in Moonee Ponds, which was alright, but I struggled a bit with feeling isolated, away from community and family. I didn't spend a lot of my down time in that environment, instead heading out to my family's place in Broadmeadows, about 20 to 30 minutes' drive away. My 'home life' at the Moonee Ponds address felt more like accommodation and was making me feel agitated and restless. My footy was fine and the boys that I lived with were good, but I was entering my third year with Carlton and I needed to get my shit together.

I guess I provided some sort of mentoring figure for Joey and Benji – something like an older brother – but *they* helped me feel comfortable outside of football, even in unexpected ways. Benji was the neatest brother I'd known around the house, other than my father. I had always been a tidy person, always had my bed made and kept my bedroom neat – I got that from Dad – but Benji was next-level clean.

That same year, after we got pumped in a game against Brisbane, Denis Pagan was, sadly, sacked as Carlton's head coach. The board decided that it was time for a change. I liked Denis as a person and a head coach. He gave me my first opportunity and believed in me in those early years when I just went out and played on instinct. I was sad that he was leaving, but I was also ready for whoever came next. I would always respect my coach, no matter who he was, where I was playing, or at what level. That degree of respect goes for everybody involved at the club. I've always just wanted to do my best for them.

I'd still be seeing Denis, anyway, because it was his house that me and the brothers had moved into. He used to rent it out to players from the club. Denis only lived about 40 metres away. You'd wake up on a Sunday morning and he'd be out in the front yard mowing the lawns. He'd get the shits if we didn't look after it ourselves.

Brett Ratten got the head coach job for the 2008 season and beyond. As assistant coach he had looked after the midfield under Pagan. Our relationship remained strong even after he got the head gig. 'Ratts' was so footy smart that he could talk about it *all day*. Footy was life for Ratts. He had played over 200 games at Carlton himself and was a life member of the club. I loved it. I trusted him completely – and in our Culture, when you trust someone, you open up to them and bond with them. To this day we get on well. Anytime I've played a milestone game, Ratts has sent me a letter or a text. Even for my 200th game, when we played against the Hawks, his team at the time, he came back to our house and celebrated with me afterwards.

I look back now and realise that, when all is said and done, Ratts has always backed me, no matter what. There was a point in my career when nothing was going right: I was getting hounded by the media, and my footy was suffering, which was devastating. Again and again, Ratts backed me and tried to pick me up to get me ready for another crack.

In mid-2008 I met Anna. I hadn't really felt so drawn to someone before. Anna was confident, smart and upfront. She didn't muck around. From early on I kinda knew where things stood between us. We were pretty much inseparable from our second meeting and, in mid-2009, after I bought my first house in Brunswick West, Scotty Wason, Anna and myself moved in together. It was a townhouse, with fairly tight living quarters, but the three of us just found a way to live together in harmony. There were never any issues, and we really loved the suburb. We felt like we belonged. Scotty, Anna and myself lived there for three years, which included a stint living with first year player Mitch 'Robbo' Robinson as well. I think Anna was fairly brave putting up with us three boys for so long.

Anna and I were – and remain – very different in character, but this has always worked for us. She was studying science at La Trobe University at Bundoora and was also working full-time nannying. She is an incredibly driven person and this trait very quickly rubbed off on my professional standards and my personal habits. My drive seemed to go up another level when we got together. We are good at talking things through and I think early on (and still) our different perspectives on things enabled us to learn from one another. We both embraced each other's families, siblings, and parents. Anna learnt very quickly the different meaning of family in Aboriginal Culture and I remember that being one of the first conversations we had.

In 2009, I decided to go back to TAFE and started studying for a Certificate in Education Support. I did my contact hours at Assumption College in Kilmore, about 45 minutes up the Hume Highway from home. I would get up really early every Thursday to get there and was never late. I'd spend my entire day away from the footy club, working at the school. I would support the classroom and often be partnered with the Physical Education team to support their footy and netball programs.

The classroom and learning support I did with the students was invaluable. I related well to all the kids and my confidence grew in terms of being able to communicate openly and provide insight. I had always been quite a shy kid in these types of environments but the TAFE course, the subsequent placement at the Kilmore campus, and the school visits helped me to grow in maturity and in leadership. The kids at the school probably wouldn't have ever known it, but they were incredibly important in my growth. The kids looked up to me, they would listen to my early childhood stories about schooling and education, and I realised I had a story to tell that could positively influence kids from all walks of life.

I was always honest with people about my journey with reading and writing, and this meant I was uniquely able to encourage kids in the classroom to just have a go. I was able to send messages to other students that weren't condescending – I just gently encouraged the kids towards learning. The more I saw how well this worked, the more this became my mantra for kids everywhere who looked up to me: Education first – footy second.

The 2009 season started well for the club. In the first game I kicked five goals in a win against Richmond at the MCG, and then we went on to beat Brisbane too.

We kept on rolling throughout that year, and – after missing out eight years in a row – we finally broke through to the finals.

We went back to Brisbane to play the Lions in a game that we should have won but didn't. I only managed one goal. We were in front for most of the match, but in the end were steamrolled and went down by seven points. It broke my heart. That game was Fev's last year at the Carlton Football

Club and it was strange to lose such a huge presence around the club due to some indiscretions.

He used to make me laugh. Fev was a relaxed figure around the footy club who I warmed to very quickly. I have heaps of good stories from my days with him in the Carlton forward line, but one I remember really well was walking out with him to play against Essendon at the MCG the previous year. Just as we were entering the race, Fev looked at me and asked me if I'd 'bought a ticket'. I didn't know what he was talking about – my first thought was that he meant the Alan Jackson concert that was happening in the off-season. I wondered how Fev knew I liked country music.

I said, 'I don't have one, brother. What do I need a ticket for?'

Fev just laughed and said, 'You'll need one, because you're going to see *The Fev Show* today.' Then he ran out and kicked eight goals.

In another game, we had just run out onto the ground and were lining up before the bounce, when Fev said to the young player who had been put on him, 'I'll bet you a hundred bucks you're not going to be on me at the end of the game.' Fev went on to kick eight that day, too – and didn't leave the forward pocket. I remember he looked up at the big screen at one point and yelled, 'I've got eight! Shit, I feel like a dart!'

NINE

In the 2010 pre-season, the playing group made a commitment to stay off the *gubby* (the drink). That went brilliantly while we were training in early December, and we were shaping up well for the coming season. But what we hadn't thought of was the post-training celebration. Back then, most clubs would have one before the squad headed home for the Christmas break. That year, we were more excited about ours than usual. There were a lot of young boys on the list that year, too, and we were looking forward to having a good time.

We got on a boat – and that's when everything started to go wrong. None of us had had much food beforehand, and it was just us players on the boat – no coaches, no staff. Each younger player was paired with an older player and we all hit it hard.

If everyone had gone home when we got off the boat, everything would've been fine. Instead, we jumped on a bus and kept drinking as it took us to a bar in Fitzroy, near the end of Smith Street, where more drinks were had until we got kicked out. Again, if everyone had called it quits then, we still probably would've been fine. But we moved up the road to a rooftop bar and carried on until we got kicked out of there, too. Finally, the group split up and we all started to go our own ways. I probably should have left then, but next up was a nightclub in the centre of the city.

At around three in the morning I finally decided to head home, so I wandered down to the street to look for a cab. There was a massive queue of people waiting for taxis outside the club. The line was so big it was winding down a side street, and the cops were there looking after everyone so there'd be no trouble. I didn't want to wait that long, so I thought I'd head across the road and try my luck there. I waited for five or 10 minutes, but there were no cabs, so I texted Chris Yarran, who was still inside the club, to get him to come down so we could try to get home together. Then I watched the club entrance and waited for Chris to come downstairs.

I kept looking at the stairwell to see if he was coming – and the police officers kept looking at *me*. I knew they were there, and I knew I wasn't *doing* anything, but eventually three coppers came over to me. The first officer asked me why I was eyeballing – which was *not* something I was doing. I was just focused on standing up straight.

They asked me for my name and address and what I did for a job. I said, 'I do nuthin.' I didn't think it was any of their business what I do. Then one of them asked me if I was still contracted with Carlton – so why did they ask who I was and what I did for a living? They clearly knew all this from the start. I said that I was just trying to get home and was waiting for 'Yazz' to come downstairs from the club.

Next thing, one of them said something like, 'This is going to ruin your career. You're about to sign a contract, aren't you? Well, not now.'

It was fucked up and I felt like they were power-tripping.

I asked the first officer what the issue was and why they had to come over 'bringing this guy and this guy', pointing at the second and third officers. That's when they grabbed me, put me up against a brick wall and cuffed my wrists behind my back. I was thrown into the back of a paddy wagon – arrested for being drunk and disorderly in a public place. I was drunk – but so were the couple hundred *wadjalas* who were also standing around outside the club. And I'd argue that waiting quietly on the street for your mate isn't being 'disorderly'.

Another guy was already in the cage of the paddy wagon. This dude took one look at me and yelled, 'Hey, EDDIE BETTS! How you goin'? Whatcha up to?'

It's hard not to laugh when I think about that now.

'Not much, mate,' I said. 'I was just trying to get a taxi home, and they've done this.'

I wasn't scared. I'd been around cops in the past – I knew this entire thing was just *bullshit*. The thought that kept revolving around my head was, 'I just can't believe I'm here.'

At the station, I had to pull all the stuff out of my pockets. Then they took my picture and put me in the cells. It wasn't until I was in there that I started to feel scared. There was a hard bench to sleep on and no blanket. Another guy was in there, too, and I felt really, really unsafe. I had to wait until they could get in touch with someone who could help me, though.

The police called in an Aboriginal legal representative, who helped get me out the next morning. As I was leaving with all of my gear, one of the coppers said, 'We don't want to see you intoxicated on the street again.' The legal rep drove me home, carrying a $234 fine.

I had to tell the club.

I called Shane-O, who wanted to know how they were going to deal with it; the news was about to become public. I knew that I just had to wear what was coming to me. I was fully aware that my career could be ended.

What I didn't know was that after that same boat trip, two other Carlton players had also been kicked out of (and banned from) the Crown Casino after having a confrontation with staff there. It's fair to say the three of us forced the club into crisis mode. Later on, more came out about the amount of drinking that had happened on that boat trip and I was told that we had almost cost the club a multi-million-dollar sponsorship deal with the confectionary giant, Mars.

I got suspended for a month. During that time, the three of us weren't allowed to have any contact with the club's playing group to train. We had to do weights at five in the morning, before any of the other players arrived, and then we'd be sent to an external boxing gym in Richmond and get absolutely smashed on the running machines. It was a hellish month – but I just put my head down and got on with what I had to do. As with my whole life I was always on time, worked relatively hard and just got it done – I remember coming home to Anna in the evenings as she was taking the dogs out for a walk and I didn't even have the energy to go for a stroll with her.

I came out of that experience with a completely different perspective on my career. I knew that I needed to grow up and start taking more responsibility for my actions. A big part of the process was making good with our teammates, so the three of us sent out a group message saying that we recognised we'd messed up and knew we had to earn back the players' and coaches' trust.

As for Ratts, we hardly spoke about it. He had a pretty simple message for the three of us: hurry up, get on with your training and be ready when you get back. Unfortunately, while Ratts didn't say much, the media said plenty – and all of a sudden, I was the 'bad boy'. I remember picking up a paper and seeing a photo of myself that they'd taken from some-one's Facebook page. It was from when I was on a footy trip to Las Vegas. I had a cigarette in my hand and was looking a bit worse for wear after a night on the town.

The headline was 'BAD BOY BETTS'.

I remember that page and that moment so clearly.

The day after being released, I went with Anna to see a local Aboriginal support worker and talk through what had happened. Upon reflection, I probably didn't deserve to be locked up but I also felt that I just didn't want to be in that situation ever again.

With Anna's support I decided it was a now or never moment. You can't always control the behaviour of people around you – whether it is cops or other people – so, to be safe, I put some limits on myself. That change was hard – really, really hard. I loved to have a drink and I was always a very sociable person.

Rather than stopping cold, I started to limit my intake. Anna and I also made a rule that we – or I, really – had to be home by 1am. That was tricky socially, because lots of players were only just getting started at midnight. I felt like I was missing out. Anna and I still tell each other, 'Nothing good happens after midnight,' and I pass that on to the young athletes we look after, who spend time with us at our house. And a question I often ask them is, 'Do you want to have a long career or a short career?'

My hope is that anytime any of them are out, when it gets to midnight they'll find a way to ask themselves that question – and then make the right decision. Since that now-or-never moment, it's a question I always ask myself, too.

TEN

TEN

In 2011, we hit the road in a big way, with 16 of us heading to Qatar for a high-performance pre-season training camp. The facilities there were ridiculous, like nothing I'd ever seen, including what was at the time the world's largest indoor sports dome as well as seven outdoor fields, an Olympic-sized swimming pool, a diving pool and a gymnastics arena – all built up out of the desert. The dust was the same, but I felt a long way from Kalgoorlie.

We were in Qatar to get ready for the season, but we were also there as guinea pigs and spent a lot of time in the purpose-built medical centre. Half of us lived and slept in special altitude rooms that had been designed to simulate living at height. The catch was that no one knew which of us had been set up in one of those rooms. We'd go out and do a heap of tests during the days – they wanted to see who would do better at training. It turns out that I was in an altitude room – and I trained and ran worse than the others who weren't. From our perspective, it was all a bit of a myth. Certainly no AFL clubs decided to pack up and move to Nepal after our results.

We were there for just over a week before heading to Doha and staying at the Emirates Palace. I remember sitting down for dinner one night and they sprinkled gold dust over our dessert. None of us had ever seen anything like it. They even had a vending machine that sold gold bars.

We trained hard, though. Our tackling coach had us crawling through the sand on the fake beach so much that I had blisters on my knees and elbows.

We also bumped into the Hollywood action-movie star Steven Seagal, and we all jumped in for a photo with him. He loved that we called him 'Mr Pressure Point', but he had no idea that nickname originated from when Fev was causing havoc and taking the piss out of Chris Judd at the 2009 Brownlow Medal awards night.

On our last afternoon in Doha we were finally allowed to have a drink and we settled in at one of the pool bars. I was wearing massive sunnies, a gold necklace and, by that point, diamond earrings. Brock McLean was sitting next to me, and the bartender wanted to know if I was a rapper and Brock was my bouncer.

In the first game of the 2011 season, all the travel and hard work looked to have paid off as we smashed Richmond by 44 points, then followed up with a 91-point hiding of Brisbane in a game where I got a couple of 'Mark of the Year' nominations. Then we won by 10 goals against Collingwood – and, all of a sudden, we were favourites for the flag.

At the end of your career there are games that you remember more than others, and one game against Essendon from that year still stands out to me. There is obviously an incredible rivalry between the two clubs and we were all pumped to have a good game. The length of AFL games means that there can be an ebb and flow to any match, but in that one, from the very first bounce, everything went our way. I ended up with eight goals – one of them one of my better ones.

The ball came in from Heath Scotland and came into a contest in the goal square. I picked it up and looked to dish it off. I slipped but got back up, then dodged a Bomber and just instinctively snapped it off my right boot. I didn't think about a single step of what I was doing, but that ended up being a Goal of the Year nomination. That goal eventually was runner up, but I should have won it. It got the public vote, but the AFL All-Australian section thought it was only second best. I still laugh about that and say I was robbed.

We went to the finals that year, but our semi-final against West Coast ended in disappointment. We lost in the last 30 seconds of the game. It was so depressing. I don't often get angry about football, but I was really angry after that game. In the end, though, Ratts was right when he told us in the rooms that we couldn't change the result and would have to learn to accept it. The red-eye flight back home from Perth is always tough, but I can't remember ever feeling so flat after a game.

Starting a family was a long and slow process for Anna and I, and it put all of my on-field frustrations into perspective pretty quickly. After about two years of trying for a baby, Anna was able to get pregnant at the age of 26. She had been diagnosed with a hormonal condition – polycystic ovary syndrome – and so we used fertility treatments which often took a physical and mental toll on her. She always had a way of making sure she talked to people about what we were going through so we didn't feel isolated, and also in the hope that it would encourage others to feel comfortable talking about infertility too.

In February 2012, after six cycles of fertility treatment, Anna suffered a miscarriage. It had been such a long time coming for her to get pregnant and we were incredibly excited, but when the bleeding started Anna knew instantly what was happening. As we had always been open about our lives, Anna and I felt well supported through the miscarriage and were able to spend a couple of days away in Wangaratta at her family's farm. We took our dogs up and spent the weekend away from the city to have a much-needed break.

We would often escape up to Wangaratta during the season when things weren't going that well with footy, or when we needed a break from the bustle of Melbourne. We're both country kids, so going back provided us with some peace of mind.

The next month, Anna was very lucky to fall pregnant again.

Our first-born, Lewis Edward Betts, entered the world on 29 October 2012 in East Melbourne. He was a tiny little 2.5 kilos and required a little time in the high dependency nursery before we carefully took him home about five days later. I remember driving the car at about 30 kays per hour down the road to get back to our house in Brunswick West – my precious little new baby was on board and we were so excited to get him home.

We were both young but fell seamlessly into parenting. Having grown up with many young children and babies around me, I felt confident handling *minya gidjas* (small kids) and Anna had nannied while finishing her university degree – so we both acclimatised to our new roles without too much fuss.

We were instructed very early on by my family that our baby must sleep in the bed with us and to always keep the baby close. Each night we would tuck our new little baby, Lewie, in between us and Anna would wake whenever he would wake for a feed.

Lewie, my first-born, was perfect. He came to footy games at the MCG with 93,000 fans and sat happily on Mum's lap – the loudness of the crowd wouldn't even phase him. Win, lose or draw, I would wait for him to come into the rooms after the game and it was those moments in my footy career that I cherish the most.

Lewis grew up to be obsessed with footy. He collected footy cards, practised kicking goals from the boundary and, before most of my home games at Adelaide Oval, he would come on the ground for a pre-game kick with me.

Lewie rode the highs and lows of footy with me and from a very early age had a deep sense of what was going on.

He understood the game very quickly and reads the game far beyond his years. As a kid, I would just play, but Lewie is *obsessed* with the game. I remember the first time he walked, along the carpet at home. I was so excited at the time, but soon afterwards I wished he was crawling again, because he was just too fast and was always getting himself into trouble. Unfortunately, I couldn't be there the first time he kicked a footy. Anna had gone away with family on holiday while I was back at home training, so I watched that kick on video. I couldn't believe he was a left-footer.

I would never put any pressure on my kids to play footy. I have always said to people when they ask that is it absolutely not on the agenda of expectations I want to add to my children's lives.

Lewie has such a different life to what I had. He has different obstacles to overcome than I did. Lewis is strong on his Culture and protective of his beliefs. He has watched me and Anna always advocate for what is right and with this he has become an empathetic and thoughtful kid. His teachers love him. There are times he attempts to decolonise his education. He will openly yarn about the true history of Australia, and for such a young kid he has a way to gently provoke people's thinking and bring everyone on a journey with him. That's Lewie.

I am so proud to raise kids that witness and learn from my advocacy. We teach our kids to care deeply for others and that there is nothing more important than the community around us. They come along to the rallies and marches that are important to our family and they use their small (but big) voices to call for justice.

I have always said to people that kids are never too young to start learning about racism. Being Black, I have no choice but to be political in order to survive in Australia. If someone is concerned about their kids being too young to learn about racism, I always remind them that I had no choice but to learn about it from a very young age.

While we were going through the fertility process, football marched on. The 2012 season was disappointing as we failed to make the finals for the first time since 2008. While it was a good year for me on paper – I played in every game, led the goal-kicking with 48 goals and 30 behinds, made my third All-Australian squad and finished only nine votes behind Health Scotland in the club's Best and Fairest – we lost games that we should have won and won games that we rightly should have lost. We finished 11-11 but had no consistency at all and faded out towards the back half of the season. I don't know if it was due to the weight of expectation or injuries to some key players.

Unfortunately, Ratts paid the price for it. The board sacked him after our stunning loss to the Gold Coast in the second-last round of the year. Ratts had a year left on his contract. I was shocked and it was a tough time for me personally as I had a great relationship with Ratts. There had been rumblings about Mick Malthouse coming in to take the head coach role, but I didn't think it was going to happen so soon. We were called in to a meeting with Ratts, and he stood up in front of all of us and simply said, 'I won't be here next season.'

He exited the club graciously. In his final press conference he put things in perspective, saying he was still very fortunate in life and that he planned to coach out the next game, our final one for the season, against the Saints. It was sad to know that our time together was coming to an end. Ratts' message before we ran out was just to go out there, have fun and enjoy playing the game.

Around the same time, Chris Judd also stood down as captain after five seasons. I can honestly say that 'Juddy' was the most professional person I have ever played alongside. He did absolutely everything he could to get his body right, and plenty of that work was on top of the official training we were given at the club. I certainly learned a lot about preparation from him. As I was coming into the second half of my career, I was finally working out that my natural skill alone wasn't going to get me everything. I needed to do the hard work.

Mick Malthouse walked into Carlton in 2013 with three AFL coaching premierships under his belt. Immediately, you knew that he was old school and that he didn't hold back. Mick became another coach who I had a great relationship with and I enjoyed it while he was there. He was incredibly focused on making the club even more family-friendly, and when I broke my jaw against Richmond in Round 1 and had to miss three or four weeks, he was more than happy to let me go home to Port Lincoln so I could be with everyone. Dad was pretty sick at the time. He'd been diagnosed with acute pancreatitis and was in and out of intensive care at the Queen Elizabeth hospital in Adelaide.

Mick was always about family. He knew everyone's partner and parents, and he always reminded us that they were the ones who would share the highs and the lows with us players. Having Lewie and my family around the rooms after a game started to become my favourite part of the week.

So I broke my jaw in the first quarter of Round 1, 2013 against Richmond at the MCG and, a month later, in my second game back against St Kilda, I broke Nathan Wright's jaw. It was the first time in my career that I was suspended for an on-field incident. Wright had possession and I tried to stop his run. He kicked the ball and I tried to hip-and-shoulder him – but I hit him front-on. I had my feet off the ground when the contact happened – only slightly, but enough. When the medical report came through and said that Nathan had fractured his jaw, I was gutted. In fact, I can't tell you how devastated I was at the thought that I had hurt someone badly.

I was sitting in the car with Anna when I got the call to tell me I was out for five fucking weeks. It was reduced to three weeks because I hadn't done anything like that before. I wasn't a malicious player and I honestly didn't care about the length of the suspension – I was just so sorry I'd hurt Nathan. I texted him, saying sorry and wishing him a speedy recovery. He ended up playing the next week. It turned out to only be a hairline fracture.

ELEVEN

It's fair to say that there were a lot of disruptions for me in that last year with Carlton, and it was at the end of that season that negotiations between me and the club broke down. I had finished the season after playing only 18 games and managing just 27 goals, and I was sitting squarely in the middle of a crossroads. We had Lewie now, so security was really important to me. I had offers on the table for four years from both North Melbourne and Adelaide. Carlton didn't want to match that, though: they were only offering two years.

A lot of people assume my relationship with Malthouse must have broken down, but from where I sit, it was good – in fact, really good. I get that every club goes through stages where they need to get new players in to try to change things up. Would I have preferred to have stayed at Carlton? Absolutely. Did I hope that would happen, right up until the last minute? Of course. My management group were the ones who spoke to all the teams. I stayed out of the negotiation process. They would just bring the offers to me and I'd sit down with Anna and try to work through them.

In the end, there were a few factors that tipped us over to accepting Adelaide's offer. One was that if I couldn't be at Carlton, then I needed to be somewhere other than Melbourne. I just didn't think it would be good for Carlton and me to be in the same town – a bit of space over in South Australia would be best. I was also keen to be closer to my family, especially Dad. I spent time in South Australia when I broke my jaw, and visited him in the ICU of the hospital. As I stood there looking at him, hooked up to endless tubes, I thought, 'If there was any way I could come back and help you get better, I would.'

So the decision was made: Adelaide it'd be. Shane-O, who was still in the footy department at Carlton, was the first person I needed to tell at the club. It was incredibly daunting to have to look him in the eye and tell him face to face. There was nothing much I could say except that I wouldn't be there next year. When I walked out of that meeting, Kade Simpson was in the change rooms, and I started tearing up and told him that I was going to the Crows. Then Jarrad Waite walked in. After telling him I was off, I started to cry even more, and he hugged me. I packed up my things, shut my locker for the last time and drove home, still crying. Anna met me at the front door. I said, 'It's done. I hope we're making the right decision.' We didn't have a clue if we were.

Despite the tears, it was a surprisingly nice exit overall. It wasn't ugly at all – just sad. I had played 184 games for the club, and they made me a life member. Mick presented me with the membership at the MCG, and Mum and Aunty Tessa flew over for it. Having played a small part in a club that has one of the richest histories in the AFL is something that is still surreal to me. I never thought I'd play a couple of games at Carlton, let alone 184 of them. To last that long was just unreal. Knowing that my name is going to be up there, next to all of those legends, for the rest of time is pretty incredible. I take that honour very seriously.

After Anna and I had collected ourselves and started to get our heads around the reality of actually moving, I had to get to Docklands to meet with the Crows footy manager David Noble and champion Crows midfielder Patrick 'Danger' Dangerfield to sign my contract. They made me feel a lot better about the whole thing. I remember Danger asked me if I liked fishing, and I told him how much I loved it. 'Well,' he said, 'I'll get you out on my boat and we can go and chase some fish.' That sounded pretty good to me at that moment. But there was a lifetime of happiness and grief to come before I'd even see that damn boat.

So I was off to Adelaide, with a 14-month-old and a partner who had never even been to the place before. After all of the ups and downs, I was excited about the new beginning.

To start with, though, Anna struggled a bit. It took her a long time to get over her homesickness. It was a different story for me: I had the club and a ready-made group of people to play with and get to know, so I had no problems. I knew Scott Camporeale and Sam 'Sauce' Jacobs from our days at Carlton, and I had also travelled to Ireland with Danger as part of the All-Australian team. Then there was Richie Douglas, whose older brother I had played with at the Calder Cannons.

At the airport we were picked up by Maria Ballestrin, the admin assistant and champion of the footy department at the Crows, who is passionate about the club. We essentially only had a couple of hours on the ground to find a house that suited us. Luckily, we found one in the western suburb of Lockleys that we liked. We signed the agreement just before getting on the plane back to Melbourne, so that was one less thing for us to worry about.

There was a lot of pressure involved in the move. Fans and the media had plenty to say about why the Crows were signing someone in their late twenties to a four-year deal, and for that much money. Let's face it: the Adelaide media scrum has a tendency to go crazy. Overall, though, the feeling was really one of excitement for me. I had to put all of my nerves aside and focus on the fresh start.

In the first warm-up match for the 2014 season, I managed to kick five goals against Port Adelaide – and immediately felt like I could breathe again. Once the fans saw what I could do in their colours, public opinion turned in my favour.

When it came to my first 'official' game, Sauce presented me with my jumper. I was the fourth Crow to wear the number 18, and the third Aboriginal player after Troy Bond and Graham Johncock.

Anna and Lewie came over to Geelong for the first game of the season, which started well enough when I took a handpass, carried it forward and kicked my first goal on the run – but after that, the Cats were too good and we lost.

We had a young Aboriginal lad by the name of Charlie Cameron move in with us in Adelaide almost straight away. Charlie hailed from Far North Queensland but came to the Crows from Perth in Western Australia. He came in on the rookie list, and he loved kicking goals like I did. After his first season he was upgraded to the senior list and was a gun. I remembered how homesick I'd been for family and connection when I was a young fella starting at Carlton, so we welcomed him into our home.

Charlie hadn't played too many games at that stage, but he was incredibly intense and ultra-professional around training. I guess it helped that he saw the standards I set by getting to training early, making sure you train as hard as you play and eating right. It was hilarious when he first moved in and we'd all sit down at the table to eat. I've never seen a bloke avoid a vegetable the way Charlie did. Even when we bought fast food, like Subway, he'd only have cheese, ham and chicken on his. So we started sneaking veggies into him. At first, Anna would chop them up really small and put them in his meat patties. Eventually, it got to the stage where he'd chop them up himself and get them down into his guts with the help of heaps of water.

We met a lot of Charlie's family and welcomed all of them into our home too. At one point we had 14 of his Aunties down for a visit, all gathered around the fire in the backyard. It reminded me of home.

Playing the Crows' cross-town rivals Port Adelaide in what the fans call 'the Showdown' was unlike anything I'd ever been involved in. I'd seen Showdowns before and I'd heard people talk about what they were like to play in, but the noise and the hype was unbelievable. Coming from Carlton and their traditional rivalry with Collingwood, I had thought I was used to massive games. But the reality of a Showdown was something I couldn't have prepared myself for. Even though you can only fit about 50,000 people in Adelaide Oval, it feels more like 100,000 in one of those games. It was just next-level.

It was Showdown XXXVII that cemented the pocket at Adelaide Oval that came to be known by fans as 'Eddie's Pocket'. In the previous weeks, I'd nailed a couple of goals from the north-eastern side of the ground, hard up against the boundary line. Against North Melbourne, I'd slotted one from there as well that had the crowd going off. This young kid in a yellow shirt had reached out to high-five me after that one. I didn't see him, so in the footage it kinda looks like I burned him. Social media went crazy, calling him 'the kid with the yellow sleeves'. Well, there I was again, this time in a Showdown, and scoring yet again from that same pocket. And *there he was again*: the same kid in a yellow jumper. I thought, 'Alright – I won't burn you this time,' and walked over and gave him a fist bump.

In the press conference after the game, head coach Brenton 'Sando' Sanderson said, 'I think we've got the official "Eddie Betts Pocket" now.' The Adelaide media tracked down 'the kid with the yellow sleeves', who ended up being in Year 8 at Henley High School. He seemed okay with his newfound nickname. I got to meet him when he came down to training one day and we took a few pictures together. I know I'm a role model to some people and that kids might look up to me. I didn't really get what that meant until I took an eight-year-old Lewie to an NBL game in 2020 and one of the players gave him his playing sleeve. For days afterwards, Lewie was still running around with it. The excitement he got from meeting one of his idols lasted for ages. That's when it really clicked for me: I realised that, even though I might never see these people again, if I could make them smile, it could make their day better.

We won by 23 points, and my good mate, Sauce, won the Showdown medal for the second time. It was also pretty sweet because we cost Port top spot on the ladder, and at that stage we were around 11th.

People ask me all the time what it's like to kick those goals, or what I'm thinking about when I'm in that pocket. It's hard to explain. I'm not actually thinking about all the little pieces that go into kicking a goal: it just comes off the boot naturally. You hear some athletes talk about doing things and feeling like everything is happening in slow motion, but it's not like that for me. It's just all instinctive. I always know where the goals are, and I just kick in that direction. Even when I look inside to see if anyone else is in a better position than me, no matter what, I always know where those goals are. I'm actually less nervous when I'm on the boundary than when I'm straight out in front of the sticks. There's more pressure when you've stopped and you're looking at a very gettable goal. I want to be on the boundary: it's fun out there, and I know that if I'm kicking goals from there, I'm getting the crowd hyped and into the game.

It was around the time of that Showdown that the crowd started chanting my name every time I was lining up in that pocket. At first, that was awesome, but it got to a point where I was a bit embarrassed by it. I'd think, 'Geez, they should calm down – I haven't even *kicked* it yet.' The chants actually started to put me off a bit. In footy, it can feel strange when people focus on an individual rather than the team. After all, there are 18 players on the field and 22 on the team, so whatever we're doing, we're doing it as a collective. When people are calling out just my name, it's embarrassing. I love that the crowd is into it though!

Around that time, we decided we wanted another baby. This time, instead of mucking around, we went straight to a fertility expert. Two cycles later, Anna was pregnant. Our second son, Billy, came into the world in March 2015.

Billy Betts is just as cool as his name suggests. He wasn't much bigger than Lewie at 2.8 kilograms and snuggled under Mum's arms in hospital. He pretty much stayed there until he was two.

You always think when you have a kid that they're going to be so much like their siblings. Billy and Lewie get along very well but they are both so different. Billy is a bit cooler on the footy side of things. He is a little gun but he couldn't really care about how many goals we won by or if I was struggling with form.

Billy shows up to his junior footy but doesn't really get involved with the discussions around structure or plans and just goes out there with no fear. He is my little in-and-under midfielder, whereas I think Lewie is the big tall forward – directing traffic, using his voice.

Billy was diagnosed with an auto-immune disease – coeliac disease – in 2019. Coeliac disease is controlled by a strict gluten-free diet. For nine months, Anna and I noticed that Billy was becoming tired and withdrawn and we were worried about him. She kept bugging the doctor to look into it and eventually, after a blood test, coeliac disease was confirmed. Billy is such a trooper though. He always grants permission for the other kids to eat McDonald's or donuts in front of him and we have this rule: 'Billy has to let you eat it first.'

Billy has a really good brain for languages. I have always used words from my mother's and father's traditional dialects around the kids, which helps with their language development. In his first year of schooling he picked up an excellence award for Japanese and I think that naturally comes from hearing other languages at such a young age.

We mainly use traditional words with the kids when we don't want others around us to understand what we are talking about. Anna has been picking up key words and sentences too and before Pop passed away in Kalgoorlie he made sure he taught her words in my language to be able to use with our kids too.

My Nanna Veda in Port Lincoln is one of many Wirangu speakers who aims to keep teaching and restoring the language for us all to pass on to our kids. Nanna teaches all her kids, my Aunties, the language and we do our best as a family to preserve it.

We finished 10th in my first year with the Crows and I led the team in goal-kicking with a career-best of 51 goals. I had made an effort to throw everything into family and footy, and it looked to be paying off. In the off-season though, our coach, Sando, was sacked. It was unbelievable that this was the third head coach to be sacked while I was playing under them. The club was clearly ready for a change of direction though. Footy can be a lot of fun – but it can be brutal too.

TWELVE

I don't often remember specific things about funerals. For me, all the details get washed away by the waves of grief and emotion. Dean Bailey passed away after a battle with cancer and hundreds gathered at Adelaide Oval to remember this wonderful man and support his family. 'Bails' was an assistant coach and a much loved character among the players at the Adelaide footy club. Even though I was only new to the club I could see how strong his relationships were with the players. The boys were devastated.

His great mate Phil Walsh, an assistant coach at West Coast, gave a powerful tribute to Dean at the funeral in March 2014. I had no idea who 'Walshy' was at the time. Listening to him talk, I was blown away by how full-on he was. He spoke from the heart – I don't even know if he had notes – and when he talked about the love he had for his good mate, you felt like he was only speaking to you. I sat there thinking, 'Wow, this guy has some powerful emotion. He's driven. He's determined.'

At the end of 2014, when it was announced that Phil Walsh was going to be the new coach of the Crows, my exact thought was, 'Who the hell is that?' It wasn't until he walked into the club that I suddenly put two and two together and realised it was the same guy from Bails' funeral. I didn't watch as much footy as I played when I was young, so my lack of recognition is with no disrespect to how good a player Phil was.

Actually, Walshy didn't really walk into the club – he more *exploded* into it. He told us exactly what we were going to do that year – how we'd play, how we'd train. He never, ever held back from trying to make us better people first and better players second. He was firm and he was determined.

During our first training session, we were doing some ball skills – a passing drill. Walshy watched for a while, then came up to me and said, 'Eddie, every time you handpass it to someone, I want you to be available to take it straight back off them.' From then on, I pushed myself to be ready as that next option for my teammates every time.

When it came time to announce the captain, we all thought it would be Patrick Dangerfield – the natural leader of our group on and off the field. He was polished and he was going to go on to be a Brownlow medallist. So I think we were all a bit stunned when Walshy said our captain was going to be Taylor 'Tex' Walker. I certainly was. Tex was rough around the edges – a mulleted, straight-up country kid. I could recognise what Walshy saw in him in terms of getting people together though. He was community minded and would think about others before himself, but he still demanded high standards from people on the training field.

Walshy was all about discipline and he demanded the best from all of us too. Team cohesion was very important to him. I remember he stopped a training session once because one of the trainers didn't have the right socks on. To him, that was about the understanding that every single person involved in the club was a part of the team. It didn't matter if you were a star player or a boot-studder: you were integral to the fortunes of the club. That kind of professionalism extended off the track, too. One day, I walked into a team meeting while I was still finishing off my lunch and Walshy barked, 'This is not a restaurant! *Put it away.*' He didn't have to ask me twice.

Early on in his first season we lost to the Bulldogs, then got on a late flight back from Melbourne, which meant most of us would probably get home around 11.30pm. Before he let us go, Walshy made it very clear that we all needed to be down at Adelaide's Brighton Jetty at 4am the next morning.

After getting home and finally shutting down, I reckon I only had about three hours' sleep before I had to get up again and head to the jetty. None of us dared miss it, though.

We rocked up, and it was pitch-black, windy and fucking cold. All I could think, looking out into the water, was that it was a great time of day for sharks. Rory Sloane had his wetsuit on, but most of us were just shivering in our budgie smugglers and jumpers. I looked around and, down the road, coming towards us, I saw this distant red shape. The thing got closer and closer – until I finally worked out that it was Walshy, wearing only his red Speedos. He had nothing else with him – no towel, nothing.

'Righto,' he said. 'Let's get in.'

We all started moving towards the water, until Walshy yelled out, 'STOP! You lot aren't getting in with all that gear on. Take off the jumpers and the wetsuit.' Then he asked us who was the worst swimmer in the group. I put my hand straight up – I've never been great at it and I was still thinking of those sharks.

Walshy said, 'Righto, Eddie. How many strokes do you reckon you can do?'

I didn't want to say a big number; I settled on 20.

'Right: 40 it is, then.'

And off he went into the water, forcing us all to follow after him. Finally, after a lot of spluttering and splashing, we got to 40 strokes.

'Are we all here, then?' Walshy called out. 'Eddie, do we still have you?'

'Yes, Coach,' I said. I was imagining that a big white pointer was sizing me up because I looked like a little black seal.

'Excellent. Another 40, then,' demanded Walshy.

By this time, we were a fair way out. I had deliberately worked my way in between two of the other boys so that when a shark came, it'd have to grab them first. I didn't have to be the fastest swimmer. I just had to be the smartest.

For those who don't know, Brighton beach has a big jetty that juts out about 200 metres into the sea. By the time we finished those next 40 strokes, we were almost at the end of it. It was still shallow enough that we could stand up – just – and Walshy, instead of letting us go back in, decided we should stand there, freezing in the waves and the wind, and do our full game review.

I don't know how long that review lasted, but every minute felt like an hour. When we were finally done, we started heading for the stairs so we could climb up onto the jetty and walk back in.

'What do you all think you're doing?' Walshy asked. 'You're not going back in *that* way. Let's go: swim it back in.'

From then until we managed to get back onto the beach, the boys kept checking on me – 'Have we still got Eddie?' 'You right, Eddie?' When we made it to the sand, I raced back to my car, jumped in and put the heater on full blast. I was shivering and just wanted to get back into bed. My memory might be playing tricks on me, but I seem to remember that there was a shark sighting at Brighton beach not long after that. Probably at the same time of day, too. One thing's for sure: that session definitely taught us that we needed to improve our tackling – and that we'd have to do it as a team, not as individuals.

In May of that year, out of nowhere, I found out that the AFL was launching an inquiry into how I'd ended up going to Adelaide. What triggered it was a rumour that I'd 'signed' more than a year before I actually came over to South Australia. That's illegal under the AFL's rules for contracting players. The media played it up like it was a big scandal – making it bigger than it actually was. I knew nothing about it. All I could do was tell them it wasn't true and that I'd never had a conversation with Adelaide until the end of the year. Certainly, nothing had been signed – Anna and I were still working out what we even wanted to do. While the investigation was going on, I just pushed on with my footy. It involved undergoing a process with the AFL Integrity Unit, but nothing came of it.

That season I got a few nominations for Goal of the Year, but it was the one I kicked in the wet against Fremantle in the Indigenous Round that actually won it. Josh 'JJ' Jenkins burst through and hand-balled to me on the 50-metre arc near the boundary. It didn't quite hit me on the full, I had to turn around and go and get it. I wasn't in the 'Eddie Betts Pocket' and I didn't have much room, but I took one step and barrelled it in with a torp off my non-preferred left foot. I've already said that when I'm doing stuff like that, it just happens on instinct – but for some reason, that one slowed down a bit and I felt completely in control. When it dribbled through, I threw my hands up and looked out at the crowd, who were all sitting in the rain. On the telecast, I think it was Hawks-great Jason Dunstall who said, 'You're not *entitled* to kick that!'

That season ticked on until Round 13, when we travelled up to play Brisbane at the Gabba. We kicked pretty horribly but still won by 13 points in a pretty straight-up-and-down game. They came out of the blocks quickly, kicked the first four and led until three-quarter time, but then we finally started kicking straight and landed six in the final term to finish them off. Afterwards, we headed back to Adelaide and started rolling through the week and training at our home base at West Lakes. And then everything changed.

I woke up at around 5.30am on 3 July and found three missed calls from my line coach and good friend David Teague. I had no idea what he could be ringing about at that hour of the morning and I was just swinging my legs off the side of the bed when he called again. I answered and straight away I could tell that he was emotional by the sound of his voice.

'You need to be sitting down,' he said. 'I don't even know how to tell you this, Ed, but Phil's been murdered.'

There was silence. My brain was trying to process what he'd just said.

He went on: 'You need to make sure you're okay. Have a shower, get your things together and come down to the club. I'll see you in there.'

Then he hung up.

By now, Anna was awake and asking me what was going on. I sat there for at least a minute trying to figure out if I had even heard 'Teaguey' right, before responding.

Anna kept saying, 'Ed, what's wrong? What's happened? Ed, talk to me.'

I finally turned around and faced her. I told her, simply, that Walshy had been murdered. I didn't know how else to say it. Anna started freaking out. Her immediate reaction went from shock to suddenly thinking someone might be going around and killing Crows players and staff – before I left the house Anna went outside to check that there wasn't anyone out the front. That sounds stupid now but the entire situation was just so foreign, so unbelievable. It's so hard to describe those moments when your mind and body go into shock; Anna and I just didn't know what to do with ourselves.

I got my stuff together and got in the car. I spent the entire drive to the club surfing the radio stations trying to find someone who could tell me it wasn't true. But finally, they said there had been 'an incident at Crows coach Phil Walsh's home'. My heart sank again.

When I walked into the club, the first person I saw was Sauce, who was crying – as were plenty of others. My overriding memory of that day is of silence. None of us knew what to say or do. We stayed in lockdown at the club for most of that day, completely lost. No one had any idea what was going to happen – or how to process what *had* happened.

Outside, Anna had started ringing the players' and coaches' partners and inviting them over to our house so they'd have a safe space where they could talk it through. They could all just sit and be with each other.

The club chairman, Rob Chapman, spoke to us. You could tell that he'd been crying too. Crows CEO Andrew Fagan also spoke. I can't remember what either of them said, though. Finally, the leadership group and a few of us older players got together with 'Fages' and spoke about our upcoming game against Geelong. We were asked if we thought that we could play. We all said we could because it was something we wanted to do for Walshy, but at the same time, we all knew we weren't in the right space, physically or mentally. We wouldn't have been able to play the way we wanted to – the way Phil would have wanted us to.

I'm sure a thousand meetings went on behind the scenes. In the end, it was negotiated that we'd share the points with Geelong. At that stage, we couldn't have cared less about competition points. It was all about doing the right thing by Walshy, his family and our own families.

The next few days were a confusion of shock, grief, media, fans and tributes. In amongst all of that, I found the time and the quiet I needed to think about Phil's wife, Meredith, and his children. It really hurt. It was impossible not to think about the 'why' and the 'how' of it.

On the day that the Geelong game was meant to have been played, the oval was instead opened up to fans so that they could go along and pay their respects. Thousands turned up. I went for a drive past the oval with Anna and the kids and it just made me so emotional to see the incredible turnout.

The following week, we were faced with the task of playing West Coast. Their football community was in mourning, too, since Walshy had spent time there as an assistant coach.

The Crows were adamant that if we were going to be able to play, we'd need our families around us, so they chartered a plane and flew everyone across.

The lead-up to that game was as normal as it could have been in a horrifically abnormal situation. It was a very emotional time for everyone. Riley Knight had been so happy in the week leading up to Walshy's death, because Walshy had just told him he'd be playing his first game of senior footy that week. He had gone from being the happiest bloke on the planet to completely devastated. Out of respect for Phil and his wishes, the team wasn't changed, and Riley debuted at Subiaco.

I think most of us thought we were going okay. We were still grieving and in shock – most definitely – but when it came to footy, we thought the emotion would actually help us.

The Eagles absolutely smashed us up.

That game was the hardest thing I have ever had to go through in footy. With our previous match being cancelled, we hadn't paid our respects to Phil publicly that week – so to stand in the middle of the ground with the West Coast boys and bow our heads was almost too much for us. We all broke down and ended up walking off in tears. The club brought our partners onto the ground to form a guard of honour for us. Looking into the stands, I could see that even the West Coast supporters were crying. I'm getting teary just thinking about it now.

If that wasn't hard enough, being in the rooms, without Walshy, was even tougher. It was silent. No one could say anything. And no one cared that we had just lost a game of football. When it came down to it, we were all there with our families – and Phil Walsh wasn't.

In the end, for the team, it brought us closer together as a group. All we had to do was survive that season. We were all feeling driven to play better footy for Phil. We were mentally tougher and more resilient than we had ever been before. We were a collective, and we relied on each other.

Scott Camporeale was put in charge for the rest of that season.

Somehow, despite everything, we made it through that year. We even finished in seventh place and made it to the finals. After winning our first one, we met Hawthorn at the MCG, and it was there that we finally ran out of legs, drive, energy – *everything*. They won by 74 points and, while that was very disappointing – we had wanted to go all the way for Phil – there was also a kind of relief there. That's how it felt at the end of that year: I could breathe again. I hadn't realised it, but I'd been holding my breath for the entire last half of the season. It only hit me after that last game that I – we – had been *just* hanging on mentally, and that, as much as we'd wanted to do something for Walshy and his family that no other club had done before, we finally didn't have to perform anymore.

When we got back to Adelaide, we all went out together for 'Mad Monday' or 'Wacky Wednesday' or whatever it was. In the middle of it, someone put on the Marc Cohn song 'Walking in Memphis', which had been played at the funeral. Most of us broke down and cried, right there in the pub. I still can't listen to that song.

In the days and weeks after Walshy's death, I kept thinking about the last time I had seen him – just the night before we all got that horrible phone call. We had done a light session that day, and I was the last to leave, packing up my things upstairs. Walshy came up and saw me and asked how I was feeling. I told him that I was good, I was ready. He said that for that week's game, all he wanted me to do was to start well. Then he gave me a fist bump.

That scene has played out in my mind over and over and over again.

When you see me on the field now, you might notice the strapping around my wrist. On one side, I have the initials of all of our kids. On the other side is 'SW' – 'Start well.'

After losing Phil, we needed a new head coach. In October of 2015, it was announced that Don Pyke would fill the role. Don came across from West Coast where he'd been an assistant coach. Before that, he'd spent some time at the Crows back in the early 2000s. He was a sharp coach and we had the list to make a grand final in seasons ahead. He spoke to all of us early on, setting out where we were and his expectations for the team – we made a clear plan for where we were headed and how we'd get there. From then on it was pretty much, 'Let's go out and train.'

THIRTEEN

The end of 2015 also saw one of my favourite teammates and closest friends depart the club. I still consider Patrick Dangerfield to be one of my biggest allies in the game. Danger was always the one advocating for anti-racism standards, not only in relation to football but in the general public too. I recognised special qualities in him during our first meeting in Melbourne when I signed with Adelaide. He is smart, grounded in good values, socially and politically conscientious, and honest. He never shies away from speaking his mind and will always stand up for the needs of others – especially other players. I always wanted to play alongside him.

There had been a lot of media conjecture about Danger's next career move. The Adelaide media always chases hard for a story, but the speculation about whether Danger would stay at the Crows or go back to Victoria once he was a free agent was ridiculous. There wasn't a single press conference where we didn't get asked what he thought he might do. It must have been hard for him.

Both of us made the All-Australian team that year. I had been named in that squad before, when I was at Carlton, but to make the team alongside Danger was an honour. We both flew over to Melbourne for the awards night. Anna came with us, while Mardi, Danger's partner, stayed in Adelaide. We are all close, but at that stage I still didn't know what Danger had decided about where he was going to play the following season. I always knew and understood how important family was to him though.

In the Uber on the way to the ceremony, he told us he was going to Geelong. It was a sad moment. I remember Anna started crying, because she loved him and Mardi so much. But we both got it – I'd made a similarly difficult choice myself. I had left Carlton, the club I loved, to come to Adelaide to be closer to family. We completely understood their decision.

When we got back to Adelaide the next morning, all the SA media was waiting for us at the Cumberland Hotel, on the edge of the city, where the rest of the team was having end-of-season drinks. The television crews and the photographers were waiting to get pictures of Danger when he walked in.

Anna drove us down to the side entrance and snuck us in. The people who own 'the Cumby' had blocked up the windows, covering them in cardboard. Once we were inside, Danger told the rest of the players. Although the boys knew that we were losing one of our best players, we all understood that it's just what happens these days in football. I know for fans that this can be upsetting, but I like to think of it as an opportunity for somebody else to step up.

In 2017, after he had moved to Geelong, we played the Cats in the preliminary final at Adelaide Oval. Of course, Danger was met with jeers from the Crows' fans. We won that match, and straight after it – as gutted and upset as he was about the loss – the first thing Danger did was find me and gave me a cuddle. This was just after I had been racially abused *again*, though I struggle to remember now the specific incident.

Danger said, 'We've got you. We'll protect you. No matter what, we've got your back.'

I'll never, ever forget that moment. He had just lost a preliminary final against his old team, and he'd been booed all night – and he was the one looking out for *me*. Everyone who bagged Danger for his decision should know about that. I will always consider him a friend. Footy is footy – but family is family.

I ended 2015 with 63 goals, finishing third overall for goals scored in the league. That's pretty good for a small forward, which is the hardest position on the footy ground in my opinion (or at least I tell everyone it is). That's mainly because 95 per cent of the time, the ball isn't going to you – it's going to the talls – so you have to hunt it down yourself. I only stand at 173 centimetres, which means my greatest asset is dancing around the feet of the talls. When they're dropping it, I'm getting it. But, if the talls are on their game, then I adjust my strategy to apply pressure defensively, which results in more forward-50 turnovers to create more opportunities for myself to get back into the game. If I do that the goals will come.

The AFL's All-Australian tour in November that year provided the selected players with the opportunity to have their partners and families join them on the trip. First stop was New York, which was partly promotional, but also to get an insight into how professional sporting teams operated over there.

We packed up Lewis and Billy (who was still a baby) and got on the plane. When we got to New York, we checked into a hotel just off Times Square. Not many of the other players had brought their kids, but the experience was pretty awesome for ours – and for us. Having said that, they were completely out of whack with their sleep patterns the whole time we were away.

On one of the nights that we couldn't go out, Lewis woke up at around 3am – which we were used to by that stage of the trip. I got up and took him down to the hotel foyer, which was big enough that we could have a little kick of the footy there. There was a Starbucks nearby that didn't open until around six, so we thought we'd have a play in the foyer while we waited around for that.

At around 4am, the boys came stumbling in from their night out. They were in a pretty good mood, as you can imagine – and they all joined in with Lewis and me. None of them could kick it even close to straight. I was laughing, and Lewis had a ball. That's one of the first things I remember when I think of that trip.

The team needed to train a little bit, so on a few occasions we'd take off to Central Park to have a run. We'd start with a little jog and then we'd find some green space where we could kick the footies around. But the park rangers would come along and kick us off, and we'd have to go and find somewhere else. We'd set up and have a few kicks in the next spot, but, sure enough, the park rangers would turn up again. In the end, the only place we were allowed to train with footballs was on a baseball diamond – complete with red dirt.

Alistair Clarkson was the coach, and he and I became pretty close on that trip, since our kids spent a fair bit of time together while they were waiting on all of us. All in all, it was a crazy opportunity. We visited the New York Jets' training facilities, which were unbelievable – a huge indoor oval, like the stadium at Docklands. We also got to go along to a Jets match to watch them play their hometown rivals, the Giants, and drank Bud Lights and ate hot dogs. In other words, we went full American.

After New York, the team flew across to Ireland and camped in Dublin. I'd first spent a bit of time there in 2010 as part of the International Rules team and again in 2013 with the Indigenous brothers from the AFL. On both of those trips I enjoyed the relationships I developed, particularly with the Irish fullas. It provided a good opportunity for cultural exchange. We attended a lot of official tour functions together and hung out socially outside of those, visiting sites that were important to Ireland and its history.

We went to kiss the Blarney Stone and also got a tour of Croke Park stadium, where they play Gaelic football and hurling. There's a museum at Croke Park that tells the history of the site, including the 1920 Bloody Sunday Massacre during a Gaelic football match which left 14 people dead and dozens more injured after British forces began to shoot indiscriminately into the crowd. The incident reminded me of similar reprisals against mob by the British back in colonial times in Australia. There were other cultural similarities between mob and those Dublin fullas too – I found out that they use the term 'deadly' to describe something that's too good, just like we do.

On the pitch, the Gaelic game is tough – and I love it. There's always been a bit of push-and-shove whenever we play the Irish, and the 2015 tour was no different, but those games always also involve plenty of skill. The way the Irish fullas can caress the round ball to make it go straight is unbelievable. Us Australian boys found it hard to hit targets like they did. We were just trying to connect with the ball – and when we did, it'd go flying off in all directions. Happily, I was able to make the required adjustments thanks to my soccer background. I don't speak Gaelic, but I swear I can speak to that round ball.

FOURTEEN

FOURTEEN

Celebrating the best goal I've ever kicked, wearing the jersey my Aunty Susie designed. This was only the second game I played after my Pop passed away, so it was extra special. (Photo by AFL Media)

My mother, sister Ella and my nieces and nephews at one of my games in Perth in July 2016. (Photo by Will Russell/AFL Media)

The kindergarten named after me in Fiji.

Co-sleeping with the kids.

Lewie with some of his cousins on my side of the family.

We would often escape up to Wangaratta to spend time at Anna's family's place. Here we're down on the Ovens River with her sister Lilly, Lilly's partner, Dan, their kids, and a beautiful Murray River cod.

Patrick Dangerfield congratulating me on the Crows' win despite having been booed by former-fans in Adelaide in 2017. I will always consider him a friend. (Photo by Adam Trafford/AFL Media)

With my boys at the 2017 Grand Final Parade. (Photo by Michael Willson/AFL Media)

Unfortunately, the Crows lost the 2017 Grand Final, but I can always count on Anna to support me through the tough times. (Photo by Robert Cianflone/AFL Media/ Getty Images)

Receiving AFL Life Membership in 2018. Anna is pregnant with the twins.
(Photo by Scott Barbour/AFL Media)

Finally meeting Maggie and Alice after being stuck in Victoria in April, 2018.

Uncle Rusty and Baby Maggie
in Adelaide.

Alice with me at the
Survival Day march
in Melbourne.

There was nothing Mum could say to soften the blow when she gave me the news that Pop had died in May 2016. I had just landed on the Gold Coast for a game that week, and we were still on the plane when Mum rang me. I broke down right there on the tarmac, and stayed in my seat until everyone else had gotten off the plane, keeping my big dark sunglasses on so no one would know I was crying. I was trying to gather all of my emotions and my thoughts, and kept taking these massive breaths to try and steady myself. I collected my bags off the carousel inside the arrivals terminal and then sat up the back of the team bus and put my headphones on.

At the hotel, I went straight to my room and cried for three hours. I rang Anna and talked it through with her and she rang a few of the boys to tell them to check on me. Some of my cousins called, like Victor, and so did Byron Pickett.

All I kept thinking about was what Pop had meant to our family. He used to put seats out at the end of that driveway on Boomerang Crescent and tell yarns. He was the nicest guy, never drank or smoked, and he steered our family through a lot of tough times. His house was a healing place. He was particularly incredible because, as Aboriginal people, we generally don't live that long – our life expectancy as Aboriginal men is 71 years – but Pop beat that by 20 years.

He was a special person. Everyone who knew him was drawn to him and felt connected to him in some way. He taught us all language and he gave our kids Aboriginal names.

He used to wear this big cowboy hat, and my sisters have tattooed drawings of it on their skin. Mum still keeps that hat with her and now she is making his bush medicine to share with everyone – the label, *Cadley's Own*, has his hat pictured on the front of it.

Pop was our connection to our younger selves too. The whole family went back to 12 Boomerang Crescent and celebrated his life – but everyone was hurting. It's tough to deal with losing a figure like that, such a respected Elder, from our lives. The funeral was huge, people came from everywhere to pay their respects. We got the hearse to drive past the front of the house so we could all walk up and say our last goodbyes. That address will always be a special place to our family. He was our connection to that place, where we'd all grown up. He was also our connection to the bush – he and Nan would always take us with them when they went out on Country, and they taught us to live in it and to respect it.

All the male family members carried him towards his resting place that day, following our tradition. Pop's role as a father figure and a protector stays with me. I know he is still looking after me and all of our family.

In some ways I didn't feel up to playing that round, but I also wanted to honour Pop's legacy and knew that he would be so proud I managed to make it out onto the field. I kicked five goals against the Suns that night. When I kicked the first one, I kissed my black armband and pointed to the sky for him.

Years later, when I went back to the Gold Coast in 2020 to stay in the AFL hub because of COVID-19, we did a smoking ceremony. We do that to cleanse and get rid of the bad spirits. It was the first time that I had done that on Gold Coast land. As I stood in front of the fire, with the smoke coming up and washing all over me, someone took a picture. The photo made it into the media, and when it did, more than one member of my family sent it to me and said they could see Pop's face in it.

When I looked at the photo, it was obvious. I thought, 'Fuck – I can *see* him. *There he is.*' It gave me tingles. I had been on that land when I found out that Pop had passed away, and now he was back with me in that same place.

For me, death is less of a final goodbye and more about feeling connected to our ancestors who have passed on. We feel like they are still here with us, looking out for us and keeping us safe. I know that all of them – my Aunties, my cousins – are keeping my kids safe. They're looking after us in spirit.

Aunty Tessa still lives at 12 Boomerang Crescent in Kalgoorlie. I don't get back there much these days, mainly as the pandemic has kept us out of Western Australia – but whenever I do, I always visit Pop's place.

A week later, in Round 10, we played a home game against Greater Western Sydney (GWS) Giants for the Sir Doug Nicholls Indigenous Round. With about four minutes to go in the third quarter, I found myself on the opposite side of the ground from 'my' pocket. Two Giants went up to spoil the ball and it fell just inside the 50-metre arc. As I got to it, I fell over – onto my *moom* – but then I trapped the ball with my right hand. Everyone else went to that side of me, but I managed to get up and to keep the ball in play and away from them while I ran outside the boundary line. I took three or four more steps, got it onto my right boot, and it sailed through for a goal. People always ask me which goal of mine is my personal favourite, and I reckon it was that one. I think it's the best goal I've ever kicked.

In celebration, I grabbed my jumper – which my Aunty Susie designed for the round – and thumped my chest. It was a special goal, but not just because of how it looked or because it helped us win a close game. There was more to that celebration than just having snapped the goal, there was more than just the pride I felt representing my Culture and my Aunty's jumper – it was a release of emotions. Four days earlier, I received a handwritten letter that was addressed to me via the Adelaide Football Club which contained a full page torn out from the local newspaper. It carried a picture of me high-fiving Jarryd Lyons on the training track at Adelaide Oval. In big black Texta right above my head some racist had written the words 'ABO FAGGOT'.

I sat there speechless for a moment after I'd opened it. Then I was like, 'Yep – again. Here it is *again*.'

Throughout my career, and more so with the rise of social media, there came more overt racist abuse towards me. Mostly I would receive monkey emojis on my social media accounts but occasionally I would receive abuse that would just stop me in my tracks. I would always look at the person behind the account that sent me the abuse. There were a lot of troll accounts, but sometimes some of the most hurtful posts would be from the social media accounts of kids. It broke my heart.

Another time, a woman shot to social media fame for her comments about me. The local news interviewed her and her partner about the reasons she racially abused me and my family. I still recall what she said in that interview. 'I just don't like him,' was her reasoning. That interview received over a million views. I know how an interview like that provides the news channel with 'clicks', but I think it was unethical journalism. Watching it, I felt a surge of emotions – I was embarrassed for the reporter and angry at the woman attempting to justify her racism, but knew I had to put on a brave face.

The letter arrived in the week of the Sir Doug Nicholls Round, when Aboriginal and Torres Strait Islander players from around the league are expected to front up to the media to elaborate on what the round personally means to them. That week, I was set to do a press conference with the Adelaide media on behalf of the Crows. I knew that I should speak up about what I'd gotten in the mail. At the same time, I didn't want to create too much hassle and work for the people around me. Anna and I had called the club and asked them for a 9am meeting, and I was due to do the presser at 11am after training. I didn't feel like I could mention the letter without at least telling the club what I wanted to do.

When we walked into the meeting with the club, straight away I was looking at all-white faces. I knew that they would not fully understand what I was about to show them – how stuff like this cuts me to the core, and in particular the effect the word 'abo' can have. For me, it immediately reminds me of what my Pop endured at the hands of the 'chief protector of the Aborigines', referring to him as an 'abo'.

I said to the club, 'Listen, I really want to take this piece of paper into this press conference and when the journos ask me why the AFL has the Indigenous Round, I want to say *this* is why.' I wanted to hold it up and maybe even just walk out – leaving the piece of paper in the press conference.

Then the club representatives spoke and Anna and I listened. These days, I would do it without even telling them, because essentially they talked us into not saying anything. Upon reflection, they were trying to minimise any type of media circus before my game, but maybe this was more important than the game itself?

That morning, as I stood at the press conference and looked out at all of the cameras, I knew I had to pretend. I was really hurting. I was answering questions about why we celebrate the Sir Doug Nicholls Round, how it highlights our Culture and our ways, while that folded piece of paper sat in my pocket.

I have kept it with my fan mail. I often think about that person, going to all that effort of cutting up the paper, writing on it and then going to the post office and posting it. Anna and I wonder what they thought as they dropped the letter into the mailbox.

An extremely loud and proud Port Adelaide crowd met me for my 250th AFL match. The local derby is huge for Adelaide. The week leading up to the Showdown is all analysis and talk about the upcoming game on any radio station you tune in to. It is a big week for the city of Adelaide as a whole: tickets are always sold out and the restaurants and hotels are booked up for the weekend. I think it's cool that footy can bring so much joy and passion to the city. The kids at school get to order donuts in their team colours and on Friday they're allowed to wear their footy jerseys. The passion of the fans is what makes the game – as I've said all along: without the fans we don't have a game. I've always been really close with the fans from both Adelaide and Carlton. I get to know them and their families and love seeing their familiar faces over the fence at the game. The fans I have got to know over the years have always been respectful and passionate.

I remember being really relaxed when I ran out. I was able to run onto the field with my two sons, Lewie and Billy, and all I could think was how amazing it was to be doing this with them. The AFL does milestone games really well. They allow families to be a part of the celebration of our individual success and I know it is a feeling I will always remember and reflect on as being incredibly special. My kids love being out on the oval and running through the banner that the cheer-squads have spent many careful hours making.

I started well and the team jumped out of the blocks quickly. I kicked three goals in the first quarter. Port Adelaide came back strongly and it was back and forth in a great game. I felt like we had it, but then Port kept coming in the last quarter. At a crucial moment, Josh Jenkins took a mark on the wing. Taylor Walker went up for the kick in, and the ball ended up falling right into my lap. I don't know how, but I wobbled it through for a goal from the pocket to clinch my fifth for the game. The boys were all jumping up and down because they were sure it went through, however I wasn't so sure and had my eye on the umpire. When he awarded the goal, I stood with my arms stretched to the sky as it sealed the game for us. JJ ran in and jumped on me in celebration – and that's when someone threw a banana at me.

It actually hit JJ, not me. I didn't even know what had happened. We just got on with the game and a minute later the siren sounded and we were 15-point winners.

Afterwards, everyone was so excited in the rooms – the Adelaide Crows change rooms are always busy after a win as all our families crowd in and celebrate with us. As always, I was quick to seek out Anna and the kids. They always help snap me back into reality, whether that be the boys whinging that they're hungry, or that they need to go to the toilet.

On the way home, we received a call from the Crows' player welfare officer. 'Listen, I don't know if you know,' she said, 'but there was an incident at the game. Someone threw a banana at you.'

My first thought was, 'Well, that's not too bad, but I guess it's not okay to throw anything at a player while we are trying to play.'

It didn't even occur to me that it might be racially motivated. I mean, what kind of person, as they're getting ready to go and watch their team play, decides to pack a banana just in case they can get close enough to me to throw it?

The player welfare officer then went on to explain that it definitely *was* racially motivated. I began to understand why her tone was so serious.

Anna and I took some time to process it. We assumed it was a mistake. *Surely* that wasn't actually what happened? Someone had to have mixed up the story? We both decided to wait and see what the investigation of the incident found before getting too worried.

Not long after that phone call, we saw the video of the incident doing the rounds on social media. It showed a woman yelling abuse, giving me the finger and then – weirdly – ducking into her bag and coming up with a banana, which she then flung at me. It also showed the Port supporters sitting in the stands around her call her out. It confirmed the incident was racially motivated. It came to light that she had even called me an ape or a monkey a few times, something she later admitted herself.

Our eldest, Lewie, was still awake in the car, and I remember he was asking for chicken nuggets as we would sometimes pull over at a takeaway shop on the way home. He just went quiet – even as a little toddler he was so intuitive. The energy in the car dropped out and we just drove home in silence.

I knew what my next week would look like and that was what drained me in that moment. It would be me answering media questions about racism, which is so isolating because a lot of people really don't know how to respond and end up tiptoeing on eggshells around me when I just need them to be themselves. I know racism is such an uncomfortable subject for people but a simple 'I am here for you' goes a long way. Over time, I have taught many people just to check in and show that you care.

The Crows media manager told me not to come in for training the next morning. He predicted – correctly – that there would be cameras down at Henley Beach for the ocean recovery session. I did my recovery in the pool in the backyard that day, just at home – in this instance, racism stopped me from being able to recover normally with my teammates.

I particularly liked those sessions too because we would be able to debrief the game, and often my kids would come down to do hot and cold baths with me, or jump in the ocean for a swim.

That day, my Aboriginal teammates and their partners came around to gather at our home. We didn't particularly talk about anything to do with racism or the specific incident, as we've all grown up with it as mob. Sadly, it's an everyday thing for us. We just sat around and yarned and tried to have a laugh. In situations like that, I always tried to stay strong for my brothers at the club as I knew that they would feed off my energy and I didn't want to let them down. It would always hurt inside but I would put a brave face on and keep strong for them.

That week our club and Port Adelaide came together and took a really strong stance, saying passion and dedication to your club is great, but racism does not belong in our game. I felt supported by both clubs and was happy to be involved in the call-out, to send a strong message to protect us in our game. I was always happy to lend my voice if it meant that future Aboriginal players might be kept safe from experiencing racism, especially when we're just trying to do what we love and play footy.

This was one of the first times that my non-Indigenous teammates stood alongside me to condemn the actions of an individual and to further add weight to our cause. Before this moment, I can't really remember this type of thing happening. It was significant and I felt suddenly that I wasn't bearing the burden of it alone this time. I had the captain of my club, my CEO and opposition teammates standing alongside me. The Showdown rivalry was set aside that day and Adelaide's two clubs stood together on the front page of the city's newspaper saying, 'Enough is enough.'

When you're in the middle of that type of storm – when you and your people have been attacked on a massive stage – it's natural to want to stay home and keep hidden, especially since the media coverage meant that just about everyone in Adelaide would have known I'd had a banana thrown at me. But we weren't going to stay home.

The next morning we went to Adelaide's Central Market, a massive undercover market next to Chinatown. We were getting some fruit from our favourite stall – Anna was on one side and I was on the other, and we needed some bananas.

Anna called across to me, 'Ed, can you grab the bananas?'

For a while, I just looked at her. Eventually, I grabbed them, quickly walked around to her and said, 'Here they are – but I'm not holding them.'

Still today, I am extremely embarrassed to touch or eat bananas and every time I do it automatically takes me back to that moment. I think it probably always will.

FIFTEEN

The Crows made the 2016 finals series that season – we smashed North Melbourne in the quarter final by over 60 points, but then lost to the Sydney Swans at the Sydney Cricket Ground (SCG) in the semi by 36. I was named runner-up in the club's Best and Fairest, led the team in goal kicking and won the Best Team Man award – which was now named the Phil Walsh Medal. Without a doubt, that's the most meaningful award I have ever won in my time in footy. It was an incredible honour to receive it in the first year that it was named after someone who had been so important to me and the club.

At the end of 2016, our family had one of the best trips of our lives. Anna and I had already taken the kids to Fiji a couple of times, and we'd fallen in love with the culture there. I saw a lot of similarities between the Fijian culture and my own. The Fijian people are beautiful. I love the way they put children at the centre of everything they do. For them, it's all about extended family and spirituality. That's no different than us mob.

Previously, we had stayed at a resort on the Coral Coast which had a program where guests could help out in local communities. We had gone to a village in the Sigatoka Valley that had been smashed by Cyclone Winston in February that year. It had destroyed a lot of the Pacific, including parts of Conua Primary School. We wanted to go back there and try to help where we could – to rebuild a kindergarten, and also to run a footy clinic in the capital, Suva. My Crows teammates Jake Lever and

Hugh Greenwood and our assistant coaches Matt Clarke and Tate Kaesler came over with us and we got to work.

Our two boys went to classes at the school while we helped build the new kindergarten. During our breaks, we'd chuck a heap of balls into the middle of the school oval and the kids would race out of their rooms and bang around kicking them towards their goal posts – which were, of course, made for rugby union, the country's national sport. It was hot work, but I loved nothing more than when one of the locals would grab a coconut and slice off the top with a massive machete and we'd drink the milk straight down.

Some of the team from Fiji AFL also joined us and they arranged for us to drive to Suva, around two hours away, to do a coaching clinic. The oval there was unbelievable; it's something like Albert Park, right there in the middle of the city, sitting right in between Parliament House and the beach.

I was surprised at how many people at the clinic knew about our game. At the end of the clinic, we had a traditional kava ceremony. Kava tasted just like they say it does – 'dirty water' – so we had a nice beer afterwards to wash it down.

When they decided to call the new building the Eddie Betts Kindergarten, I felt embarrassed but incredibly touched. I knew it was only because we had come over as a collective that we had gotten so much done, and other tourists had given us a lot of help, too. When the kindergarten opened, the activities manager at our resort, Kin Sarai, pointed out,

'For ordinary villagers, raising funds to send their kids to school is already a struggle – and raising funds to build a building like the kindergarten would take years.'

The thought that young kids would start their education in that building is pretty incredible to me. I love that I played even a small part in that. When we finally left, the locals sang us goodbye, and there were tears on both sides. I'll forever feel connected to that community.

We flew from the Pacific to join Anna's parents in Italy. By the time we got to Rome, we'd endured a couple of long flights with Lewie and Billy, and we only had four days there, so we did all the touristy things straight away. To go from building a simple village kindy to standing outside the Colosseum was weird.

After we paid for our tickets and went in, we ran into another family from Adelaide – the father turned around to us and said, 'Well, *hey there*, Eddie Betts! How are you?' You can go all the way to the other side of the world and still run into AFL fans.

We saw the Trevi Fountain, checked out the Vatican and did as much sightseeing as we could. We then caught the train to Florence and hired a big bus to get us around. I was the nominated driver and this thing was a manual. I hadn't done too much manual driving in Australia, so maneuvering that bus across Italy through all the little winding streets was full-on. I'm sure it was also terrifying for the locals who had to get around me.

The villa we stayed in was an old house in the countryside outside a small village called Lamporecchio. When we first arrived, I thought, 'What the hell are we doing here?' To me, the place looked haunted. We ended up staying for two weeks, though, and it was the absolute best. We used the villa as a base and did day trips to the Leaning Tower of Pisa and Siena. The kids particularly loved going to Collodi, the town where the author of the original Pinocchio grew up. We discovered a little restaurant there that served up the best pasta I have ever tasted in my life. I ended up having a photo with the chef and getting the recipe. We tried to soak up everything we could.

We finished up our trip in the south of France, where I ate about three Nutella croissants every morning. Actually, I was a big fan of *all* the pastries and the cheeses. Anna's mum and dad love to try different foods so they were in their element too. I was already close to Anna's dad, Barry – he hadn't missed a game of mine since Anna and I met, and always provided feedback after the game (where I could do no wrong) – but being able to share those experiences together was invaluable. It was great to provide our two boys with that kind of adventure early in their lives too. Lewis and Billy were natural travellers and tagged along with us everywhere we went with no issues whatsoever. Without a doubt, that off-season was one of the best we'd ever had as a family.

SIXTEEN

Back at clubland, the 2016 off-season was a pretty quiet one. There weren't many personnel changes to the team. I think that says a lot about where we were at as a club – especially after everything we'd been through together. The biggest change to the place that year was the launch of the AFL Women's league and the establishment of the Crows' women's team – a combined Northern Territory and South Australian team based out of West Lakes' AAMI Park. What a great pathway for women playing footy!

We went to every game of the AFLW that we could. In fact, it'd be accurate to say that we – our family – wanted to be involved in every way. For women to finally be able to play footy at the highest level was a critical step towards gender equality in professional sport. The players were unbelievable on and off the field and were awesome role models for our kids. We were so lucky be so involved in the inner sanctum of what would soon be a highly successful team.

Their training and competition space was a completely different environment to the men's. When you play men's AFL footy, pretty much everything is provided for you – and, in all likelihood, it's been provided for you since you were much younger, coming up through an established system. For women's sport to prosper, men have to show up and give their support. I wanted to get the women's players more involved in and around the club, but it was tricky – they all had jobs, so they trained at night, whereas we were able to be there during the days. Instead, I loved taking my kids down for some of their night sessions and kicking the ball around with them on 'the shed' floor.

The team was incredibly successful, winning the inaugural AFLW grand final in Brisbane that year. I remember watching them that day. We were at a friend's house for his son's birthday and I kept walking in and out of the speeches and the cake-cutting to keep an eye on the game. I think there's actually a video clip of me yelling at the TV and jumping around because I was so excited when they won.

The men's team started the season on fire. We won our first five games, including beating Hawthorn for the first time since 2011. Everyone was interested in what would happen when we met Richmond in Round 6, as they were also un-defeated. We absolutely smashed them. Of course, footy is pretty up and down. The next week we played North Melbourne, who had only won one game. No one was tipping them, but they kept us scoreless in the first quarter and ended up beating us by over 50 points. It was a complete annihila-tion and just one of those games where you can't seem to do anything to change the momentum.

I couldn't wait to get home after that loss. On the Sunday, while watching our Crows' reserve side play in the state league against the Norwood Redlegs, I began to feel an ache developing in my tummy, but I didn't really think anything of it. That night, I started sweating. Not normal, run-of-the-mill sweating – it was full-on. The pain in my stomach had gotten so bad that I could hardly stand up and walk.

I rang the club doctor, who came over and gave me some morphine. Knowing me and that I don't like to complain, he didn't muck around. When the morphine didn't ease the pain, he sent me straight to hospital. We rang our development coach Tate Kaesler and his wife, Colleen, who we were really close with, so they could look after the kids for us. When Tate came to pick them up, I tried to walk down the hallway and he started laughing at the sight of me hunched over and crying from the pain.

'What the hell is wrong with you?' he said.

The doctors at the hospital diagnosed me with appendicitis. It turns out my appendix had been leaking into my stomach cavity. I was rushed into surgery and out it came. Apparently, the first thing I asked when I came out of the anaesthetic was whether I'd be right to play Collingwood at the MCG that weekend.

'Nah, mate,' the doc said. 'You'll miss two.'

So, the next week I stayed at home on the couch and missed my first game as a Crow in over a hundred games. I found that really difficult and struggled to rest up like the doctor had advised. I ended up watching the game with a notepad and pen, jotting down forward-50 pressure, leading patterns of the forwards, and costly turnovers that resulted in goals . . . but also did a bit of yelling at the TV. I reckon I paced about 10 kays back and forth through the lounge room that day. Every time I screamed, the pain in my appendix was like somebody stabbing me – but Anna was quick to provide some perspective, regularly reminding me of the laparoscopy procedures she went through for us to have the kids.

We started the game against Collingwood like a house on fire, but by the third quarter were down by 50 points. Then we started to claw our way back. The momentum swung our way, we had less turnovers and moved the ball quicker, like we had all year. The boys kicked goal after goal after goal. That year, as a group, we felt that no matter how far we were down, or who we were playing against, we could always turn things around and beat anyone. In the dying stages of the final quarter we found ourselves within six points. With eight seconds to go Jake Kelly took a mark at the top of the 50 from a Collingwood kick out. I was up screaming at him to get the ball in because I could see the time ticking down. Jake launched it into a pack 15 out and straight in front of the goals. As the siren blew, Mitch McGovern flew through to take a big mark from the side of the pack. He needed to kick it for us to draw. Showing great composure he put it straight through, to top off a classic game. It was as good as a win for us, after coming back from such a deficit.

The week after missing that game, I knew I had to get myself up for the next one – Round 20: the Crows versus

Port Adelaide Showdown. Us Blackfullas can heal quickly, so in my mind, I could probably halve the time the doctor had told me I would be sidelined for. My mum sent across some bush medicine and late in that second week my body felt right to line up against Port.

It was tough conditions for footy, driving rain and windy, and, as always, the match-up was very physical, but we came out on top by 84 points. I managed to slot four, including a couple from both pockets. The win kept us on top of the ladder, but we started to get shaky in the final three rounds that year and finished the home and away season with losses – first to Sydney, who were also challenging for a top-four spot, and then away at West Coast. Somehow we still managed to finish as minor premiers. Of course, there was chat outside the club about how we had dropped our final two games, but I felt we had things under control.

We met GWS at Adelaide Oval in the qualifying final and ran out 36-point winners. That sent us straight to the preliminary final, where we lined up against Geelong – again at Adelaide Oval. And that meant the return of my good mate Paddy Dangerfield, after he had left the Crows the year before. Paddy coming back to play against his old side and to get into his first grand final was a massive game in the context of everything: for the Adelaide supporters, for the Adelaide club, and for us as players too. There were also a lot of my teammates in that Crows side vying for their first grand final spot as well.

Again we got off to a really strong start, kicking 6.3 in the first quarter to their 1.2. I bagged two of the goals and that kind of start set us up well for the rest of the game. Charlie Cameron also turned it on and kicked five goals. I watched one from the interchange bench which had me jumping for joy. I was pumped knowing that he was dominating in one of the biggest games in his career at that stage. We went on to win by 61 points.

After the game, I found Paddy and gave him a hug. It's always tough when you play against mates. Especially when one of you ultimately has to miss out on a grand final opportunity. I was emotional but Paddy kept a brave face. He just said, 'You deserve this.' I felt his disappointment and just wished he was still playing with the Crows at that stage so we could go to the big dance together.

Shortly afterwards, it was back to business for our team. We had a brief celebration in the rooms but knew we couldn't get carried away. Anna and the boys were there to share in the moment and there's a photo of me and Lewie embracing after we'd all finished singing the team song. I'm telling him there's just one more game to go. That photo always reminds me of what I cherished most about playing the game.

So there we were: minor premiers and now headed to the MCG for that last Saturday in September, 19 years after Adelaide's last grand final appearance.

It was a hectic week. We were supposed to treat it as just another lead-in, but that was impossible. Unfortunately it came at the same time as our family received some distressing news: our longtime friend, John Hall, lost his battle with cancer. John and his wife Josie were surrogate grandparents for us in Adelaide. We called them 'Nanna' and 'Poppa'. They were the greatest support for Anna and I, and a close part of our kids' lives too. We really felt for Nanna Josie that week, knowing that we had to fly out to Melbourne only an hour after the funeral.

On Wednesday we were doing our 'main training' – full contact ground drills and short match simulations. The fans poured into Adelaide Oval to watch us train. My kids were sitting on the bench the whole session and all the players' families were welcomed to enjoy every moment that they could. This grand final was for everyone in our club. Having families involved in clubs has always been a positive for me. No matter how serious things can get, kids being around helps me relax.

There was a real buzz in town. The Crows' team colours went up everywhere and expectations began to build. The media hunted down both my Nanna's place in Port Lincoln and my Poppa's place in Kalgoorlie – my family obliged the media, standing loud and proud and provided lengthy interviews decked out in their Crows gear. Some Crows fans even changed the Betts shoe stores in Rundle Mall to read '*Eddie* Betts', which I also thought was funny.

On Thursday, after the funeral, we flew across to Melbourne and stayed at the same hotel as always. The club was doing their best to follow routine because we wanted to try to keep everything as normal as possible. The message from our coaches that week was simple: 'Business as usual.' We all had to accept that the build-up was different, but do everything we could to make sure the week wasn't draining for us. The red, blue and yellow fanfare followed us to Melbourne, but was triple the size. It was the first time I'd ever seen so many Crows supporters in Victoria. There were Crows flags flying everywhere.

On the Friday morning we did the captain's run on the MCG. Even though it was a closed stadium, it was still madness. Located right next door was Richmond's training ground on Punt Road and helicopters were hovering and circling. From outside the ground you could hear large crowds and PA systems blaring at the different events happening around Yarra Park.

I'll always remember the Grand Final Parade later that day. I had Lewie and Billy in the car with me, and Charlie Cameron was there, too. It felt so surreal to be in that situation. The Crows fans were yelling out not only our names but also the *kids'* names, and the boys spent the entire time waving furiously at everyone they could. I caught sight of Mum and Aunty Tessa at one stage, but I lost them in the swarming crowd just as quickly.

When the parade finished at the MCG, the players moved into one area and the families into another – but I kept Lewie and Billy by my side and they came up on stage with me. I wanted to share every moment I could with them. The club wanted to keep the partners separate to give the players their space – but my family *is* my space. It was the same situation with the hotel. Anna and the kids had been put up in a hotel across the road, but I brought them over to stay with me in my room.

I was also still sorting out tickets for my family. In the end, I had to round up 18 of them – Mum, Dad, my cousins, and I also wanted Anna's family to be there as well because they've been incredibly supportive, and an important part of my journey.

I was okay the night before the game. I was even fine when I woke up the next morning. I did exactly what I normally do on the morning of a game – went and got myself a coffee and hung around in the foyer chasing the kids. Then it was time to board the bus and get to 'The G'.

I can't speak for everyone, but to me it seemed like the over-riding feeling on that bus was one of excitement, not nerves. We'd beaten Richmond by plenty when we'd played them earlier in the season, so we were pretty confident. I just kept thinking, 'We can do this. We can win this. Just two hours. Play the way that we played all year for two hours.'

The nerves kicked in when the bus arrived at the MCG. We pulled into the bay beneath the Great Southern Stand. I get butterflies in my tummy before every game, and they were fluttering in full force that afternoon. I take two Imodium before every game – to stop me from shitting myself – and two Panadol (I joke with the boys that I need all that to keep my bones strong because I'm too old).

Running out onto the ground in front of 95,000-plus people was like being hit by a wall of sound. It was similar to a Showdown at Adelaide Oval, but way louder: the noise just kept swirling around and around. It was pretty amazing, because up until we ran out, we hadn't heard a thing – we had our own music playing in the change room, so we didn't even hear any of the pre-game entertainment. Running out into the sun and all that noise was deadly. Just a little Black kid from Kalgoorlie and Port Lincoln living out his dreams.

We lined up again for yet another national anthem – but when that song plays, it's in one ear and out the other for me. In those last moments before a game, when the crowd is standing and most of them are singing, I'm already thinking about my first contest, my first touch, my first tackle. We came together before the bounce and told each other we just needed to play our way – our ruthless and aggressive style.

Being out there for the first bounce of a grand final is breathtaking exhilaration, particularly when the ball bounces your way. The ball came down our end for a stoppage, and Rory Sloane got on the end of it and kicked the first goal. 'Fuck yeah – let's *go*,' I thought. When the ball came in again and

I got it and kicked a goal, I was thinking, 'Here we go – we're going here. Let's do this.'

But by the second quarter, Richmond was playing good footy and had started kicking goals of their own – and by half-time, it genuinely felt to me like we had already lost the game. That might sound stupid, given we were only down by nine points – but when we went into the rooms, we were flat. We were trying to get each other up and we were saying all the right things. The only way I can explain it is that there seemed to be some deep, underlying feeling in the room that we'd already lost it. In all of the other finals, we'd sailed through. No one had really tested us. Now, here we were, down by less than two goals at half-time of the grand final and it felt like we were gone.

In the third quarter, they annihilated us. It was a blur. We couldn't stop their run and I felt completely helpless. We were all trying, but nothing was working, and at three-quarter time it was impossible not to realise that we had just let our entire season slide in one quarter. We were *gone*.

Again, we said all the right stuff in the next huddle. We wanted to earn some respect in that final quarter – but we knew that it was over. It's then that the words 'Why?' and 'How?' started revolving around my head, over and over. As the clock counted down those last minutes, it was like my physical body and a part of my brain were still on the field, but another part of me, existing somewhere else entirely, just kept saying, 'Fuck me – we've let this go.'

When the siren sounded, the Richmond Tigers were AFL champions. They had won by 48 points. At that moment – and even when I look back now – no other game in 2017 mattered.

I sat down on the MCG grass, still not able to believe that it had played out like it had. It had *never* played out like that in my mind. To me, we were always going to be the ones holding up that cup. I still believe we should have won it – but we let one game define our season.

In the rooms, we just sat quietly. You could hear the *click, click, click* of the news photographers who had been allowed in. Sam Jacobs had lost his brother Aaron on the eve of the finals, and I remember him crying and falling into his mum and dad's arms when we could finally get to our families. Anna and my cousin Victor were in there, as were the kids. The entire time, they just kept kicking the footy to one another. In some small way, that lightened how I was feeling.

After spending some time just being with my family, I went back into the change rooms to have a shower – when, all of a sudden, I heard this voice saying, 'I'm Eddie Betts. Let me in, I'm Eddie Betts.' I quickly got dressed and went out to see what was going on – and there was my dad, who had somehow gotten himself down to the change rooms. Yep: he had managed to talk his way past three security checkpoints, with no ID, by telling people he was Eddie Betts, my father.

We all went to a Crows function that night – which was fairly low-key – and then headed out, but our hearts weren't in it. Finally, there was nothing to do but go back to the hotel and wish we could have the entire day over again.

Have you ever had that feeling that once one thing goes wrong, everything else goes wrong, too? Well, the morning after the game we headed to the airport, only to find that our flight had been delayed because of some sort of glitch in the plane. So we all made our way to the Virgin lounge, which they had done up with decorations – but those red, yellow and blue balloons were just about the saddest things I had ever seen. When we finally arrived at Adelaide Airport, half of our bags hadn't made it. Then we were straight onto a bus to Adelaide Oval, where our supporters had been waiting for us all that time.

It was impossible not to feel like we had let them down.

It was impossible not to feel like we'd let *ourselves* down.

We stood in front of them, and it was obvious how flat they were. All I can say is that we were feeling it, too. We promised them we'd come back bigger and better next year – and I hope we all believed it. But for me, it was impossible to look past the next minute or hour. We went to a function in a room at the Oval later that day, but no one stuck around for long. Afterwards, Anna, the kids and I headed home to our place at Lockleys.

There was a surprise waiting for me at home: my dad's bag out in the backyard, with a blanket folded up neatly next to it, plus some of his clothes. He was always like that, with everything in its place. So there I was, with Anna and the kids, feeling like shit and planning on going out with the boys to drown our sorrows as a team, and my dad's belongings there unexpectedly – but him gone missing. I took a guess and headed to the nearest pub, the Lockleys Hotel down the road. Sure enough, there he was, propped up at the bar – 'Eddie Betts, the dad of Eddie Betts' drinking with the manager. There was nothing I could do but find it ridiculously funny.

I finally made it into town, and there we sat, as a team. The shock had worn off by then, and we were angry. In two hours, we'd undone an entire season of good football.

Anna and I were keeping a secret. Well, *two* secrets. We had been trying for another baby to join us and the boys, and we'd been going through fertility treatment again. It can be tiring and emotional, and it was definitely taking its toll. Anna ended up needing a break from it, so she told her doctor that we were just going to put things on hold. She had already bought the medication she needed for that cycle, so in the end she decided to go through the drug process but not any of the monitoring or scans. In her head, she was more than happy to take all the medication and listen to the doctor; she just needed some time away from the appointments.

After just over a month, she realised her period was late, and so she went in for her six-week scan. She wasn't necessarily thinking much of it – so much so that I didn't even go to the appointment with her.

When they did the scan, there, on the screen, were not one but *two* babies. Anna says she started crying right away, then she rang me with the news. By chance, that same day I had signed a three-year extension with the Crows and when Anna told me we were about to have twins, my first reaction was to say something along the lines of, 'What? There are *two*?! Are you fucking joking? Thank God I just signed a three-year deal!'

I rang my mum, whose immediate reaction was, 'Good – the more mob the merrier!' I was so happy. Anna was very nauseated early on with the babies. We didn't necessarily hide the news because we're very open with our lives, but the pregnancy wasn't easy. Anna was really sick in the beginning and was extremely unwell for the first 12–14 weeks. She was nine weeks pregnant at the grand final, and so Anna always says, 'I couldn't even have a beer to numb the pain of that loss.'

We didn't really make a huge fuss about it, obviously our number of children was doubling but we knew we had such a good team around us – including two helpful older siblings – that we would just get on with it.

In April of 2018, Anna went into labour – she was 36 weeks pregnant. For the four weeks around Anna's due date, I was only scheduled to be out of the state and away from home for 48 hours. We had to get through one game against St Kilda in

Melbourne and then I would have the remaining three games at home.

The day before the twins arrived, Anna went to the boys' school sports carnival just down the road and remembers that she could barely walk for the pain. She thought it was all part and parcel of carrying the two girls. That night, the pain started to get more intense and she was alone at home, with the boys in our bed. She spent the night climbing in and out of the bath, trying to soothe the pain.

At 5am on the Saturday morning, Anna called me in Melbourne and said, 'I don't think I am going to be able to hold on to these babies, for some reason I think they're coming.'

I was under huge pressure from the external footy world to play that weekend, as I had played shit in three games to start the 2018 season. Anna told me to stay and play and put the team before anything else.

At 7.30am that morning, sitting on the couch in the lounge room, her waters broke. She called me straight away and told me, then called her doctor to notify him about her impending hospital admission. Nanna Josie came over and was running around with a towel behind her, mopping up the fluids, while Anna was hurriedly packing her hospital bag.

I was a confused mess about what to do. There were no flights to Adelaide and there was nothing I could do for her in Melbourne. I called up my good friend Lyndall Down, who would come visit me for breakfast before most of my

Melbourne games, and I told her that Anna was in labour with the babies. 'I think we better get some breakfast,' I said.

I ordered my regular two poached eggs, salmon, mushrooms and regular latte, one sugar – and I just could not sit still through the whole feed. Anna kept calling me to give me updates and told me to stay by my phone and get a secure wi-fi connection. I decided to head back to the hotel and for some silly reason chose to use the free internet in the lobby. I don't know what I was thinking – I could have just paid the 12 bucks for secure wi-fi in my private room.

Anna had some meds to try and stop the contractions but as they were already two minutes apart the decision was made to continue. Anna was booked in for a caesarean and they scheduled the time for around 10am. So, I sat in the foyer at the team hotel and watched my twin girls being born into the world over FaceTime, while Anna's friend filled in for me at the hospital in Adelaide. The fact that I wasn't able to be there wasn't a major issue. Most of my cousins' partners had their babies surrounded by other women and for me that is beautiful and important as well.

Alice and Maggie were born into the world on Saturday 8 April 2018. I will never forget this moment. I will also never forget the guy who wandered over and asked for a photo as I was watching their birth on my phone. It was first time I ever refused a photo with a fan. I want to find that person one day and give them an opportunity for a do-over.

That night I ran out against St Kilda in Round 3 and kicked three goals to get our team a win for the first time that year. I also accidentally announced our girls' births on live television during my post-game interview. I remember the facial expression Channel Seven's Matthew Richardson made when I casually dropped that I missed the twins' birth for this game and that I was glad to be able to contribute to the team's win. Anna hadn't had time to tell many people about the arrival of our girls, but I was just so excited. Anna wasn't too worried, she just said, 'Oh well, saves me having to text people.'

For some reason, the girls were put into the hospital's special care nursery, but Anna – a fierce advocate for our children's health – insisted that was an unnecessary intervention. By the time I arrived home to Adelaide the next day, Alice and Maggie were back with Mum, tucked up under her arms in her room.

Alice and Maggie are a little mix of all the good things about our personalities. They are professional negotiators and strongly assert their boundaries. Alice is sensitive and caring, while Maggie is more robust and spends a lot of her time trying to keep up with her two older brothers.

Alice looks like her mum, with blonde hair and green eyes, and Maggie looks like my sister's kids, with her brown, curly hair and dark eyes. People that don't know us spin out when we tell them they're twins. We often have people ask us many questions about our family dynamics as all the kids look quite different from each other.

SEVENTEEN

The 2017 grand final still haunts me to this day. Often when I'm asked about the day, I develop this deep feeling of dread. Even years after that particular match, I still find it hard to watch grand finals generally. They make me feel a bit sick.

About halfway through that season, but particularly in the lead up to the finals series, we had started working with 'mind training and leadership' people. Over the years, we've always had outsiders come in to the club to try and implement programs that are supposed to give our club the edge over others. In my head, I used these sessions as an opportunity to kind of switch off. For me, it never made sense the way people throw a one-size-fits-all approach over a bunch of players from completely different backgrounds, experiences and environments. I was never the type to challenge these mob though, as that's not in my personality, but I would always check in on the other Blackfullas around the club to see if anything these people were doing made them feel uncomfortable.

To me, leadership needs to come from those within the club, not from external forces. It doesn't always have to look a certain way, but I believe leadership is fundamentally based on relationships and community, and good teams should allow everyone to have some type of role in being a leader.

People coming in to fix leadership issues, or improve existing leadership, often do so with their own bias and without sufficient previous relationships in place. I always found these programs a little fucked up – they didn't know me or have any understanding of the backgrounds of other players at the club.

At the Crows, we started working with a 'leadership specialist' training group that the club had engaged to implement programs that would apparently better our minds for on-field success. This mind training was centred, mainly, around us being 'warriors' – they talked about things like inner-voice, dominance, mindset and other long words that sound like corporate jargon. Their goal was to teach us how to train our mind to work best under pressure, but actually, with some of the stuff we did, I didn't even understand what they were talking about.

Meditation was one of the things we had to do and I didn't really enjoy it. A psychologist has since explained to me that sometimes meditation isn't always good for people who've had significant trauma from a young age. My philosophy is that I'm always moving forward: I don't like to reflect too much. I've always been taught to just get on with the job at hand. The reflection and meditation in their program didn't really benefit me.

At one stage, we'd lost a couple of games in a row and the leadership specialists reviewed videos, identifying where they thought we had lost the match. One of the trainers from the program told the playing group that we'd lost the game because of the way we'd run through the banner onto the field. Apparently, our facial expressions weren't up to game mode. Straight after that feedback and video review session, the whole team was made to rehearse our facial expressions for running through the banner. I was thinking, 'What the fuck are we *doing* here?' but I was obligated to keep trying to buy into their mindset.

Part of the in-club training sessions involved all of us players forming a circle, making awkward eye contact with one another and screaming 'Fuck you!' at each other as we thrust our groins in the other person's direction. I vaguely remember this was about increasing our masculinity or something. I look back and think to myself, 'What? A club full of footy players isn't masculine enough as it is?'

I shake my head laughing now about how ridiculous and shameful it was.

Another activity they had us perform supposedly originated with the ancient Japanese sumo wrestlers. It involved standing in a circle with our hands in front of the crotch of the person standing either side. Apparently the old sumo wrestlers used to grab each others' *garluus* to show full trust in one another. We never went the full cupping, but it all had the potential for disaster.

In my head, I felt compelled to participate in these weird exercises. I just used to try to find something to get me through it all. But I also had been around long enough to know myself and what drives me to play footy, and most importantly, how to prepare myself to perform well on-ground.

My energy and my performance don't come from within the walls of the club: I get my mindset and drive from my mob, especially my own little family. I didn't feel safe thrusting myself and shouting 'Fuck you!' at a bunch of young kids. I wanted to do the opposite and protect them.

My performance on the field was always inspired by the women in my life – my Aunties, my mum, my sisters and my partner. So for me it didn't make any sense for the leadership specialists to try and increase my angry man energy, or whatever the fuck it was they were after.

Before the leadership specialists became prominent that season, my family and psychologists had provided me with the strength of character and cognitive tools to prosper both on and off the track. The AFL is lucky enough to have some of the best sports psychologists in the country. The good thing about seeing an evidence-based psychologist, is that the mind stuff is customised for the person. It's also private. You can go have a yarn with a psychologist and it doesn't mean that every person in the club has to know about your past or current issues.

I used to do things during the groin-thrusting exercise. I'd watch other players and try to make them laugh. I remember making eye contact with big sexy man Scott 'Thommo' Thompson during one session. Thommo didn't buy into the male thrusting session either and we were laughing at each other. His big smile beaming across at me got me through that one.

I always made an effort to debrief with the young Blackfullas at the club after these exercises, and after this session specifically, one of the young fullas said to me, 'I see you as an Uncle. I don't really like screaming "fuck you" at you.' In our Culture, from a young age, our older people are a model of respect to our kids and we quickly learn to reciprocate that respect back towards our Elders. In my view, some of the younger brothers were getting *wala* with these leadership specialists.

I kept pushing through the sessions, just trying to get them over and done with. I was part of the leadership group, so I saw my role as having to provide a buffer for these young fullas. If they told me they were feeling uncomfortable, I'd try and downplay things by making light of the exercises and the experiences we were being put through.

Right before the finals series, the leadership specialists implemented a set of rules for us on game day – one of these was called the 'power stance'. It dictated how we were to stand during the national anthem, a ritual that already didn't sit well with me. We were instructed to stand with our chests puffed out, our arms straight and wide of our body, and our fists clenched firmly. We were to stare down our opponents in an attempt to intimidate them. We also weren't allowed to break the stance and walk away until the other team began to move off to their pre-game warm up. We even practised it at training. We had different options of stance too, and there was even an Eddie Betts version of it – which was arms outstretched and smiling – but I was like, 'Don't bring me into it.' I cringe a bit even thinking about it all now.

We did this for all three games in the finals series, including that last agonising game in September. We debuted it in our qualifying final against GWS, but I really can't attribute our win in that game to it. We won because we had an awesome team playing for each other. Our hard-working coaches, fitness staff, medical staff, psychologists, and ultimately our teammates were responsible for that win as well as the next one in the preliminary final against Geelong. That so-called power stance wasn't responsible for either of those wins. And as everyone knows, it didn't do much good at all for us in the grand final that year.

The club continued the mind training in the off-season – in fact, it wanted to step it up based on our two hours getting beaten by Richmond on grand final day. Apparently we weren't mentally *resilient* enough – an assessment I disagreed with privately, both at the time and now. Our team was absolutely mentally strong. I felt like we were all also closer than ever. The death of our much loved, much respected coach Phil Walsh had bonded us together. We also had established close relationships between players and coaches, club staff and families – everybody that was involved in the Adelaide Football Club. That strength and cohesion isn't common in footy clubs.

In the 2018 pre-season, word circulated around the playing group about a camp we would be going on to help us improve our mindset. I was used to camps where army people would yell at us and make us do gruelling things like 100 push-ups at 3am, so I wasn't too worried about those rumours. I just kept pushing forward with my pre-season training so that I could come back stronger and fitter to have another crack at a premiership.

We had some weird sessions pop up. One consisted of us training while the Richmond club song blasted around AAMI Park. It kind of made me angry and I never want to be an angry person. I always tried to bring an upbeat, positive feeling to training, so I could feel myself getting drained. I lacked energy and I also started to lack motivation. To be honest, I couldn't be fucked listening to people yell at me while the Tigers' song played too loudly through the PA system – but no big deal, it just didn't do it for me.

Then the chatter about the camp got a little strange and I decided to ask some questions. We were split into three groups and my group was told we were going away and were to have no contact with our family members during the course of the camp. The idea of a camp didn't bother me, but the idea that I couldn't remain in touch with my family certainly did. I don't take anything in my life more seriously than my family, so I wasn't at all keen on being told that I couldn't talk to Anna and the kids. Lewie was going to be starting his first day of school while we were away and Anna was still pregnant with the twins. Also, I am 30-something years old and I didn't sign up to be in the army. So, if I want to call my partner and kids to check how they are going, I will.

I still agreed to go on the camp as I was part of the leadership team, but I had serious reservations, and together with another player I went to plead my case for changing groups so that I would be allowed to communicate with my family. I was told that I would come back a better husband and father, a better teammate and that I'd get a lot out of the camp. I'm not perfect but I reckon I was already going pretty well with all of those things. So, ultimately I agreed and we came to a compromise that I would be allowed a two-minute phone call after Lewie's first week at school to check how it went. The fact that I found most of the shit we were already doing at the club pretty weird, as well as the prospect of spending four nights away with no contact with my family, meant that I had a bit of a gut feeling not to go; but, as I have in the past, I just shut up and went along with the process.

Before we left for the camp we were told we had to have an interview with a counsellor. It was essentially a one-hour psychological assessment by phone. We were told that we weren't to do the interview with our partners in earshot and that the objective of the questions was to build a profile about us that we would work through on the camp.

I'd been generally pretty open to people about my upbringing and my life. I thought disclosing this same information to

This was the 'miraculous' goal I kicked from the boundary line in the last few minutes of my 300th game. It earned me my fourth and final AFL Goal of the Year (see photo on the next page). (Photo by AFL Photos)

With my fourth Phil Manassa Medal for Goal of the Year in 2019.
(Photo by Daniel Pockett/AFL Photos)

Being chaired off for my 300th game on 21 April 2019. (Photo by AFL Photos)

With my family
after the game.

Unfortunately, my last two years with Carlton coincided with the COVID-19 pandemic, so a lot of games were played for empty stadiums (left). (Photo by Darrian Traynor/Getty Images via AFL Photos)

The hardest part of the pandemic was having to spend so much time away from my family. It was such a joy to see my kids again after spending so much time locked up in the AFL hub on the Gold Coast (below).

Shaking hands with Syd Jackson during a game in 2021. (Photo by Michael Willson/ AFL Photos)

Some of the team wearing special tribute T-shirts that were made to commemorate my 350th and final game. (Photo by Darrian Traynor/Getty Images via AFL Photos)

Being chaired from the field after my 350th and final game in 2021 (above). It was sad to play my last game without a crowd, but I made up for it with a lap of honour at the MCG in 2022 (below). Unfortunately, my kids missed the lap as they were stuck in traffic! (Photos by Michael Willson/AFL Photos)

I feel so lucky to have met so many great people through AFL. Me and Tyson Stengle (right) and all the brothers from Adelaide (below). From left to right: Wayne Milera, Cameron Ellis-Yolmen, Tyson Stengle (back), Ben Davis and Shane McAdam.

Now that I have retired, I have more time to spend with my beautiful family. Here is all seven of us (from left to right): Alice, me, Lewis, Billy, Maggie, Anna and Eddie (we call him Sonny now). (Photo by Kristina Wild)

the counsellors would allow them to understand me a little better and to appreciate the cultural complexities I'd experienced in my life. I thought it would be used to build a profile about me that showed obstacles I'd overcome to be successful and to play AFL. I hoped this would get them off my back with all the talk about resilience and all the other bullshit that came up in the sessions with them.

In retrospect, I was too trusting with the information I provided and I really regret giving it to them now.

The phone call with the counsellor took about one hour and the dude told me that he 'understood' Aboriginal Culture. He tried to make out as though he was like me, as though I should feel comfortable disclosing to him my trauma around growing up Black in Australia.

We flew up to the Gold Coast and to begin with the camp was pretty straight-forward, involving a lot of normal footy-type training on the first day. After the first run, we all went back to the hotel where they assembled us together on the grass outside and told us that the camp was about to take an unexpected turn. All the groups were to change up based on some injuries within the playing group. The group I was in was led into the hotel's foyer where we surrendered our phones and then were escorted in pairs down to the basement car park. Some dude waiting down there was decked out head to toe in the Richmond stripes, called himself 'Richmond', and was employed to jump out from behind a wall and scare us, before taunting us about the grand final loss. After that, two army dudes with fake guns escorted us up a ramp and onto a bus with newspaper taped over all its windows. As each of us stepped onto the bus, we were blindfolded.

In my head, I was laughing. 'Here we go again,' I was saying to myself. 'Another camp where army men yell shit at me and I have to obey orders and just do whatever physical shit they ask before falling into my bed at night and getting some sleep. Same shit, different year,' I thought.

My memory is that the Richmond theme song and some other heavy metal music was playing on a loop inside the bus. It also reeked of off food. We weren't allowed to ask questions, instead the army dudes ordered us to sit down with bowed heads, our arms holding the headrest of the seat in front of us. We were also told to shut up while they bagged us out about the grand final result, again.

I did get uncomfortable when they questioned other players' leadership during the game and thought to myself, 'Fuck, you've gone a bit far there with your role playing.' But mostly I sat through their shit wondering how my 14 years in the AFL had come to me being blindfolded on a smelly bus with the fucking Richmond theme song blasting in my ears, again.

I wanted to know where we were going, just cos it's in my nature to have an awareness of where I am. I sneakily pressed my watch to record how long we were driving for and in which direction. I knew we'd skipped south across the border into

New South Wales as my watch clicked forward an hour with the daylight-saving time difference. We were blindfolded on that bus for at least 45 minutes.

When we finally got to the secret destination, and after listening to them carry on for a while longer, we were allowed to take off our blindfolds to discover 10 or so men dressed in black, up in our face doing the fucking 'power stance' at us.

'This is where your journey begins,' they said, and we were ordered to walk single file through some smoke from a campfire and then enter a marquee that had chairs positioned in a circle. We had to walk anti-clockwise and then sit ourselves on a chair and endure an induction to the camp by two of the facilitators.

Some rules were given to us. For example, we weren't allowed to shower, they were 'out of bounds' – we had to stay sweaty and smell 'manly'. We also had to keep what they described as 'noble silence'. This meant we weren't allowed to discuss any element of the camp with each other. We also had some rules about the processes and how we had to commit to participation as best we could. After the induction they led us in single file to a row of timber cabins where we would sleep in groups of four that night. We were given 10 minutes to unpack our stuff before the camp counsellors came and took us from our rooms.

We walked single file down a slope to a secluded area to witness one of the camp dudes go through an 'initiation process'.

This was extremely uncomfortable for me to watch. Apparently, the guy had been mistreating women and needed to 'remove his childish boy'. The process involved the other camp dudes slinging the initiate around by a rope attached to a climbing harness he was wearing. There was plenty of aggression. His objective was to fight his way towards a knife to cut the rope, and they kept toying with him, letting him get closer before they slung him back. All the dudes on the rope were yelling profanities and by the end of this 'initiation' session the guy was bawling. As he was crying, they all continued verbally abusing him and thrashing him around. Then they started to re-build him up with encouragement again, and he had to commit to better behaviour. I was quietly thinking, 'What the fuck is going on here?'

I remember walking single file back to our hut again and Josh Jenkins saying, 'This is a fucking cult.' He wanted to leave straight away but he was pressured to stay, even though he made it clear that he objected to what we'd all just witnessed.

I remember that evening all of us snuck a wash from the little tap behind the cabins. I think we all looked at each other and asked, 'Should we?' And then went, 'Yeah, fuck it.' We all stripped down and washed our *mooms*.

That night, we kept getting told off for talking inside our cabins – the camp dudes would march past and angrily hiss for us to 'shut the fuck up'.

The next morning, we were told that we would have to participate in the 'initiation process' ourselves. It started with the group of us that had been selected to attend 'group one' camp. We were all sitting on a mat and one of the camp counsellors would walk up to each of us one by one and say, 'It is your turn to go.' Theoretically, it may have been voluntary, and apparently the harness they put us in could have been unhooked at any time, but that's not the way team dynamics work. So eventually it was my turn for the initiation. Just like the guy we saw the day before, I was told it would get rid of my 'childish boy' and I would become a man. I was put into the climbing harness with the rope attached and told that I needed to get to the knife and cut myself free. I crawled through the dirt while the camp-dudes held the rope and yelled abuse at me. At one point I thought I was getting close to the knife but they dragged me 30 metres back over the gravel and mud. When I got close again, they instructed two of my biggest teammates to jump on me and push me onto the ground and not let me move, while the camp-dudes continued to yell abuse to me.

I heard things yelled at me that I had disclosed to the camp's counsellors about my upbringing. All the people present heard these things. By the time I got my teammates off my back, I was exhausted, drained and distressed about the details being shared. Another camp-dude jumped on top of me and started to berate me about my mother, something so deeply personal that I was absolutely shattered to hear it come out of his mouth. I was in a compromised situation, with some dickhead literally on my back yelling private information I thought I'd disclosed in confidence. Here they were now using that against me.

Among the really awful things he said was that I'd be 'a shit father as I was raised by only a mother'. This wasn't the worst of it either, but I don't want to go there in order to protect the people I care about.

I've never been violent, but in that moment, I elbowed the guy in the head as hard as I could. I remember looking up at someone who knew me and I could see the dismay and embarrassment in their eyes. For me, it was traumatising. I was broken to tears and looking back now I was put into a fucked situation that I never should have been subjected to. I was put into a situation that was psychologically and culturally unsafe.

This scenario was repeated for each and every one of the boys and we were all recruited to provide the verbal abuse aimed at our teammates. I'll live with this shame for the rest of my life. I never want to be in that position again, where I am forced against my will to physically and mentally abuse someone I care about.

The camp ended up appropriating a First Nations peoples' ritual of a 'talking stick' and attempting to apply it to all of us, even the non-Indigenous players and coaches. In my view the talking stick was used incorrectly, and I was not aware that any Elder had given permission for it to be used either. There was all sorts of weird shit that was disrespectful to many cultures, but particularly and extremely disrespectful to my Culture.

I feel like a piece of me was brainwashed. I was sucked into it. My ability to switch out was replaced with a weird aspiration to belong. In the fatigue and pressure, I started to think that I had somehow grown stronger with the boys on that camp by having details of my past traumas aired for everyone to hear.

At the end of the camp, we were told that the group members provided our safe place now. Any issues we were faced with were to be raised only with the group members. Then we started an exercise that consisted of roleplaying our responses to our partners when they inevitably asked what we did on the camp. That's when I started to get super suspicious about things again. One of the responses suggested to us was: 'I feel like a better father and husband, having been on this camp.' Anna and I have always had a really honest relationship and there was no way I was going to be able to go home and lie to her.

When I got home, I felt drained. I'd even lost my voice. But the weirdest thing was that at some point over the past four days I'd somehow bought into the thinking that had been promoted at the camp. When I started to talk to people around me about my experience, I started to realise that what we'd been put through was all just a bit fucked up, and I rightly became angry. I actually went through so many emotions and was pretty overwhelmed to be honest. I also started to feel a bit paranoid about what people knew about me, how I acted on the camp, and how I'd been told to treat my teammates. It all made me feel really sick. The stress made me anxious, and I started having weird, unsettling dreams. This is when it all went downhill for me.

Other players – those who weren't in the same group as me – started to worry about me. I was too scared to confide in anyone and just kept playing some of the camp scenarios over and over in my head. It was making me feel embarrassed. Some of the boys were getting stuck into us, but instead of laughing about it, it just made me feel more angry. Anna noticed I was starting to get snappy at the kids and I was experiencing really bad anxiety. I was worried that I was the only one feeling like this out of the whole group that went.

Obviously, the first person to notice the extent of my distress was Anna. She sat me down and together we went through what had happened to me. We needed to understand why I was feeling angrier than ever, being weirdly secretive and anxious, and feeling so drained and lethargic. I was not okay.

I leaned on Anna a lot. Worried about me, she started to put some questions to other people involved in the club as well. She was mainly asking other players' partners if they had noticed anything unusual about us after we'd returned, and if everything was okay. By this point, Anna was becoming increasingly concerned that the camp was too cult-like.

I chatted to some Elders about the specific practices being used in the camp because I had started to feel more and more uncomfortable with what I'd observed there. Some references to Aboriginal words that are very sacred and culturally sensitive to us as Aboriginal men were used in the camp process, and the fact those words were chucked around in such a carefree manner started to play on my mind. I also felt a deep sense of regret for what had happened and I felt I couldn't allow it to continue at the club. I didn't want those responsible for what had happened to keep working with our team.

Anna and I finally decided we needed to bring the entire matter up with the club. We felt as though it was time to try and do some things internally to support the players affected by the camp. I wasn't ever resentful towards the Adelaide footy club. The mind training people though, that was another story. How dare you take me through a cultural protocol saved for particular men in my Culture? How dare you share parts of my private life with my teammates without my consent and while I'm in a vulnerable situation?

After a meeting with all the Blackfullas at the club, I decided to address the playing group and talk about how

I found the camp, mainly addressing the cultural safety implications for us brothers. I sought permission to remove all the Aboriginal boys from any further interactions with the 'leadership specialists' and their mind training exercises. I told the club I wouldn't be involved in any more mind training exercises at all. Instead, I was more than happy to do meditation with the yoga teacher – that mainly involved me falling asleep.

During the meeting there was quite a lot of discussion but something that would always stand out for me was the support I received from Josh Jenkins. Josh stood up when we needed a louder voice. I wasn't as confident as JJ in terms of being able to express how I was feeling and how I thought this camp was tearing us apart. He was a strong support for me and asked everyone to consider listening to what I'd just said – and to stand with me, not against me. Finally having someone else open up gave me some sense of relief, that it wasn't just me feeling isolated and paranoid. I also recall my teammate Hugh Greenwood – another great leader and a gun on the field – asking other members of 'group one' to disclose what had happened so he could work out a strategy to support those players that were hurting. Hugh's vocal leadership always helped to give me a safe space to yarn.

From then, everyone knew I opposed the camp and therefore when stuff started being leaked to the media, Anna and myself began to cop it. People within the club blamed Anna and myself but we weren't leaking anything to anyone. We loved the club and the players and we wanted to try to protect them from any more fucking weird interactions with 'leadership specialists'. In my opinion, that stuff doesn't belong inside a footy club.

Three weeks after I addressed the team about my concerns, I was told that I hadn't been re-elected to the leadership group. I was devastated. I came home and Anna met me in the driveway, where I broke down. I was so fucking tired. I was also angry. It takes a lot of work for us Blackfullas to prove to other people that we're capable of leading. Most often we acquire these roles by modelling behaviours, which is why we hold our Elders in such esteem. I always tried to uphold those same values in footy clubs. Our leadership qualities also look different to others – I'm not the loudest leader, but I grew up caring for big family groups and navigating a big mob of cousins, so being one of a team is a natural part of my being. I had been so proud to represent my brothers in the leadership group. I felt I could add weight to topics or issues that might not be as straightforward for us Black mob. It took me 14 years in the AFL to prove my leadership qualities, so to lose my position in that group flattened me. I felt like I'd let myself down and disappointed everybody I cared about.

My on-field form also slumped in the wake of the camp. I found the opening weeks of that 2018 season a really tough slog. It wasn't until about Round 3 that I managed to kick a goal. I knew I was falling out of favour with a few of the coaches and some of my teammates too. Caring for the newborn twins on top of all of that had us staggering around the place like a pair of zombies. That entire year was tough to get through.

We spent a lot of time at Tate Kaseler and his wife Colleen's place that year. Anna was, by this stage, also an emotional mess. The stress of our babies, as well as copping the blame for the leaks to the media took its toll. So we were both super anxious and paranoid a lot of the time. We felt we couldn't really talk to anyone, as we were worried someone close to us might start leaking and people would hate on us even more. Colleen and Tate often made these big batches of butter chicken for us and we'd just sit there and watch our kids play with their kids, nurse the newborns and try get through the days.

The media were hounding us all day every day for the camp story. I had a regular spot on my radio show, but I just had to keep showing up and trying my best to put on a brave face, downplaying most of how I was feeling about what was going on.

The Crows failed to even finish in the top eight that season. Personally, I felt like I'd lost the drive to play footy, and to be honest I'm not sure I ever had the same energy I did before that camp. I sought the help of a psychologist during the season, but even then, it was really difficult to speak to somebody who had no grasp on the cultural implications that experience had for me. When the season concluded, we packed up the kids and got as far away from it all as we could.

A SafeWork SA enquiry conducted much later found that no work, health or safety laws had been broken at the 2018 pre-season camp, but my view remains that the activities there were inappropriate, counter-productive and culturally unsafe.

EIGHTEEN

The escape to Italy at the end of 2018 was exactly what our family needed. We were physically and emotionally wrecked. We packed our little mob up and asked Nanna Josie if she wanted to come with us. It'd been a tough year for her too following the death of her husband, Poppa John. We looked like a small circus getting through international airports with all of our kids tagging along. I noticed a lot of other passengers had that nervous look about them whenever we boarded their international flight with a couple of five-month-olds and our boys, but our kids are good travellers and little legends on planes. Whenever the girls would start crying Anna would immediately be rotating them for a feed. We're incredibly fortunate to be able to give them those experiences too, as these will enrich their lives forever.

We spent two weeks in Sardinia, where the boys played soccer all day in a camp there. We wanted to be able to just park ourselves in the one spot and for the kids to be happy with heaps of things to play with. That soccer camp gave them the opportunity to meet lots of other kids from all 'round the world. They spent long days communicating through football instead of language and they made the best little buddies ever.

I spent my days rating which restaurant made the best tiramisu and which region in Italy produced the best red wine. It was great having Nanna Josie travelling with us too, and she helped us fine-tune our Italian, which added so much more to the experience.

I got right back into the soccer too while I was there, even managing to convince a local friendly game to let me join in. Before long I was recruited to one of the sides. Every evening we'd get together and have a soccer match. I think they were wondering, 'Who the fuck does this Australian kid think he is asking to join in?' but before long, and probably thanks to my soccer skills as an 11-year-old, I was accepted to play.

These guys were not there to muck around either, and pretty quickly I took it fairly seriously too. It was incredibly hot but it was so good for me to be playing, having fun and rediscovering my love for having a kick. The games also counteracted all the tiramisu I was eating and provided a really tough daily training session to prepare me for the upcoming pre-season. As my career went on, I learnt to have a good balance between eating and drinking and maintaining my fitness in the off-season. I would always take a solid three-week break before the club's pre-season program started up again.

During that off-season I also launched a passion project I'd been working on with former Collingwood and Sydney player Jesse White. Jesse is an expert designer and we discussed the idea for a children's book series, which eventually emerged as *Eddie's Lil' Homies*. Like those soccer games in Italy, the project helped me deal with a lot of what was going on elsewhere by putting things into perspective and reinvigorating my energy in general over that period. I was excited by being able to connect with kids and enthusiastic about inspiring them with my own storytelling. Those books authentically represent me and my mob and I'm proud to read them to my own children. We also made the books into raps and had heaps of cool, relatable characters to represent all different types of kids.

Most of the characters are based on kids we know.

The day I released my first children's picture book, *My Kind*, I went on a journey throughout Adelaide, hand delivering copies to people I had randomly chosen from the book's pre-orders. It just gave me so much joy to see those people's faces when I showed up at their doorstep. Being able to connect with fans through that special project made me so happy, and it was encouraging to see how well they were received by parents and little readers.

My Kind was quickly followed up by the next book, *My People*. The concept behind *My People* was to support the early introduction of our Black Culture in early learning settings, like kindergartens and pre-schools and, most importantly, in the homes of these little readers. The books are fun and people started to really get onboard. I even started to do reading events in hired halls and travelled out on Country into communities just to give back. Connecting with people, especially mob, is incredibly important to who we are. Doing that also increased my confidence in my voice outside the arena of footy. I started to feel like people wanted to hear from me. The fearless questions from the young fullas I visited helped me to get back on track mentally and rediscover my form both in terms of my personal life and my professional career.

Hopefully, the books continue to be important conversation starters in many homes across Australia. It's probably too hard to measure but I hope that at least one child out there is able to take something valuable away from the *Eddie's Lil' Homies* books.

Right before the 2018 pre-season, another family member joined our home. Tyson Stengle is a nephew, in Blackfulla way, on my Betts side of the family from the far-west mob in Ceduna. Richmond had traded Tyson back to Adelaide and the young fulla was looking for a place to camp. We were thrilled to welcome him into our home and he remains a close and important member of our little mob. We always love it when family members are able to live with us. Tyson also grew up navigating big families, helping to raise his many brothers and sisters, and he is always putting his hand up to help us with the twins and the boys.

He quickly settled into our house and I remember he was babysitting within the first few days there. He's a funny and caring fulla and my kids just absolutely loved him. Tyson would do school pick-ups for us, hold the babies when we didn't have enough hands and even watch over Anna while she was cooking for us all, just to offer her his rating on the quality of food that night. Sometimes Tyson can be a shy, misunderstood kid but he's overcome serious adversities to be where he is today. He's a leader, and both footy-smart and street-smart. We could see instantly that he had the potential to be a great man.

He and I would have arguments occasionally, as he liked to walk a fine line in getting to the club on time for training or whatever – whereas I've always been that early bird. We developed a routine where I would make a coffee for him before I'd leave and sing out real loud just as I was walking out the door: 'Get yer hole up!' I like to think that's why he was never late to training, but it was probably me just over-compensating for my own nerves.

Tyson was playing reserves for the Crows, and as a family, our weekends became even more so all about footy. We would take the kids to watch every one of his local games and then the little mob would come to my games as well. But even from day dot, Anna would always bring all the kids to as many of my games as possible. They'd certainly never miss a home game! The car trips were absolutely hectic, but I wouldn't have had it any other way.

I didn't have any set pre-game routines when I had kids. Most nights they'd be in and out of the bed with me and I'd always make an effort to be around to support Anna with the parenting before I was due to play. As we know, it's a kids' world and they don't care that Dad has to go to work. As with my whole career, I'd always account for every possible unrealistic scenario in my planning, which often meant we'd be the first to arrive. I always made sure we were heading out the door at least three hours before the game started.

On the drive there, my mind would often go back to my childhood days and I'd play songs that my mob back then would sit around and listen to, singing real loud, at 12 Boomerang Cresent. It'd usually be country music, occasionally mixed with some R'n'B, depending on the kids' noise levels in the car. Most of the time my music would be hijacked by the kids screaming for Peppa Pig – so I'm well known to give in to that as well.

Adelaide Football Club made attending the home games as easy as they could for us with a creche for the little ones to go into with all the other kids from the club. It was near the change rooms, so Anna and I were able to drop off anyone who didn't want to sit out in the stands and watch the game. One ritual that was always important to me was Lewie and I going out on the oval for our pre-game kick. Lewie didn't really have an 'access all areas' pass but he quickly got to know all of the security guards at the oval and would give them high-fives as he walked out for a kick with me. As we got closer to the start of the game, and it was time for me to head to the rooms to get ready, I'd hoist Lewie over the fence to Anna and they'd then go up and sit together to watch me play.

Every game I played, no matter where I was, I'd always try to make eye contact with Anna and the kids before the game.

I could spot them at The G amongst 90,000 fans, no problem. They helped me get into game mode. During the 2017 grand final, amongst all that noise and the tens of thousands of people, I could see my mum and Aunty Tessa sitting on the fence. It was so weird that I just instinctively knew where they were inside the ground.

Obviously I didn't get to watch too much footy sitting with Lewie during my playing career, but he soon became an expert on my game. I didn't need to yarn to my line coach to receive the most brutal feedback, I just needed to listen to my son! For a young kid he could read the game so well. Actually, he's gone on to be a really keen observer of all sport – especially basketball and footy.

NINETEEN

NINETEEN

Anna and I have always had a policy of keeping an open house, a place for us mob to come together in times of adversity or celebration, whether it be the families from the club whenever they needed anything or young fullas coming through in their early seasons of AFL. This environment was invaluable to us all, particularly the young fullas. I've always believed that if young kids are feeling settled off the field, they're more likely to have success on it. Gathering together is what us mob do best and we thrive from the bustle of heaps of people. Everyone knew we had this open-door policy too.

We would put on a special 'mob night' every ten days or so, which generally consisted of cooking in bulk, especially large pots of Keen's chicken curry. These nights provided safe spaces for all the mob to get together and share a feed and a laugh. Everybody helped with the cooking amid passionate debriefs in the kitchen about what was happening that day or week. There were always volunteers to listen to the kids' school readers too.

Our kids are so fortunate to have had so many wonderful role models come through our door. They learnt lots of different languages and lingo from everyone's mob. In Adelaide we all would communicate in the language that Tyson Stengle, Cameron Ellis-Yolmen and Anthony Wilson grew up using. The other boys like Shane McAdam and Curtly Hampton would still use their language but quickly picked up words in ours so that we could have laughs together or just be able to still feel connected to one another. It brings me so much joy that they're able to grow up exactly how I did – with a strong sense of community. Our house is still a gathering place today.

Over the years now we have had quite a few players from the AFL, AFLW and NRL stay with us. People wonder how we do it with so many extra kids, but the truth is I wouldn't have it any other way. They became such an important part of our family and we try our best to support their journey as much as possible. You will often find me on my phone, switching between the games of all the kids that have stayed with us. My kids have nine different team jumpers to wear that we pull out when they're playing.

Having extra hands around the house is also a help to me and Anna too; we never have to worry about one of the kids crying as they'll be soon picked up by one of the mob. It works both ways – the nurturing and challenges of raising a family is shared between everyone.

I warmed into the 2019 season and by Round 5, for my 300th AFL game, I wound back the clock against the Gold Coast Suns and booted six goals and three behinds, with fourteen disposals – my sixth goal that afternoon eventually went on to be recognised as Goal of The Year, the fourth time I'd collected that award. That week was the best week of my AFL career, just having all my family and friends fly in from all across the continent, including Mum and Dad together in the same room. That all meant a lot to me.

After the game we held a big gathering upstairs in one of the function rooms at Adelaide Oval. The club put on a massive spread for everybody. It also gave us the opportunity to have Mum and Dad meet our girls for the first time. In addition to our mob, people from Carlton footy club like Shane-O and Lyndall Down came across. Shane-O has been like my second dad from the moment I stepped into the Carlton footy club as a 19-year-old kid from Port Lincoln and Kalgoorlie; and Lyndall, as a wellbeing officer at the Blues in the earliest days of my career, has been one of my strongest supporters and remains important in my family's life to this day.

Mitch Robinson and Charlie Cameron came down from Brisbane which meant a lot to me and especially my boys, who look up to Charlie as an older brother. I'd lived with Robbo while I was playing for the Blues, and with Charlie when I was at the Crows. Scotty Watson from my Templestowe days flew in, as did Tyron Maher, my brother from the Phil Krakouer programme when we first moved over to Melbourne as footy wannabes. Rusty Carbine stuck his head in too.

Crows legend and 200-gamer, Graham Johncock ('Stiffy') was also there. Back when I was first considering signing with the Crows, Stiffy called me to say I should take on the legacy of the number 18 jumper. Stiffy had inherited it from Troy Bond, and when I departed at the conclusion of that 2019 season,

I would pass it down to Tyson. Which meant the number 18 jumper would remain Black for 25 years. The number 18 has remained vacant since Tyson left in 2020.

The Crows had designed a guernsey especially for my 300th, which was awesome, and on the morning of the game we got all of the kids in their Crows jumpers – except Maggie, who wore a Carlton jumper with the number 184 on the back, representing the number of games I had played for that club up until that point. I really wanted to do something to thank the Blues for giving me my start in the AFL and having Maggie wearing that jumper was just something small that we could do to acknowledge their part.

There had been plenty of build-up in the Adelaide media that week and it was all positive. I was able to share my AFL journey with footy fans and there were lots of well-wishers and congratulations going around. Driving to the game, we were thrilled to see swarms of Crows fans headed towards the oval much earlier than usual, thousands of them wearing the special 300th edition Eddie Betts jumper, which carried a nod to the 'Betts' Pocket' on the chest. The club had invited a lot of its past Indigenous players along for the game too.

I had all of the kids with me in the rooms before the game, and I asked Cam Ellis-Yolmen – one of the brothers who had spent a lot of time with us, particularly on those 'mob nights' – if he could help to get them all out through the banner with me. Cam carried Alice and I carried Maggie because she was wearing the Carlton jumper. It was the first time I'd ever taken the girls out onto the field with me. Lewie and Billy walked beside us. The two of them walked so slow too – Lewie especially – and I could tell the Suns players just wanted to get past us and out onto the field. But Lewie was soaking the moment in, and I loved that he did. After giving all our kids a kiss, I handed them back to Anna and her sister Lilly, who were already on the boundary line at the top of the race.

We came out of the blocks strongly and were never really troubled by the Suns. The boys in the midfield were dominant and made sure there were plenty of entries into our forward line to give us opportunities to boot goals. As I've mentioned, I usually enter games looking to assist teammates in scoring which gives me as much joy as doing it myself, but on this day I just wanted the ball in my hands – all I had in my head was goals. I had kicked three before three-quarter time. Early in the final quarter I got a free kick for high contact, which I put through for my fourth.

My fifth goal was a gift from Lachie Murphy, after he was down hurt and had a free kick. I was quick to line up and grab the ball. Then my sixth goal: at the 20-minute mark a ball came into the pocket and was punched away by the Suns' Jarrod Harbrow. It almost sailed over the boundary line, but I spun, caught it and then off one step, kicked a left-foot check-side goal. To be able to do that right in front of where all my friends and family were watching was incredible. I didn't go over to them, but I could see them up in the stands. When the siren sounded shortly afterwards, nobody left the ground. There were 50,000 people watching when I was chaired off the field by Cam and Bryce Gibbs, who I'd played footy with for seven years while at Carlton. I was able to give my good friend and Gold Coast Suns assistant coach, Tate Kaesler, a big hug as I walked off. I felt the love from the Crows fans that afternoon and from the Gold Coast Suns. They shared the moment with me and my mob that day.

Usually, I would have gone home after an event like the official club function at the oval. By the time you get to 300 games, you know that a six-day turnaround – we were up against St Kilda in Melbourne the following Saturday – means you have to start getting your body right pretty soon after a match. We had a self-imposed policy to stay away from the beers with that short of a turnaround, but this time, I thought, 'Fuck it. You only ever play in your 300th game once in your life!' So we went to a friend's pub for a few drinks with our closest mob before heading home. I reckon that week and that game was about as perfect as you can get. Everyone in my family and all my friends still talk about it. It was just the best week of our lives. The weather was perfect, the twilight game had an awesome atmosphere, and the outcome of the game was just the icing on the cake.

*

There was another highlight later that season in Round 17, again against the Gold Coast Suns, when Tyson made his debut with the Crows. I presented him with his jersey before we took the field. Those presentations to the young brothers were always an honour for me. Tyson had played a couple of games with Richmond the year before coming across to Adelaide, but never really got his opportunity with the Tigers as they had a lot of small forwards who were ahead of him at the time.

We beat the Suns again, this time by 95 points, and once more I managed to kick six goals. Tyson kicked three and a behind, which is a strong debut for a small forward. It wasn't enough to keep him in the starting line-up the next week against Essendon, but he made his return in Round 19 against Carlton, which involved me making way for him. The team, like my form, had been inconsistent all season – we'd lost a couple before beating the Suns, then lost again to the Bombers. I was looking forward to lining up against Carlton, but I was happy that Tyson was getting another run, even if it was at my expense.

The club was under pressure to find consistency and I knew I wasn't playing my best football at the time. I had a meeting with the coach and I knew from quite early in that meeting that I wouldn't be running out that weekend. When the coach told me I was out, I asked him if Tyson was in. I then asked him, 'Does Tyson know?' The answer was no.

'Well, go ring him and let him know,' I said. I didn't want Tyson to feel awkward about replacing me. I think it was the first time in 12 years I'd been dropped for form, but I was excited that Tyson would be back in the side and getting a game. I think he should have been there all along. I'd been watching him in the SANFL all year and thought he had plenty to offer our team.

His debut against the Suns was memorable for another incident as well. There was no question that Anna and all of the kids would come up to Queensland to cheer him on, but as we were going strong on the field, unfortunately, things weren't going so well on the other side of the fence that day. Anna had started to feel really unwell – so unwell, in fact, that she ended up being taken from the ground to a hospital. Clearly, she wasn't able tell me, since I was out on the field at the time.

She just had to leave our two eldest kids with the sister of someone she knew who was also watching the game at the ground. As I was walking off with a Gatorade in my hand, I heard someone yelling at me from the crowd. When I looked up, there was this woman literally throwing the boys over the fence because there was no one else there at the game who could look after them and take them off her hands.

Anna was diagnosed with a serious case of mastitis and ended up in hospital for three days – for a long while they couldn't stop the infection spreading down her rib cage and were trying to find the right antibiotics to treat the infection. That night of the game our friend Colleen Kaesler took Anna from the oval to emergency at the local hospital. When she arrived her heart rate was alarmingly high and she was taken straight through to start treatment.

I went to see Anna immediately after the game and sat with her in the hospital. The girls were older by this stage but Anna needed them to come up and feed to help with the infection. So it was a bit of a production line, bringing the girls up to feed and see their mum that they all missed so much.

We ended up staying on the Gold Coast for five days. Tyson went back to Adelaide with the rest of the team and – again – Tate and Colleen Kaesler came to our rescue, looking after Lewie and Billy so that I could visit Anna in hospital with the girls. If they hadn't been there, I don't know what we would've done.

TWENTY

TWENTY

In the same meeting that I learned I was dropped for the week and that Tyson was back in the team, the coach asked if I was thinking about retirement at all. I was completely straight and said, 'Nah, not thinking about that to be honest.'

'Good, get it out of your head,' he replied. But in that moment a seed of doubt had been planted in my mind.

I was still working hard and thought I had a lot left to give, plus I had a year left on my contract, so I was focused on playing that out. However, I got a feeling from that meeting that maybe the writing was on the wall for me.

That weekend I was excited to be able to go back and play for the Crows reserves in the SANFL. The game was down at Glenelg footy oval, in the western suburbs of Adelaide. At that particular game a heap of my good friends from the Crows were also playing in the reserves – Bryce Gibbs, Hugh Greenwood, Sam Jacobs and Richie Douglas. We all went in with a really positive mindset and a promise to do our best to support the development of the young kids in the team and to try to get a win for the reserves as Glenelg were one of the best teams in the SANFL league that year.

I probably wasn't supposed to enjoy it as much as I did – fans might expect that I was filthy about being dropped to the reserves. But in fact, the pressure that had been building all season was relieved momentarily. I kicked four that day, but it wasn't enough and Glenelg beat us by two.

My family came down to support me, like they always do, and I could hear Lewie cheering for me on the wing. As you would probably expect it was a much quieter atmosphere than the Adelaide Oval.

Our AFL team was playing at the same time as the reserves against Carlton, so I wasn't able to watch much of the game. I managed to catch the last five minutes on my phone with my teammates in the change rooms.

That night we had a flight to Melbourne as we had an engagement party at the Footscray bowls club. We arrived three hours late but it was just so good to be back in Melbourne with family and friends.

I was re-selected back into the AFL team and towards the end of the 2019 season, I kicked my 600th AFL goal, in a Round 22 loss to Collingwood. Our team missed out on finals football, winning only 10 games to finish 11th in the league. My year was fairly strong for a small forward, playing 21 rounds out of 22 and kicking 37 goals and 21 behinds, with 18 goal assists.

Despite having a season to run on my three-year-deal, the last game I would ever play for the Crows would be Round 23 against the Western Bulldogs in Ballarat, where I could only manage to kick three points. It was a typical Ballarat day, cold, wet and windy and we were thrashed by the Bulldogs.

*

At the end of the 2019 season, we had an offer put in front of us from the Blues. Their offer, of one year, obviously involved leaving the Crows a year earlier than I'd anticipated, but we always knew that we weren't staying in Adelaide forever. We had a house and other obligations in Melbourne; Anna and her family are Victorian, and I'd been there since I was 15, so we consider it to be home. Melbourne is a city that always gives you that urge to return to it. I was raised in the desert and that is where I belong, but I feel incredibly connected to Melbourne as well. It is hard to explain – maybe it's just the coffee?

We were settled in Adelaide, but if belief in my ability was waning, then I wanted to be somewhere where I would be able to keep adding value to the team. It had been my intention to stay at the Crows and finish my career there, but I also wanted to keep playing well and contributing to the team.

I loved the club and the people at the Crows, and I loved South Australia and our supporters and I will be forever grateful to them. It was an incredibly hard decision – but it was the right one for our family at that time. Publicly, the narrative was that the Crows had an ageing list. The club was trying to refresh the group and giving a lot of the younger fullas their break, which meant a few of the older players had to make way. To the older players' credit, they all took that on board and supported the younger guys coming through.

If any other team had offered me a contract to leave the Crows and relocate to Melbourne, I wouldn't have been interested.

The fact that it was the Blues meant that it was a homecoming for us. Not many players get the chance to do that. I also felt that I could repay Carlton for giving me my first opportunity to play at the highest level after I'd been overlooked in the draft as an 18-year-old, by coming in and providing leadership and guidance to their talented, though still emerging, playing group. There were also still some older players going around for the Blues that had been there when I left six years earlier, which added another appealing element for my return. David Teague was coaching the team by that point too – as the Crows' assistant coach, he had been responsible for the unstoppable forward line we had in the 2017 grand final.

None of it was about money – not in the slightest. In fact, I took a $350,000 cut to finish my career with Carlton.

My decision to go home to the Blues was separate to the outcome of a club inquiry into the 2018 pre-season camp. There had been so much external media noise that we underwent an interview with the club around the camp.

Once we had made that decision to head back to Victoria, I had to break the news to the players, but also, heartbreakingly, to the fans in South Australia, who had done nothing less than embrace me for my entire Adelaide stint. I think they were originally a bit suss on me coming across, but then it was nothing but love from Crows fans.

The first people I spoke to were the brothers at the club. They mean so much to me, so I felt I had to sit down with them first. When I did, I told them that I wasn't going to be around the next year and that one of them was going to have to step up and look after everyone. Without a doubt, missing them is the hardest part of being back in Victoria, even now. Our bond was and is so special that we'll be connected for the rest of our lives. I'm so sad that we can't just call in on them, and they can't just drop in on us. They are all like our little sons – and that's how we'll always see them. No matter where we are, our house will always be theirs.

Next, I told the other boys in the team at our end-of-season drinks. I just said, 'Listen, boys, this is pretty hard for me to say, but I'm not going to be here next year.' They were all really supportive, like the brothers had been. They said that as long as my family and me were happy, they'd be happy. That's the way it is in footy these days: players understand that at the end of every year, you'll be saying goodbye to some and welcoming in a heap of others. Everyone understands that AFL is business and often times that means you have to do the right thing for yourself and your family. Yes, you can still love your club – and it's a real privilege to be able to play for a single club for your whole career – but there are so many factors involved now that most people just won't be one-club players, no matter how much they'd like to be.

It was great to sit with my teammates and for everyone to finally know what was happening. A lot of us had been through so much together – the loss of Phil Walsh, the 2017 grand final, the camp – and, in different ways, change was coming for all of us.

Unfortunately, I did not get to tell the fans myself, as a journalist I had worked with on radio in Adelaide, and trusted very much, decided he would break the story. That moment for me was very disappointing, that someone I had worked with very closely and spent a lot of time getting to know revealed my news. I understand that journalists have a job to do but I didn't like the announcement being made before I was ready.

I spent one of my final weeks in Adelaide at the Royal Adelaide Show. We had a stand there for the *Eddie's Lil' Homies* books I had written. I spent long days taking photos and signing books for people and I felt like it was a good way to say goodbye to the community and be able to reach as many people as I could.

On my very last day in Adelaide, I went back to the club with Anna and took a couple of massive hampers of nuts and chocolates up to the commercial and office staff. I really wanted to thank them for everything they'd done for our family. I'd worked with so many of them on community and commercial projects and member initiatives, and so after six years I knew a lot of them and their families really well. They all stood up and clapped – and I shed some tears. There were a lot of hugs. These are the people who keep a club running. Without them, we wouldn't be able to achieve the things we do. As players, we get the recognition and the support and these guys are too often overlooked. It was just a few chocolates and nuts, but I really wanted to convey to everyone at the Adelaide Football Club how I felt about their support over the years.

Afterwards, I went downstairs and said goodbye to the footy admin team and thanked them as well. The footy department at the Crows had worked so hard with me and my big family to make our time in Adelaide easy. My flight back to Victoria for away games would always involve extra kids on the plane, or needing extra tickets for family members to come watch a game, and the footy admin team were always so accommodating to me. I really appreciate everything they did for us in Adelaide.

The stats say that I played six seasons and 132 games at the Adelaide Crows. I led the team in goal-kicking in the first four years that I was there, averaging 55 goals a year. While wearing the blue, red and yellow, I kicked three Goals of the Year – all from my pocket – and I was selected to three All-Australian teams. Those are the numbers. When I think about it, I went through some of the toughest times of my life while I was at that club, but I'd also say I played the best footy I've ever played while I was at the Crows. In my mind, though, those are the smallest parts – the tiniest bits – of my experience there. When I think about my time at the Crows, I think about the friendships, the laughs and the tears. I'll always look back and have the club and the supporters in my heart. Adelaide Oval is also, without a doubt, my favourite place to play footy.

I get sad sometimes when I think about the people I miss around the club. One of my kids might get an opportunity to take us back to the oval someday, though, if they decide to go down that path of playing sport when they're older. It'd be great to sit back and watch them kick goals from the Eddie Betts pocket too.

TWENTY ONE

I headed over to Melbourne to start pre-season with the team in November. Anna and the kids had decided to stay in Adelaide to finish off the school year. I was flying between Adelaide and Melbourne each weekend, training at Carlton and sleeping on Lyndall Down's couch in Richmond.

Lyndall was my old player welfare manager at Carlton and had stayed in contact with me and the family when we moved to Adelaide – but she had left Carlton by the time I got back. She was a really supportive friend for our whole family when things were tough in South Australia. She understands the industry. At the drop of a hat she would fly over to Adelaide just to be there for me – she came over the week I had to play after the banana was thrown at me, then again for my 300th game, when the twins were born and every other family crisis where we needed an extra set of hands.

Anna managed in Adelaide until about the end of November before a nasty head knock and a hospital visit for one of the kids told us it was time to just get back to Melbourne.

I went back over for the last night we would spend in Adelaide and we had a dinner outside with all of our mob crew. We stayed at the local caravan park as the house had been packed up and all the brothers and their partners came and cooked fish on the BBQ before we left early the next morning.

We played rock paper scissors to decide who had to fly with the one-year-old twins and Anna's dad, or who got to drive back with the older two kids. I lost. So I flew back with the twins on the plane while Anna drove the car and the last of our things over.

I was slightly nervous walking back in through the gates of the Carlton Football Club. I hadn't been back there in seven years and I didn't want to let anyone down. I wanted to do a good job for the club that had given me my first big opportunity when I was young, and I took the responsibility of coming back very seriously.

It was probably one extreme to another from Eddie walking in as an 18-year-old compared with Eddie walking in as a 32-year-old. There had obviously been a lot of changes since I left the club but there were a core group of players who were still around from my time there in 2013. One thing that hadn't changed were the fans, and some of the cheer squad who I became close with during my earlier days had skipped work to come down and greet me back on my first day. It was so good to see them all.

It was also kind of like an Adelaide reunion too: a good friend of mine, Mitch McGovern, had moved over to play; Matt Bode was our strength and conditioning and fitness guy; one of the ex-Crows physios, Rohan Hattotuwa, was heading up medical; and then of course Teaguey was in the head coach role.

I remember we had a meeting in the club's theatre where they've got the student seats with flip-up tables that sit over your lap. Lachie Plowman said, 'Hey, Ed, check this out: your name is still on this one.' I went over and, sure enough, there was my name which I'd scratched into the wood years before like a cheeky school kid. I'd completely forgotten about that.

Melbourne was just the same as I remembered it. We slotted back in like we'd never left. The kids don't mind where they are, they make friends easily and have no troubles being in and out of different kindergartens and schools. I was in at the club each day training and Anna continued to work from home on her business, as well as helping to manage my *Eddie's Lil' Homies* business.

Being a country kid, I love getting back to the open spaces. Anna's family live up in the country and they have a little boat, so we often go fishing on the river, and her sister lives on a kiwifruit farm in Whorouly, about 45 minutes away in the north-east of the state. When we're up there visiting Anna's parents, we spend a lot of time at her sister's place having bonfires, fishing and swimming. It's peaceful and beautiful – and such a good change of pace from the city. Sitting there on the riverbank, you're miles away from it all.

Our two dogs had moved back to Anna's family's house as one of them had got a bit grouchy with our small kids. Poor things were sick of the kids climbing all over them so we used to go back and see our dogs a lot. They transformed quickly from city dogs to farm dogs and absolutely loved the move to Anna's parents' place. Every time we got in the car to return to Melbourne the kids would be begging for the dogs to come back with us. Sometimes they would sneak them over the back seat of the car and we'd pretend we couldn't see them.

That year I had been approached by a network to do a doco series for the 2020 AFL season. They had pitched the idea first to my manager, and then the AFL and the producers came to me.

It was a series based around a few AFL players, coaches and teams and would follow them for the entire footy season. The series would follow us at training and games but also at home. So I talked to my family about being involved and they were all cool with it.

The Blues seemed okay with it too – I guess they saw the positives of the exposure that it would bring – but for me, I wanted to make sure that all players were okay with it as well. I didn't want any of them to feel uncomfortable. After all, we were there to win footy games, not shoot a TV show. I said I'd only do it with their backing. They did a survey, and everyone agreed.

I injured my calf during training a week out from Round 1 while doing some one-on-one contested stuff that involved a push off and sprint. It felt like somebody had kicked me – but when I looked behind me no one was there. I knew I had hurt my calf pretty badly and after seeing the physio and doing some scans, we discovered it was a grade-two tear. That injury was set to sideline me for six to eight weeks. I was gutted knowing I wasn't going to be playing the first game of the season against Richmond, the reigning premiers. I so badly wanted to play and do well for the club in my first game back.

At the time, people were throwing around the words 'old-man injury' but I had just had a really great pre-season and my body felt good.

Due to COVID restrictions in Melbourne, the opening game of the season was to go ahead in an empty MCG. Like everyone else, I had to stay home and watch the boys play that Thursday night, which ended in a 24-point loss. The documentary crew recorded us watching it on the TV at home and it was weird for me to not be there, but the strangest thing about it was that empty stadium and so clearly hearing everything that happened on ground that night. After that round the AFL paused the home and away season to try to work out how to continue with the threat of COVID hanging over everything. All players in Victoria were instructed to only train in small groups, so I finished off my rehab commitments that week and then Anna and I packed the kids into the car and headed up the Hume Highway to Wangaratta.

On the drive back to Melbourne a few days later, we heard Gillon McLachlan on the radio saying the AFL season was going to be postponed for a couple of months.

After that announcement, we were still allowed to go into the club, but everything was modified. We could still run in parks and train with two or three people. But then Melbourne entered its first hard lockdown, and we weren't allowed to even do that. We had to remain at home and couldn't do anything for fitness other than backyard exercises and riding stationary bikes. I had a treadmill too, so there were plenty of slow jogs as I rehabbed my calf. Lockdown certainly made it tougher to keep fit, but given what others were going through, it was nothing, really. In fact, I loved being able to spend time at home with my family – and it was pretty cool to be able to train one on one with the kids.

Everything at the club involved video meetings. The club set up some group chats where us players could all speak together, and even the brothers from right around the country had our own chat group, which was great. I could spend hours speaking to Nic Naitanui in Western Australia and when that little party was over I could jump across and yarn up to a brother in Queensland or South Australia. They all had it pretty cruisey compared to Victoria, which had the strictest lockdown.

I also decided to have a bit of fun with my social media following. I put up three pairs of my boots as prizes, to go to whoever sent in videos of the best trick goals. I wanted to do my part to keep kids in the community as active as possible. Lewie, Billy and I filmed a few trick shots of our own, and then I got others to do the same. Some awesome goals were sent in, and it was great to hear from parents thanking us for the fun.

We took a pretty relaxed approach to home-schooling during the pandemic. As Billy was only in his first year of school and still so young, we didn't push anything. We felt like their lives had been changed so much anyway so we didn't want to make them stressed and upset at home, trying to complete their school work without the usual support of the classroom. We would usually aim for about an hour a day where we would do some reading and writing with the kids and then it would be either outside or, as kids do these days, gaming on the PlayStation.

We loved our local park – every day, at the same time, the same parents and their kids would be down there, so we started to have a regular exercise crew for the kids so that they could keep up their social interactions. Occasionally I would run COVID-safe kicks of the footy for them. I really enjoyed that people in the community were getting to know each other and that kids were just playing freely. It was one good thing to come out of the pandemic for me, kids just getting out and about and not having to rush off to activities. It reminded me of how I was bought up. Just playing.

The documentary filming didn't finish, though – they sent me a camera so I could keep recording everything that was going on. I filmed quite a lot on a hand-held device and captured the madness of our house with four young kids at home during a lockdown.

Finally, the call came that footy was coming back – but it wouldn't be as simple as just running out and playing anymore. We'd have two weeks to train together before Round 2. We had to be very careful whenever we were coming to and going from the club. There were also strict travel arrangements and we could only train in certain groupings and meet in certain ways.

The production crew and cameras followed me to get a COVID test – the first of many. It felt like they were sticking a swab in my brain and down my throat at the same time. Throughout the season, we were initially tested twice a week, then that slowed down to once a week. COVID tests became just another routine for everyone I imagine.

After a start to a season unlike any other, I was ready for my second 'first' game for the Carlton Football Club. As is tradition, I was presented with my jumper beforehand – and, as became COVID tradition, I presented it to myself. I recorded myself giving myself my new guernsey, and they showed the video at our team meeting. It was good to have a laugh with everyone during that abnormal time.

It was weird not playing in front of a crowd. You could hear everything – the kick of the leather ball off our boots made a loud thud. When we lined up at the start of the second quarter, I looked around, and Jake Lever was on Mitch McGovern.

I could also see David Teague on the sideline and Matty Bode nearby. I said to Jake, 'Well, isn't this a nice little Adelaide reunion?' Then I turned to the guy beside me and asked, 'And where are *you* from?'

That game against Melbourne brought another loss, which meant we were none from two to start the season – which is always tough.

Next we were up against Geelong, at Geelong – which is, without a doubt, one of the hardest fixtures in footy. You have to travel down there in a bus, and you just know that whatever happens, it's going to be a tough fight. Not having a crowd was going to be an advantage for us there though. Once the Cats get up and going in front of their supporters, they are bloody hard to stop.

We started like a house on fire and played, without a doubt, the best footy we'd played all year. They came back, but we held on to get the win at the famous 'Cattery'. Afterwards, the boys all wanted to get me in the middle of the team song – like we do with first-time players – and throw Gatorade on me. I said, 'Hang on: I've played over 180 games for this club. This is *not* my first win for the Blues.'

But it didn't matter – I got drenched anyway.

We managed two more games – a win against Essendon and a loss to St Kilda – before we all got a call to come into the club for an extraordinary meeting. While we had been concentrating on football, the world around us had been unfolding into a health emergency. The AFL was desperately trying to work out how to keep the competition running, given different states and territories had different rules – and people were getting really sick. They knew that we were only hanging onto the competition by a thread. Now that we had played everyone in Melbourne, the challenge to play those interstate was ahead of us.

During the lockdown a miracle occurred. After years and years of previous fertility treatment, Anna found out she was quite far along naturally, pregnant with our fifth child.

It was initially a shock for our family but on the other hand we also weren't overly stressed about it as we knew that once you had more than three, an extra one wouldn't really make a difference. We always got the older kids to be involved in looking after their siblings so they would be able to help us out with care anyway.

We were excited but nervous about people's reactions – when I called my mum she again said straight away, 'That's good, Edward, the more the merrier,' and was really excited for us. My mum always wanted a big mob of 'grannies' and now that was definitely what was happening. My sister Lucy has five kids and my other sister Sarah has two – they live in Kalgoorlie near Mum so she always has plenty of kids at her house.

In contrast to the happy news in our little family, Brad Lloyd, our head of football, ran us through the implications of the difficult situation that was unfolding across the rest of the country. Essentially, we'd been due to go to New South Wales and play Sydney – but, since that state was closing its borders, the AFL was instead going to send us to play on the Gold Coast.

That afternoon, players from all around the country had a massive meeting with the Players Association and listened to their head, Paul Marsh, talk about what was going to happen for the remainder of the season. He threw out a heap of different scenarios and asked for our opinions on things like how long we thought we could live away from home. At that stage, having our families go with us was not an option.

For me, it was tough hearing that we'd be away for four weeks (it was only going to be four weeks, at that point). I had never been away from Anna and the kids for that long. We talked about it and we were keen for the kids to stay in school and their kindy programs, so the plan was for Anna to stay in Melbourne and manage things from there.

Packing my bags for a month away was incredibly hard. I took everything I needed to play, plus all my laminated photos of the kids and Anna. That way, whatever hotel room I was staying in, I'd be able to stick them up around me, so it'd at least feel like my family was close.

I was really emotional saying goodbye to Anna and the kids. It was only four weeks but in the 15 years we had been together we had rarely been apart. I was crying as I was getting into the car to take me to the airport. Lewis was probably the only one out of the kids that really understood the concept of time so he was crying too. I was upset as I felt incredibly guilty leaving Anna with all the kids, pregnant and trying to run her busy business.

After touching down on the Gold Coast, we went straight into quarantine. We were staying in a resort complex with the North Melbourne and Western Bulldogs players, but we couldn't mix with them. We were able to train with our team-mates, as long as we stayed within the hotel. We had to have masks on whenever we got on a bus to the training ground, and from there it was always straight back to the resort.

After two weeks on the Gold Coast we were on the move again, this time to Perth. We had another two weeks of quarantine there, this time at a hotel with a golf course. By then, there were over 100 daily cases in Melbourne, and it was hard to think of everyone back there. Because of the time difference, that was about all I could do for them: with the kids' school and our training, by the time I had the freedom to call, they were usually in bed or at school. Every morning I'd get up somewhere between four and five and wait for the hotel café to open so I could get a large coffee and go for a walk around the golf course. I was doing that because I was missing my family so much. I needed something to take my mind off it. I would walk and walk and walk. I wasn't into playing PlayStation or watching TV and it felt so strange not having the non-stop environment of being at my home with four kids under seven.

Our high performance manager, Andrew 'Jack' Russell, started to get worried that I was doing too many extra kilometres on my old-fulla legs but if anyone ever needed me they knew where to find me – I would be pacing around the golf course, it was the only thing to keep me sane.

I would call Anna and the kids frequently. I was missing them all terribly and I felt very conscious of the load on Anna, without any support allowed in the house and with such young children. I longed to be back with them and I was finding it harder and harder to concentrate.

We did find a new sort of normal. We had a lot on – meetings, training sessions – and I still had the documentary camera crew chasing me around (but by that stage that was normal to me, too). Josh, Matt and Terry from the production team were great guys, and they were staying in the room next to mine – so I pretty much couldn't fart without them knowing about it. We all became really close and even all the other Carlton boys made them felt like they were part of our team.

*

While I was in Perth, there was talk of us potentially being away for longer than four weeks. So, Anna and I decided that she'd head to the Gold Coast and do two weeks of quarantine with the kids so that by the time I got back there, they could all be with me. That was always going to be extremely tough – but if anyone was going to give it a go, it was Anna. Just imagine it: two energetic boys, plus the twins – plus being pregnant. Not only that, but her room was on the top floor of a three-storey hotel that had no lifts, so she had to manage the prams, the carriers, the luggage, the kids and everything else by herself while around 26 weeks pregnant.

She got through the first week okay – but she couldn't do the second. It was getting to the stage where every time I spoke to her, she was in tears. The girls were challenging little three-year-olds at that stage, and, being pregnant, Anna just wasn't feeling great and was so tired anyway. She seemed completely drained. I told her that she needed to do what was best for her – for her mental health and for her body. I was worried that she was at her breaking point.

The AFL and other players, coaches and staff partners were really supportive but Anna was also trying to run her business and was having issues with part of her supply chain. She just had to get back to Melbourne, where she at least had some support with the kids as they would now be allowed to go to kindergarten and childcare. In the end, I missed her by a few days. She was so sorry, but I understood completely.

It was hard when we got off the bus at the Gold Coast: all the other families were there and waiting for the players, and it was impossible for me not to see them all reconnecting and feel the absence of my own family. I put my head down, walked into a bathroom and cried. I actually couldn't stop crying until finally the CEO, Cain Liddle, came in and gave me a hug. I just missed them all so much.

There was a lot of footage in that documentary, but you didn't see any of that moment in the bathroom. I needed those minutes to be just for me. To their credit, the producers respected that. One of the provisos of me agreeing to it all was that we could veto what went in the final edit, and they never pushed that. I know the people who watched it won't like to hear it, but there was some pretty funny shit that got left on the cutting-room floor.

There's no doubt that, for so many people around the world, 2020 was an incredibly tough year. The sorrow that the pandemic has brought to those who have gotten ill or passed away is devastating to think about. In that context, I don't want to talk about how tough my year was. I know that others were doing it far worse.

I did find the hub life hard, though. For me, of course, that was mainly about being away from my family. It wasn't like we didn't have any support – we certainly did. We all had each other, and we had a team psychologist and others who we could talk to if we needed. For me, what was hardest was the stillness and the quiet. Originally, I thought being on my own for a while could be a good thing. Maybe I'd be able to concentrate solely on my football. But I completely underestimated how important it was to me to be constantly busy, and to have a busy house around me as well. Because of the toll of missing my family, I wasn't playing footy at the standard I thought I could be.

Without any crowds there for each game, it'd also felt a bit like a training run. Afterwards, we'd just go straight back to the hotel. To the boys' credit, we'd never sulk after a loss – we'd embrace and look after each other, playing cards and drinking the occasional beer – but we all knew how frustrating it was to lose.

The short turnarounds between the games – sometime four days, sometimes five – also started to stress my body. Being older, it became tough to get myself recovered and ready to go physically. I felt like I was playing catch-up with my body the whole time.

That period changed the way I thought about my football. For the first time in my life, I began to let the critics get into my head. Before games, I started to think about how I was going to play – and wonder whether I was going to play well. I had never been like that before: it was always just about going out and having fun, just playing on instinct. Now

I was thinking a lot about stuff like not having a contract for the next year.

The pressure kept increasing – and it was taking away all the fun.

Through all of the ups and downs, Anna had noticed that I had been getting more and more reclusive. At the same time, the situation in Melbourne was getting worse, with schools closed and more restrictions. When we found out we were actually going to have to live that way for up to *12* more weeks, Anna decided to come up with the kids and try to get through quarantine again.

It was easier this time, since heaps of players' partners and other staff members from the club were doing the same thing. That meant they could all support each other through it. Also in that group were a few AFL players who hadn't gone initially, for various reasons – people like Shane Edwards, Dan Hannebery and Gary Ablett. With so many kids running around, my boys were in their element. They'd have a 'scratch match' most nights, which meant Lewie got to play with Gary a fair bit (he was pumped).

Finally, they finished their 14 days and I was due to see Anna and the kids. I woke up early and nervous that day. I couldn't believe it was happening – and I couldn't wait. I was there and waiting for them 45 minutes before the bus had even left their hotel. I was worried the girls wouldn't remember me. Even though they'd been seeing me over FaceTime, it just wasn't the same.

Billy was the first one out of the bus. He jumped into my arms and we had the best cuddle we'd ever had. Next came Lewie, who just jumped straight on me too, and then came Maggie. By then I was sitting on the ground, and I was really unsure if she would run up to me. She did, and Alice came bolting over, too. Then, to see my beautiful partner step off that bus as well, made me the happiest I'd been in weeks.

There had been some changes in the time I'd been away: my little girls were speaking and Anna was showing (you could definitely tell that she was pregnant now). I'd only heard them say little words before I left, and I kept freaking out when Alice would say whole phrases. 'Hi, Daddy. Hello. How are you?' I just kept looking at her. It reminded me how quickly kids change in that time of their lives.

We stayed on the coast for a while, and from there it was up to the Northern Territory for the Sir Doug Nicholls Round. It was awesome to be in Darwin, because for the first time since COVID hit, we were back in front of a crowd – only a few thousand, but after silent stadiums, it was brilliant. Most of the spectators had come in from the communities, and they didn't necessarily follow Carlton – they just love their footy. Looking out and seeing the big, bright smiles of all the kids as they cheered and shouted made everything worth it.

A lot of them probably won't get the chance to see AFL footy rounds played in Darwin again – or if they do, not for a long while as Darwin rarely hosts AFL games – so to give them that enjoyment after being welcomed onto their Country was really special. We won, and after the game I swapped jumpers with Izak Rankine, a young and upcoming Aboriginal boy, also from South Australia.

Finally, in the second-last round, I got to play against my old side. It's funny to me how the media and others build up matches like those as being about revenge, or 'righting wrongs'. Honestly, it was more like a family reunion. It was *so* good. Before the game, we all came out on the ground and said hello to each other. I slapped Tyson Stengle across the head and had a laugh with him. The off-field staff came out and said hello too, and Brodie Smith presented me with his Indigenous jumper with a note attached. He knew I loved them all and so handed me his from that year. There was no revenge, just joy and happiness, even though we lost and I didn't play my best – I think I only finished with one goal. I got to play on Luke Brown, though, who I had worked with a lot, and I enjoyed every minute of it.

When we finally got to the end of that shortened season, we'd finished-up with seven wins. I went into my exit meeting knowing I didn't have a contract for the next year. I had no idea what the future would hold. I felt frustrated with my season but I was injury-free and knew I still had the potential to play some good footy and support the younger forwards out on the track, more like a playing-coaching role. The season took its toll on me but I was grateful to be able to continue doing my job, even if it was under immense pressure at times.

TWENTY
TWO

TWENTY TWO

I was offered another contract with the Carlton footy club for 2021 and was looking forward to playing again – but I was also hopeful of adding some off-field leadership as well for the young fullas coming through. I really enjoy working with the small forwards and naturally I was drawn to teaching the younger kids. The decision was made in my exit interview but they waited quite late to announce what was happening with my career. There was some speculation around what was going on but truthfully nothing really was happening, we were waiting to sign up everyone else and then I was given what was left.

We had a huge off-season as a family. At the end of 2020, on 18 December, little Eddie Betts IV, our fifth baby, came into the world delivered by one of our best friends, Vicki Woodward, in Melbourne. Eddie's name has since evolved from being called 'Son' to 'Sonny'. Bubba was tight in Mum's arms after he was born and like all the other kids still hasn't left her side since.

We managed to have him in a period where COVID infections were relatively stable here in Victoria and the kids were able to come up to the hospital and see their baby brother. One night Anna wasn't feeling very well so I spent the night with her in hospital and Anna's mum stayed at home with the other kids – it was like a little holiday for us with one child in a quiet room. Of course I feel bad saying that, and anyone who has stayed in a hospital room as a visitor knows about those little fold-out beds that are too short for even my little legs.

I made sure this time to stay off the hospital food – I'd learnt with my eldest son Lewie that an extra five kilograms going into an off-season wouldn't be good for my preparation.

Things didn't change too drastically after bubba arrived – he was just taken around to all sorts of activities and drop-offs as any fifth child would be expected to. Anna and I decided to do a renovation of our house in Melbourne and get it ready to sell. We spent six weeks with tradies we knew and we tried to do as much of the work ourselves as we could. I spent one day picking 5,000 staples out of the floorboards, mostly with the kids running around and making more and more mess.

It was good to be focusing on other projects and doing things to keep me busy. We had been so lucky over the years to be able to go and travel in the off-season but due to COVID we stayed in Victoria and spent time together as a family. The house renovation was so much fun for me. I loved watching the place transform. Anna and I are really shit at knowing what to do when it comes to renovations, so luckily we worked with some talented tradespeople and I was just the labourer under strict instructions.

I had signed a media deal in 2020 with Fox and had started to find my voice in the media landscape. I really enjoyed doing some regular radio and TV spots in Adelaide from about 2016, even though it was something I didn't initially think I would get much joy out of – I was such a shy kid when I entered the AFL that there was no way back in 2005 I would ever have pictured myself having a voice in the landscape of Australian media.

It turned out, I loved being on radio and TV so much that you couldn't shut me up. Sometimes it was stressful for the footy clubs I would play for as I had a tendency to be too honest about things. No one ever told me off but I think they did sometimes get worried about me and have a listen in to check on what I was saying. I loved being on a commercial radio station in Adelaide as well as I was able to talk about lots of things *other* than footy. I love talking about the game, but I equally love talking about my kids and family and just having conversations with people about things that are important to me. This experience in the media gave me confidence in my voice and helped with the internal walls of a footy club. I could really feel myself growing and, even though it was sometimes uncomfortable, I loved the challenge and the responsibility it gave me.

The weight of this job is huge for me. I am often called upon to respond to incidents that impact my people and I want to do all Aboriginal people justice by having our issues heard. I take the role of talking about racism in the media landscape really seriously but I also am not an expert on racism, so I have learnt that all people can really see is how it directly impacts me, and I don't have to have the solutions to the questions people ask me.

The next year started again for me with a minor calf injury in the pre-season which was really disappointing. I was ruled out for Round 1 and then I didn't get the chance to play until Round 3 against the Dockers, but that was my 200th game for the Carlton Football Club, and we won. Afterwards, I was presented with a trophy and my five kids were in the change rooms with me. It felt good to have my kids around the footy rooms again. It has always been my favourite part of the game, and COVID had meant we hadn't had our kids around the change rooms for almost two years.

During the season we were relocated to Sydney as COVID infections in Victoria started to rise and Anna and I started to panic a little at the thought of another forced separation. We were promised that this season we would not be away from family for longer than four weeks. We had a plan in place for COVID restrictions this time as it would be impossible for Anna to stay home with the five kids alone and try to work. Being able to have the kids in school and childcare took some of the pressure off both of us – it still meant the nights were hard but it wasn't so relentless.

Lewie started playing footy this year and I couldn't believe how much I enjoyed watching the Under 10s play. It was becoming the highlight of my week, I get so much joy from watching my kids play sport. Billy was also playing Under 8s but managed to fill in for a few extra games in Lewis's team too.

I don't know how we will do kids sport on weekends when we have all five playing at once; it was already like a puzzle trying to get to watch each kid play and get them dropped off in time. Remembering which child needed white shorts or who was on oranges was a struggle – I really am just starting to learn how busy kids' sport is and I take my hat off to all the parents and coaches and friends and family who manage to pull it off every weekend. It finally made me think about my family, who managed to get all of us kids to everything despite many barriers, and gave us the best opportunities. Kids in Victoria hadn't really played much sport the previous year so it was just so good to see them back out with their friends playing again.

I tried to be an assistant coach but I would get too excited and start pacing up and down the side of the ground. I was just so excited for the team that I couldn't help myself. Lewie had a good little crew with an awesome bunch of coaches and their team ended up top of the ladder, which meant they were premiers when the league was again shut down due to rising COVID infections.

Coaching and teaching young kids brings me so much joy. I love the challenge of getting the best out of people and problem solving to make things better for the team or individual. Coaching was never something that really crossed my mind throughout my career, but it was something that I just naturally fell into doing while I was playing and ended up really enjoying.

Towards the back end of the season, while we were still playing footy, there was a report and investigation going on into the operations of the Carlton footy club. For this reason, and others, our season didn't end as we would have liked it. We missed the finals and the pressure was on our senior coach. We managed to win eight out of our 23 games. I finished with 29 goals from 20 games and came seventh in the Carlton Best and Fairest.

TWENTY THREE

'I'm done Bub' was the three-word text message I sent to Anna. It was three weeks out from the end of the 2021 AFL season and I had just walked out of a meeting with the head of football – Brad Lloyd. He had informed me that they wouldn't be offering me a contract for the following year.

I went into the meeting not knowing which way it would go. I had earlier in the month informed them that I felt I was ready to play on and that my body physically was in the best condition it had been for that year.

My position was that while I wasn't kicking 50-plus goals as in previous years, I was still contributing to the scoreboard while also adding value in coaching and development to some of the young forwards coming through. I had developed really close relationships with those fullas and wanted to keep working alongside them.

I chatted to Brad about where I thought I sat within the club and he informed me that they were going for youth. I was a bit flat but I also said to him it was a bit of a relief – since turning 30, every year people had been questioning whether or not I still had it in me to play footy. So the idea that those conversations wouldn't happen anymore made me feel somewhat better.

I walked out of the meeting and sent Anna a text and then just got on with weights.

It was good to hear that news from Brad directly as we had a really good relationship at the club and I felt it was really easy to have honest conversations with him. He was a very caring footy manager and I would often spend time in his office. He was approachable and considerate – so it was good that the person ending my career was someone I respected really highly. He probably wasn't entirely responsible for the decision, but I appreciated him having that yarn with me and being the person to deliver that news.

For so many years in footy you always wonder what position you will be in once you retire. It's easy to stress a lot throughout your career about whether you are doing enough off-field to be prepared for that next stage. I felt really confident in myself that I had gotten enough experience over the years to make a smooth transition out of footy and the more time that passed after my conversation with 'Lloydy' the more comfortable and relieved I felt.

I told some of the people who I was close to in the club that I hadn't been offered a contract but I was careful not to make a big scene as I also wanted to respect that a few other team-mates had milestone and retirement games coming up. Other than a few people around the club, I told Anna, my family and a few other footy friends. At home, it wasn't a big deal. COVID restrictions had meant the kids had barely been to the footy in two years and had somewhat lost a bit of interest in the game. Lewie was a little teary when I told him but it wasn't something we dwelled on or made a big deal of. It was all very conversational and matter of fact, then back to what was for dinner.

I sensed Anna's relief as well. Footy had taken its toll on her over the last couple of years – especially after the eleven weeks I was away and she was in lockdown in Melbourne. She was really excited for me to start my next chapter and was quick to reassure me of the importance of my voice around the game in Australia for years to come.

I wanted to be honest with the public and fans about how the conversations around my retirement went too; I was never really worried about rejection or being told that I was no longer required – it is just part of the industry. So when I went public with my news I wanted to be honest with the fans that I wasn't offered a contract, but that that was okay. I didn't feel the need to act like my retirement was my own choice – keeping with my values was to always tell the truth of the story.

The Monday of my last week of footy I announced to the playing group that I was retiring. I had managed to have a private conversation with most of them over that weekend or the week before, so it wasn't really a surprise anyway.

For so many years I had watched people announce their retirement to the team, with their kids or partners alongside them, and I often wondered how mine would go. That day Victoria was in lockdown, so there were very few people other than my teammates and staff in the room, and Anna and the kids were at home.

From when I first arrived at Carlton to where I was finishing up I couldn't have been happier in my footy journey or the voice I found. To stand up confidently and talk about my retirement and what it meant for me was something I loved doing. To be honest, the urge to talk to groups of people rather than actually get up and play footy was a natural evolution of who I was becoming and what I was beginning to feel more comfortable doing.

Footy was something I had enjoyed doing for so long, but I think a part of me was ready to finish up. The development of my instinct to care for others and coach and be a voice for my mob in the media was happening so naturally. Like most things for me throughout my life, I just transitioned to where I was meant to be at that time and didn't overthink it too much.

The week leading into my final game was one of the most emotional weeks of my life. We were still in lockdown in Melbourne but I heard from so many people across my 17-year career that it was like reliving those years all over again. It was heart-warming to have so many people reach out, and to get to hear stories about what I meant to them. I tried to make sure I really took in every message that I received and made an effort to write back to every single person who contacted me.

I heard from people I respected so much in the game of AFL, including former and current players and club presidents.

I played my last game against GWS. I managed to kick a couple of goals but mostly I just went out to have fun – and I enjoyed every last moment. I will never forget what GWS footy club did for me: they wore their Aboriginal-designed jumper, presented me with a signed jumper of my own, and gave me a nice bottle of wine as I was carried off. It was such a kind gesture and represented what was most important to me – my Culture – in such a moving way.

I remember for my last on-field interview I couldn't think straight. I went back to how I felt as an 18-year-old entering the AFL and having to do a media spot. I was mumbling and fumbling my way through the interview and my thoughts were all over the place. I was trying not to cry but I also didn't really care if I did cry. I was mostly trying to remember who I needed to thank, emotional that my family weren't there with me, and I was so overwhelmed that, on reflection, I don't think I made much sense.

We were the last game on the Sunday night and after that game I was presented with the match footy on Zoom, with a computer screen holding the faces of all my family members back home. Anna and Lewis (the younger kids had apparently become disinterested in the first two minutes of the game), my mum and Aunty Tessa and all of the nieces and nephews, my sisters, Anna's family and a few friends all showed up online to watch me in the change rooms. The connection was poor, they could barely hear and once Zoom disconnected we all just left and I went home. There wasn't any crowd or fans and I could hear a pin drop in the stadium.

When I got home, Billy was awake with Anna and he greeted me at the gate with a big hug, Anna with a champagne in hand. I didn't know what to do with myself, so I just went off to bed.

I hadn't even been retired five minutes when I received a phone call from Glenn, the footy operations manager of the Palmerston Magpies in the Northern Territory, seeing if I was keen to have a kick in the NTFL in Darwin. I had a laugh with Anna before she said, 'Well, you do realise you don't have to be back for pre-season now?' I had become so conditioned to not being able to do things due to footy re-starting that I didn't even think it was a possibility to go and travel for three months to play football.

I realised that I would love nothing more than to go up to Darwin, with a footy club with a high population of mob, to give back, play, coach and do some community work. I was so excited. We decided we would all go up as a family, and so I signed, alongside my friends and distant family through my Port Lincoln mob, Alwyn, Russ and Aaron Davey, at the 'Palmy Maggies'.

As the borders to Northern Territory and Victoria were closed due to COVID restrictions, it was going to be a mission to get up there. I needed to have government approval, which I got as I was relocating for a few months and was going to be adding value to the Northern Territory by working as an educator in communities. Then I needed to complete a 14-day quarantine with my five children in the closest thing to jail, the Howard Springs quarantine facility.

This showed the resilience of my kids as they were confined to very small rooms and balconies. It was actually terrifying for me. We were patrolled by police officers and I was extremely uncomfortable in this setting.

NT police issued me a warning, via three police officers marching down to our four single bedrooms with five children, for getting off my balcony. I had jumped off to grab one of the kids' toys that had gone under the portable houses we were living in, but I think they also said it was 'cos I had also kicked the footy to another one of my kids. It felt like living my childhood all over again, being afraid of being caught by the cops. Some of the police in the facility were really nice but it wasn't the easiest thing I have ever done. I felt really nervous for the full 14 days but I didn't want my kids to feel that unease so I tried my best to put on a brave front.

After our 14-day quarantine it felt so good to be in Darwin. It was really hot though and I was thinking to myself, 'How the fuck am I going to play footy in this?!' Darwin in October and November is going through the 'build up'. According to locals, it is the worst time of year to be in Darwin, weather-wise. It is so hot and humid – it was sitting on 36 degrees most days and if you tried to even go for a walk you would almost pass out from all the sweating. At about 3pm every day there was a huge tropical storm. It always seemed to come from nowhere and it brought flash flooding, lightning and thunder like I have never seen or heard before in my life. It took us a few weeks to get used to the weather and to not freak out about the storms. Back in Victoria we now laugh at the storms that happen here and all say to ourselves, 'This is nothing like Darwin life!'

Almost immediately I was full swing into the footy club. As a player, coach and member of the footy club I didn't hold back on wanting what was best for everyone. I wanted us to win but also to have tight connections off-field and to build a community around us that made people want to come play for the club. Those months playing at Palmerston, being in Darwin and connecting with local and remote communities was one of the best times of my life. I loved playing footy freely, coaching young kids, giving back to the community and being able to go and see places with the Davey family that no one else could take you to. It was a sigh of relief to play footy for fun again, and to not have the scrutiny that often professional footy can bring. I was out having a great time and just doing it all with a smile on my face.

We didn't have much success as a club on-field but my family made some really strong connections in the Palmerston footy club community and that experience so quickly after retiring allowed me to remember why football is so important for so many people. Local footy clubs are what keep our kids engaged and are sometimes the lifeline for youth seeking stability and connection within a team environment. I don't think I can accurately describe how much I believe that footy saves lives here in Australia, and that having just one strong role model in your local club can inspire a whole team. I believe football is what saved my life. Without something for me to do, I could have quite easily fallen into a trap, and the trap of the justice system here in Australia for people who are in my demographic is not safe. So to football I am endlessly thankful.

The whole family unfortunately caught COVID with only one week left before we were due to come back to Victoria. We were pretty unlucky to get it, as in Darwin at that stage only about 180 people in the community were COVID-positive. We caught it from a friend who had been visiting from Brisbane, as borders had just opened.

It took us 16 days for every kid to eventually get it and for us to be able to leave isolation. We extended the stay in the house we were in, which was much nicer than the previous stay at the quarantine facility – so we didn't complain once! I reckon the only thing we truly missed was our daily coffee from the local café, so we had to ask friends to drop us in a takeaway cup each day.

Prior to leaving for Darwin I had received a phone call from my good friend Paddy Dangerfield. He asked me if I would consider doing some coaching with Geelong. I kept laughing it off when he sent me pictures of houses in the area that he thought I should buy. My urge to coach and be involved in the game was still there but I also knew I had a passion for working in the corporate space and telling my story, and I loved my job in the media.

I had to work out how to plan my workloads and where I would best fit after my playing days were over. I was out walking my usual daily route on a Friday afternoon when I decided to just call Paddy. I said to him, 'I'm interested in doing some part-time coaching with Geelong.' Paddy got me on the phone to the footy manager and by the Monday I had a verbal agreement with Geelong Football Club to do some part-time work with their development.

I thought it would be a good idea to do lots of small things that keep me happy. Coaching, corporate talks and media. It gives me a good mix of things that I am passionate about – I still don't know what I like best out of all three, but it is really good for my weeks to be varied, as it makes the transition out of playing professional footy easier.

I have enjoyed working with corporates and giving presentations on racism, leadership, diversity, resilience and allowing people to ask questions. I always like to make my presentation a mix of funny and serious. My favourite part of the talks is having the space at the end for people to yarn to me. I call it a yarning circle. Sometimes when I am with younger kids the questions about what car I drive or how much I get paid are funny, but I love having conversations with people of all ages. I feel that the more people I can reach, the more I can reduce the biases towards and stereotypes of me and all Aboriginal people here in Australia. I can explain my story, why I do things a certain way, what our leadership systems and practices look like and how they are still crucial in conversations about Australia as a nation – about how and why Aboriginal people deserve space, voice and leadership in this country.

My last game on the field that night in August 2021 was quiet, but I am determined that the next stage of my journey will be quite the opposite. I have worked so hard to get where I am today, but I remain full of a sense of responsibility to continue to work to shake the stereotypes of my people. And there is no better way to break down barriers and build communities than through the game of AFL.

FINAL WORD

The year I retired, the AFL mandated Aboriginal Liaison Officers in every club for 2022. It was a bittersweet moment but it certainly lifted some weight from my shoulders and I felt like my advocacy, along with other senior Aboriginal and Torres Strait Islander players, had been heard.

As of 2020 the AFL had about 11 per cent Aboriginal and Torres Strait Islander players, which means we are over-represented in comparison to the population, which is around three per cent.

I want the AFL to be a safe place, where our people can thrive, not just survive. Where our differences are accepted, not questioned, and our ways are celebrated. Where our unique leadership style is recognised and supported.

The introduction of Aboriginal Liaison Officers is a small step in the right direction and I am hoping that with internal support at club level we can see more Aboriginal and Torres Strait Islander players drafted and maintained long term, to then go on and lead clubs. Who knows? Maybe we still might see an Aboriginal senior coach in the game?!

I must admit, it took me a long time to find my place in AFL. It took a long time to find my voice, to be brave. But everything went well for me as I always maintained my core values that I was taught when growing up – care for one another, be honest and be respectful.

I did all of those things, mostly, with a smile.

A NOTE ON THE ILLUSTRATIONS

The illustrations used on the cover of this book, and in the chapter headers, are from an artwork called 'Women's Ceremonial Body Paint' by Aunty Debra Nangala McDonald II. Eddie and Anna are lucky enough to have this beautiful original piece hanging in their family home.

Debra Nangala McDonald is a Pintupi artist, born at Papunya in 1969, who has been practicing since 1999. She has become a highly respected, and strongly collected, artist both locally and internationally. Debra hails from a long line of established Indigenous painters and she keeps ancient stories alive as part of the new generation of artists working in the Pintupi tradition.